Due Return	Due Return
Date Date	Date Date

The Shrine of Party

THE
SHRINE OF
PARTY Congressional

Voting Behavior 1841-1852

JOEL H. SILBEY

University of Pittsburgh Press

To
my Mother
and the
Memory of my Father

PREFACE

S I N C E the end of the Civil War, American historians have repeatedly examined the political situation of the two decades preceding the disruption of the Union. Most of them have particularly concentrated on the influence of sectional factors and the role of sectional leaders in shaping and determining national policy, while stressing the concurrent decline of nonsectional political forces. However, despite the enormous quantity of research published by several generations of scholars, many aspects of the political struggles they describe remain confused and unclear. There is, of course, a large measure of agreement on the broad factual outline of events between 1845 and 1861, but there is also a profusion of interpretations concerning the nature, strength, and importance of the political forces present. How and why the American scene crumbled into internecine warfare is still clouded by what one writer has called a "confusion of voices."[1]

Fortunately, several scholars have held out the hope of eventual general agreement about ante bellum American politics as they have engaged in the difficult process of re-examining their own methods and approach. Finding much to criticize in the conceptual narrowness of many monographs, these historians have suggested that the actual nature of political history has been distorted because of overconcentration on the careers of prominent statesmen and "the classic controversies over great national issues," rather than on mass political behavior and the social conditioning of political action.[2] Moreover, some historians have also questioned the overdependence on certain types of evidence. The almost exclusive use of newspapers and manuscript collections as primary sources has led, they believe, to a "kind of documentary determinism"—conclusions have been inevitable given the nature and scope of surviving documents, and yet these documents do not accurately approximate the realities of past political behavior.[3] For example, in discussing the causes of the Civil War, American historians have made many general statements based on these sources concerning the state of public opinion and its effect on political action. But because of the limited field of vision, the prejudice, or the lack of complete knowledge of the editor or letter-writer involved, we have conflicting, incomplete, and limited accounts. Thus it has been impossible to determine precisely what public opinion actually was at specific times on most of the issues discussed.[4] The result has been the historiographic "confusion of voices," as different documentary sources stress different factors in ante bellum political behavior.

Such being the case, how can one more accurately measure the state of public opinion as a crucial first step in analyzing political behavior? The answer may be found in the adoption by historians of ideas and techniques borrowed from other social sciences. For example, some recent historical applications of simple statistical methods, ranging from attitude scaling to simple and multiple correlations of different political variables, suggest that we can derive more precise measurements of public opinion in different political situations and thereby move towards a better grasp of the relative importance of different political forces in American history.[5] Several periods have already undergone re-examination with such methods.[6] There has been, however, little focus on the ante bellum political crisis, and my intention in the following pages is to alleviate part of that deficiency. My aims are limited: to apply one kind of quantitative analysis to one level of the political arena over one period of time. In the United States Congress between 1841 and 1852 many representatives vigorously expressed predominantly sectional points of view on political issues. At the same time, however, other congressmen just as militantly articulated nonsectional points of view and affirmed their continued devotion to such long-standing nonsectional institutions as the two national political parties. Consequently, it has been quite difficult to determine precisely which of these two points of view best reflected the predominant political forces of the day. Nor can we ascertain from the debates and reports the substance of any changes in the importance and relative strength of these conflicting forces over the course of the forties, a period when some new and apparently disruptive conditions appeared on the American political scene. My work attempts to solve these problems by carefully measuring how much either sectional or party considerations affected a prime reflector of public opinion—congressional roll-call voting. In so doing it is hoped that a fresh start will be made towards comprehending the politics of the pre-Civil War era.

Certain qualifications should be stated at the outset. This is only a first venture into the application of social science techniques to the political problems of the ante bellum period. The focus on Congress during one important decade produces only possible guidelines for understanding other periods and other levels of American politics. Obviously these other institutions and periods have to be examined in a similar manner before we arrive at any complete portrait of the forces shaping American politics in the period which culminated in the events of 1861.

I have incurred many debts in the course of producing this book. At an early stage in its development the Social Science Research Council became interested in my work and extended substantial financial aid. I am grateful for their help. While I was a faculty member at San Francisco State College, the Graduate Division there contributed the cost of typing and clerical assistance during the preliminary preparation of one part of this manuscript. The secretarial staff of the Department of History of the University of Maryland coolly and competently typed the final draft. The staffs of the many libraries used during my research were, at all times, courteous and considerate. I am in debt to all of them, but wish to particularly thank those of the Library of Congress, the New York Public Library, and the University of Iowa Library.

The stimulating criticisms and judgments of Professors William O. Aydelotte of the University of Iowa and Samuel P. Hays of the University of Pittsburgh, materially shaped and clarified my thinking about political behavior, legislative activity, and the implications of much of my material. I have also benefited from conversations over the years with John L. Shover of San Francisco State College, Seymour Drescher of the University of Pittsburgh, and Don S. Kirschner of Roosevelt University, as well as from the critical acumen of my former colleague,

Allen Weinstein of Smith College. On several occasions the suggestions of Professor Lee Benson of the University of Pennsylvania were most helpful. As a fellow student in the field of behavioral research as well as a long and close friend, Samuel T. McSeveney has contributed more to my thinking than I can ever hope to reciprocate.

My greatest debt is to Professor Allan G. Bogue, now of the University of Wisconsin, who directed this work as a doctoral dissertation and who has maintained a deep interest in it ever since. I can only say that without his friendship, concern, and sound advice this book would not have come as far as it has.

My wife Rosemary worked with me at every stage of the development of this manuscript. For her clerical and critical abilities as well as her unlimited patience she deserves the recognition but not the onus of co-authorship.

CONTENTS

The Shrine of Party

1. SECTIONAL COMPLEXITY AND INTERPLAY

T H E American historical experience, Frederick Jackson Turner wrote in 1925, has been the product of a "sectional complexity and interplay not unlike what goes on between European nations." This country, he continued, is "an empire, a federation of sections, a union of potential sections,"[1] in which historians must identify and analyze the conflicts and accommodations between the always-present sectional forces in order to fully understand American development. Political historians, for instance, could certainly see much sectional interplay in the voting of the United States Congress where, on fundamental issues, there has been "a persistent sectional pattern."[2]

Turner did not originate this concept of sectional forces in American history, nor was he the first to point out the necessity of using it in historical studies, but he did popularize the sectional approach.[3] His emphasis on the persistence of sectional patterns provided a framework within which succeeding generations of students analyzed American history. Their many books and articles reinforce the assertion that the sectional concept has been a major theme of American historiography in the twentieth century.[4]

Turner believed sectional interplay existed in every era of American history, but the years between 1815 and 1860 particularly fascinated him.[5] His research into this period in which sectional differences produced a civil war led him to identify the two primary forces of the era as the conflicts between the East and the West, and between the North and the South. But he also suggested that such broad sectional patterns were oversimplifications. For more precise understanding, he identified six regions within the sections: New England, the Middle Atlantic, the

South Atlantic, the Southwest, the Old Northwest, and the Far West. Each of these regions had distinct geographic and cultural characteristics that in some degree separated them from each other. None of these sections or regions, however, could dominate the country by itself. Therefore, statesmen working through political parties built coalitions between sections or regions based on mutually accepted programs. When these national accommodations broke down in the 1840's and 1850's, American politics dissolved into its sectional parts.[6]

Despite his interest in sectional problems in this period, Turner never developed his ideas in detail. Rather, he left behind a body of general concepts about the nature of sectional forces in American history that needed precise development and demonstration to clarify how sections worked together for so long, and perhaps more importantly, why they split asunder in the 1840's. Other historians took up that task. Many of them paid primary attention to the factors in American life that produced, first, different sectional institutions and outlooks, then two distinct civilizations in America, and, finally, an inevitable conflict between the North and the South.[7] One of Turner's graduate students at Harvard, Avery O. Craven, focused on the major problem of how American politics actually sectionalized before the Civil War.[8] Craven was primarily interested in the breakdown of the national political process, first into two antagonistic sections, and then into two warring countries.[9] He centered his work in the 1840's, the decade in which the differences between the various sectional forces in American life were dangerously intensified by the slavery question. He suggested that before that time, although the regional elements identified by Turner had hardened into three major sections—the North, the South, and the West—there still remained a superstructure of two national parties through which the sections worked out necessary accommodations. In the early 1840's, however, a group of concerned Southern leaders, led by John C. Calhoun, tried to awaken Southerners to the danger from the growing antislavery sentiment of the Northeast.

Craven indicated that Calhoun and his supporters wanted to accomplish two things: to unite their section as a coherent and independent area, and, since a united South would not be strong enough to defend itself alone, to work out a political alliance with the Upper Mississippi Valley region. They succeeded briefly in their second goal during the early 1840's with the formation of a Southern-Western alliance. During James K. Polk's presidency, however, the Westerners did not achieve certain things they desired: the Oregon territory north of 49 degrees latitude for one, and rivers and harbors improvements for another, both of which they considered necessary for their well-being. They had expected the Polk administration to respond to their needs in return for Western support of Southern demands for Texas and a lower tariff. When Polk, a Southerner, compromised the Oregon boundary at 49 degrees and vetoed the internal improvements bill, the Western leaders angrily criticized the South and moved towards poltical cooperation with the Northeast.

In response to Western criticism, Southern leaders intensified efforts to unite their section in defense of their system. Thus began a process which culminated in a decade-long crisis over slavery, and then civil war.[10] Although national parties moderated sectional influences some-what throughout this period, the different sectional interests soon became too powerful for the parties to remain important factors. Militant sectional politicians clashed bitterly with one another and ultimately viewed all issues in terms of sectional advantage only. When this happened, rents in the fabric of national unity appeared, sectional leaders injected moral issues into politics, and the sections moved irrevocably apart. Although there were some dissenters from the majority position within each section, the growth of sectional unity in support of an articulated set of demands overwhelmed them.

This interpretation of the last fifteen years before the Civil War, as developed by Avery Craven, demonstrates the working out of Turner's sectional thesis. Other historians have also adopted this view of the 1840's and 1850's in their writings, so that it has become one of the dominant themes in ante bellum studies.[11]

II

As a result of the work of Turner and his followers, historians have widely accepted the overwhelming importance of sectionalism in the pre-Civil War era, especially in the years after 1846. Yet, it is possible that such acceptance has been too readily given. Historians may have looked at the period in light of what happened later and deduced what must have been significant at an earlier point in time from these later events. The breakdown of the country into sections was complete by 1861. This immediately raises a question as to when the breakdown began.[12] But the search for beginnings can lead the research scholar into a methodological trap. In looking for facts to fit the particular pattern of the coming of the Civil War he may ignore or play down other facts, which although not a part of the sectional breakdown, were important to the people at the time. In his effort to discover historical continuity the historian may construct an artificial framework and superimpose it upon a historical development. This, I believe has happened to many historians of the ante bellum period. They have neither dealt concretely with certain problems about the different sections, nor have many of them given detailed attention to the existence and possible influence of nonsectional elements in American life even though such forces may have modified sectional behavior.[13]

In approaching the sectional problem most students have noted the existence of more than just the North and the South, even after 1846. Turner, for example, also studies East-West sectionalism, as well as the various subregions existing within the different sections, each with different needs, ideas and values.[14] Both Henry Clyde Hubbart and Avery Craven indicated that in the Old Northwest there were two subregions, the Ohio Valley area and the Great Lakes region, with different values and policy needs. Furthermore, one of these regions, the Ohio Valley, was closely tied to the South while the other was not.[15] Other analysts have demonstrated the presence of other sub-areas as well.[16] All of which raises several problems about the sectional concept. For, if there were many lesser groupings within a section with antagonistic viewpoints on public policy, how could they unite so completely in the relatively short period between 1846 and 1861? If it was through a series of sectional "alliances" in which individual differences were submerged for the common good, how did these alliances act together, and were there strains and stresses which weakened their effectiveness and made it possible for other factors to operate in the political arena?[17]

In his discussions of the formation of sections in the United States, Frederick Jackson Turner stressed both the importance of mechanistic factors such as geography and climate, and of "ideals and psychology, the inherited intellectual habits derived from the stock from which the voters sprang."[18] But this list raises another question. Given the natural geographic limitations and the different cultural heritages present, could men transcend such factors and act in a nonsectional manner? If so, why could they not then continue to work with men from other geographic regions? The possibility of people from different sections cooperating was posed by Turner as an important problem, but most later students, while noting the point have concentrated on what seems to them to be more important—the growing political unity of the North and the South. They have not stressed as much the possible existence of interregional cooperation between groups in the North and groups in the South.[19]

The nature of human behavior raises another set of questions concerning sectional influence in American politics. Although we may accept the presence of important sectional forces on the American scene, it is also true that there were other, nonsectional factors which limited the free working of the sectional elements. Several American historians have commented on the presence and occasional importance of these nonsectional influences. Both Avery Craven and Charles Wiltse have noted the difficulties encountered by John C. Calhoun in the late 1840's when he attempted to unite all of the Southern congressmen against the North.[20] And, in an article in the *American Historical Review* in 1954,[21] Charles Sellers pointed out the tenacity with which Southern Whig leaders maintained their traditional party ties in the 1840's. Reluctant to cast aside their party allegiance to work with members of the opposite party in their section against whom they had fought so long, they preferred to continue to work with Whigs from the North and West rather than with Southern Democrats. Even after the sectionalizing issue of slavery extension was introduced into politics these Whigs continued in this vein, for Whigs and Democrats in each section had desires in common with their party allies which they could not forego. Thomas P. Govan has added to this argument by criticizing the assertion that the old South was different from the rest of the nation because of geographic, economic, or cultural factors.[22] Rather, said Govan, national economic and political ties transcended sectional lines and weakened sectional feelings. Govan vigorously challenged the thesis that two antagonistic sections developed because of immutable physical forces, and argued that the presence of slavery, pure and simple, produced sectionalism.

Such suggestions from Professors Sellers and Govan that the sectional theory has to be modified to a great extent if we are to fully understand the political processes of the time, lead into a deeper probing of the question of how and why men acted as they did in mid-nineteenth-century politics. If they did not react automatically to sectional stimuli, what other factors influenced political behavior?

The recent research and findings of students of political behavior can be useful for the student of ante bellum politics.[23] For example, it is a truism, confirmed by recent work in political behavior, that there is a great deal of difference in the rate of response of individuals and groups to the introduction of new influences in the political arena. However, most historians have not really given detailed attention to this difference in response rate. We know that a John C. Calhoun perceived and reacted to sectional factors quite quickly but that the average Southern representative did not. Similarly we know that some groups in a particular constituency noted and responded more quickly to sectional forces than did other groups in the same place. And we know that such differences in the rate and intensity of reaction probably had important consequences for the growth of sectional loyalty and the willingness of many to act in sectional terms. But we have not really spelled out exactly when each group and political level responded to sectional stimuli, how fast each did, what were the differences among the various responses, and most importantly, the implications of such differences for the whole sectional concept.[24]

The question of rate of response leads to a second set of questions: What are the things that move men to act or react in a particular manner—for instance, sectionally? Does everyone perceive the same facts in the same way or consider the same things as most important to them? Political behavioralists have suggested that the many factors which moved men to action—economic, political, cultural and social—transcend sectional lines. A farmer in Northern Georgia would not see all problems in the same way a Virginia tobacco planter would. Similarly a Louisiana Catholic and a North Carolina Baptist probably differed in many of their political reactions. Such factors indicate that we must know more about the context in which men perceived and reacted to the political forces—both sectional and otherwise—affecting their lives.

A third problem in understanding political behavior is in grasping the limitations placed on the operation of geographic or cultural influences by the formal institutions through which men act. At the formal level in the political realm are national political parties; the party, state and national leadership; and the machinery of Congress itself. Research into the interactions between these institutions and the individual legislator suggests that many representatives follow behavioral patterns having little to do with the demands of their sectional constituents. In one of the most fruitful areas of behavioral research in recent times, Campbell et al. have suggested the power and importance of the political party in human behavior.[25] Men see in particular parties the way to achieve desirable things. It cannot be overemphasized how limiting the presence of strong national institutions to which men reacted positively would have been on sectional reactions and behavior at any time. Frederick Jackson Turner noted the presence of two apparently strong political parties in the mid-nineteenth century and indicated that they were the product of sectional and regional alliances. Avery O. Craven had many of his students trace the breakdown of the old parties into their sectional components. But, if national political parties were important as behavioral determinants in the 1830's and 1840's, would all men easily give up their party allegiance in favor of sectional ties? If political leaders disagreed as to whether or not they should take heed of sectional influences rather than party influences, the whole political scene from the mid 1840's onward must have been complex and conflict-ridden with much hesitation, exhortation, and articulate disagreement, all of which affected the growth and importance of sectional influences in American politics.

The influence of traditional political institutions on the development of sectional points of view can at times be clearly seen. For instance, a few Western Democrats voted for the Rivers and Harbors Bill of 1846, but after President Polk vetoed it, they reversed their votes and refused to try to override the veto.[26] Apparently they placed party loyalty and the wishes of their party leader above sectional needs and loyalties.[27]

Students of political behavior have shown that cases similar to the Congressional behavior on the Rivers and Harbors Bill occur quite often. During presidential campaigns, for instance, interested people often see two distinct and meaningful behavioral factors. On the one hand voters are stimulated by traditionally relevant determinants such as party. But on the other hand, they are sometimes confronted with powerful new factors which could modify their perception of what is important and thus how they should vote in this election.[28] Such a description is relevant to our discussion. Sectional animosity arose in the mid 1840's and apparently disrupted existing political patterns. Political behavioralists have demonstrated that people react differently to such new forces. Some abandon their old allegiances while others do not. The important consideration is that differences between people do exist and prevent the immediate replacement of one set of behavioral patterns, in this case, party adherence, with another, such as sectionalism. When that is the case there are obvious limitations to any such wide-ranging concept as that concerning the importance of sectional factors in American politics.

Thus, there are many questions unanswered or imperfectly answered concerning the sectional versus the national factor in ante bellum politics. The sectional concept is vague and loosely defined. There were nonsectional variables present that appear to have been important. And, unfortunately, there is much imprecision in our scholarship as to the relative strength and importance of the conflicting forces present. All of which suggests that we have to clarify both our definitions and our understanding of political processes if we are to understand fully American history in the period before the Civil War. We can do this only by accurately ascertaining how much sectionalism existed in the period and whom it affected and to what degree. We need to discover also, who was affected, and to what degree, by nonsectional forces; and, to discover *which* nonsectional forces. When we have ascertained these things we can then determine why people reacted as they did to the phenomenon of sectionalism. The sectional concept may well be important to our understanding of the 1840's, but its full meaning at this point is obscure and only by turning back to that period with a fresh perspective can we overcome the existing fuzziness.

III

In the 1840's the American people entered a period of rapid industrial and commercial development. The two political parties of the day were quite strong and each had a clearly defined program for achieving the fullest development of the country's prospects.[29] Americans thus entered the 1840's concerned with national problems which could be solved, they believed, by using national institutions, particularly the political parties. However, the 1840's were also a time when Americans saw the rise of significant new problems. In the middle of the decade, expansionist sentiment of long standing, especially in the West, produced the Mexican War and added vast new areas to our territory.[30] These acquisitions quickly caused new problems. The demands of both Northern and Southern leaders for the fruits of the territorial conquest revitalized the slavery issue. Coupled with this, and intensifying the sectional tension, was the disappointment of Westerners at not gaining all of Oregon.

From these sectional disagreements came the Wilmot Proviso limiting slavery, the birth of the Free-Soil party, the crisis of 1850, and the compromise legislation of that year.[31] Several years of hectic activity and tension apparently sectionalized American politics to the point where the Union was endangered. Although sectional animosities abated after 1850, especially around the election of 1852, they were never again completely dormant.

The swift succession of events and the sectional problems and crises produced by them, suggest the contours of a case study. In little more than a decade Americans faced a political situation in which new forces challenged long-standing political patterns. Although we know the broad outlines of what occurred in the period there is still much we do not know about the reactions of Americans to the sectional crisis. Did mass Southern and Northern pressure build up along sectional lines in response to events and, despite the contemporary presence of nonsectional influences, cause a sharp rise in sectional unity in American politics? Or were there differences of response to the events of the 1840's, and if so, which political leaders and groups responded which way? In other words, how much or how little was American politics sectionalized by the Wilmot Proviso and its aftermath? It is in dealing with this question that our scholarship is most imprecise, conflicting, and contradictory.[32] There are various answers offered to the question of the impact and importance of sectionalism in politics. Only when we have exactly pinpointed who reacted most strongly and most rapidly to sectional pressures and who did not, so that we know precisely what the patterns of response were, will we have a more accurate knowledge of this particular period, a better understanding of the sectional process in particular, and of American political processes in general.

In his essays on sectionalism, Frederick Jackson Turner advocated the study of Congressional history as a particularly fruitful source of evidence of sectional politics and the growth of sectional discord.[33] This was an excellent suggestion since, as Turner pointed out, Congressional records are a convenient and useful source of historical knowledge. They are convenient because the actions of Congress and congressmen are to be found quite readily in the debates in which positions are outlined, and more especially in the voting on the various phases of legislation. Roll-call voting is particularly useful since there, as contrasted with the debates which precede the voting, most congressmen irrevocably commit themselves on the issue under discussion.[34] And with the voting patterns of congressmen determined as the first step, we can then proceed to carefully correlate these votes with the debates and reports of Congressional activity. We will then be in a position to understand the context in which the voting occurred, what factors apparently influenced congressmen, and how individual congressmen viewed themselves, their functions, and their relationship to the different influences present in American life. When all of these things are put together a clear picture of the facts of Congressional activity should emerge.

The study of Congress is also useful for understanding the impact of sectionalism on the American people in the 1840's. Whatever pressures and tensions exist in a country in any period, as well as any changes taking place in these pressures, are reflected in the chief legislative body of the country. In the 1840's, as always, the unorganized and organized groups in society brought pressure to bear on congressmen. In most Congressional districts each party maintained a newspaper which was read by its congressmen. In Washington also, the newspapers were primarily party organs. All of them were filled with reports of local and state party rallies and meetings of the electorate. The individual congressmen were therefore keenly aware of opinion among party leaders in their districts and states. The 1840's were also the heyday of petitioning. Through such activity individuals and groups in the electorate presented to their congressmen their views on the issues of the day.[35] United States senators also received instructions from state legislatures in this period, although the practice was dying out.[36] By using all of these contacts carefully, we have a picture of the interplay between electorate and representatives. We can follow, in the newspapers, petitions, and written instructions, any changes occurring both in the problems of individual people and in their legislative desires. Finally, when we correlate this material with the voting patterns of the individual congressmen we will have a picture of the interaction of men on different levels of political life as they confronted new issues.

Obviously, the use of roll-call votes, legislative debates, and related source material is not new. Turner, Craven, and Orrin Libby, among other historians, utilized such data and found them to be very valuable.[37] However, historians have used these sources and votes unsystematically, not covering all issues where congressmen voted. Most often historians have discussed only the few "highlight" votes they considered important after reading in an impressionistic way contemporary speeches and newspaper accounts.[38] There is a danger in such a method. Deductions based on debates and newspapers can be very misleading. In the 1840's as always, many congressmen did not speak during any given debate. Those who did were not necessarily leaders of substantial blocs of congressmen. If a series of speeches actually reflected only the public views of speakers not supported by other congressmen, then the whole sense of Congressional activity is distorted by any great reliance on such speeches. Loquacity can be mistaken for power or leadership.[39] Therefore, it is vital to begin the study of Congressional behavior with the voting itself, and then to turn to the speeches for amplification and clarification of the patterns found.

The analysis of only a limited number of roll-calls also distorts our knowledge of Congressional behavior. In any given set of circumstances, a historian may satisfy himself by selecting one or two key votes. These are usually the final votes on a particular bill. But there can be only two positions on any particular roll-call, *aye* and *nay*, and the congressman appears therefore to have been either for or against a particular bill. There is more to a congressman's position than that, however, because the question can be asked about each congressman: How much was he for, or how much was he against a bill? Congressmen may view any legislation with different quantities of approval or disapproval. Some may be absolutely against a bill under any circumstances. Others may not be so committed against, since they would accept it if it were slightly amended. Another group of congressmen may accept it only if it is amended substantially. On the other end of the scale, some congressmen may be in favor of the bill under any circumstances. Others may not be as favorable but will vote for it depending on how it is amended.[40] The number of congressmen voting for or against a measure varies depending on the nature of the amendments to the bill. Thus the maneuvering over a bill is important because the result of the fighting and amending determines the number of votes the bill will receive.[41] The voting on all of the amendments to a single piece of legislation is more important in revealing the attitudes of individual congressmen than just the single final vote.

In addition to analyzing each issue separately, we must also include as many issues in our analysis as is necessary for us to see the whole of Congressional behavior. If congressmen reacted to sectional forces in their voting on one issue, does this necessarily mean that sectional forces were important on all issues? And if sectionalism was important only on certain issues, what other influences were present? The only way we can have a complete picture of the congressmen's behavior as well as of the nature of the sectional challenge is by answering these questions. And to do this we need some method of bringing together and studying all of the pertinent Congressional votes.

IV

In recent years social scientists have developed several methods designed to reveal and rank people's attitudes towards particular subjects.[42] One of these methods, the Guttman scalogram, has been particularly useful in the study of roll-call behavior.[43] Central to the concept behind the scalogram is the assumption that the individual congressman is usually quite consistent in his voting behavior. A senator, for example, unless unusually quixotic, or suddenly confronted with new pressures or conditions, will almost certainly not vote in favor of a national bank on one roll-call and then reverse himself and vote against the bank at the next opportunity.[44] Similarly, his attitudes on foreign affairs or other matters of domestic policy will not suddenly be reversed from one roll-call to the next. He will be consistent because the pressures influencing him in the first instance will also influence his next and most of his subsequent votes as well. Although his attitude may change over time, the change will probably be gradual, not sudden.

However, a legislator's attitude towards a particular measure is only one dimension of his total behavior. We may know the senator favored a national bank or was quite militant in foreign affairs, but we do not know how strongly he favored the bank or how militant he was in comparison with all other senators. The Guttman scalogram meets the problem by showing how each congressman voted as compared to all other congressmen along a scale of attitudes ranging from most in favor of some particular area of legislation to most against. This is done by first ascertaining the individual congressman's votes on all of the amendments to and versions of the type of legislation under consideration—financial matters or foreign affairs or slavery—and then placing him and his responses on a scale along with all of the other congressmen and their responses.[45] The result will be a summary chart of a great deal of crude data. The advantage of this chart and of the scaling procedure is that it incorporates into a single, readily perceived pattern a large amount of otherwise unmanageable and complex information. And the scale does more than this. It also serves "as a kind of ideological measuring stick which divides a group of men not just into two categories as would happen if only one division were used, but into a series of graduated steps which are defined in the concrete terms of the votes men cast for or against various proposals. It thus provides an instrument for measuring . . . attitudes which is both comprehensive in the amount of information it includes and refined in the number of gradations or nuances that it reveals."[46] The scale, in other words, permits us to go beyond the usual gross and impressionistic assertion of a man's attitude (for example, that so and so is a liberal) to accurately delineate where and with whom a legislator stands.[47] With this information in hand we can then proceed to ascertain why congressmen voted in these patterns instead of in some others.[48]

It should be stressed at this point, of course, that the scaling procedure is simply a mechanical device for ordering a certain type of material. It does not pretend to answer the basic question of why a particular pattern occurred. Such ordering of quantitative data is only the important preliminary operation which lays a foundation for understanding the vast amount of qualitative data available concerning the 1840's. To determine why the voting patterns occurred as they did, we still must isolate the determinants of legislative behavior present and correlate them with the voting patterns. Since most historians consider sectionalism a major, if not the most important, influence in American politics (at least after 1846), we should compare the voting of the individual congressmen with their sectional affiliations. As noted above, some historians have also emphasized the importance of subregions and intersectional and sectional alliances as well as the main sectional breakdown of North versus South, and East versus West. Therefore we should test for these patterns as well. Finally, since most historians agree that national political parties played an important role in American history in the 1820's and 1830's[49] and recent research further suggests that parties, despite their nonsectional character, are perhaps the most important political influence shaping people's behavior, we also have to measure the extent of party voting in Congress.[50] This is especially important since the historians of sectionalism claim that the events of the 1840's disrupted and sectionalized the two major parties. If this was so, the roll-call voting should reveal it.

Although historians have identified sections and parties as the two major political influences of the 1840's, local and district problems and conditions may also play a role in political behavior that lies outside the framework of parties or sections. Such things as the narrowness of political contests and the ecological makeup of districts could be involved. In addition, irrational and emotional factors may influence behavior; however, the extent to which we can determine such influences is limited. In the case of irrational factors we can perhaps suggest some and guess at others. In the case of purely local considerations, our knowledge is limited and is likely to remain so until local historians have looked more thoroughly at political behavior on levels below that of nation and section. But knowledge of local and personal influences on political behavior may not be as vital to our work as it appears at first glance. We have to ascertain the importance of such factors to be sure, but it remains moot as to how many of the actors on the Congressional stage reacted to variables other than parties or sections. Further, many of these irrational and local factors were probably part of the larger influences that made up the sectional and party variables. And until historians have completed more work in the area of political influences in the 1840's we cannot refine the question *why?* more than we have here. Until then, it is hoped that the level of analysis in this study will be an improvement over our present knowledge and may, as such, serve a useful purpose in historical scholarship.

2. PARTY CONFLICT IN AMERICAN POLITICS, 1840–1850

I N recent years political scientists have repeatedly demonstrated that in the United States the party loyalty of individual voters is deep-rooted and tenacious.[1] Contemporary students of Congress have added that "at least in the act of voting, the party label is consistently the most reliable predicator of a legislator's actions."[2] All of this is, of course, because political parties serve a purpose. They are agencies in the words of V. O. Key, "for the translation of mass preferences into public policy."[3] Obviously, then, in order to understand the politics of an era as thoroughly as possible, we should evaluate the role played by existing national political parties.

Unhappily, most studies that stress the importance of political parties draw their evidence from recent times. The work of the University of Michigan Survey Research Center is based on the period since 1948; David Truman's work is on the 81st Congress of 1949–1951. We may assume that what they say about recent politics is true; but can we apply their generalizations to the 1840's? Had political parties developed by 1840 to the point where they fulfilled the national role which political behavioralists give them today, or were they just meaningless coalitions unable to withstand the pressure of sectional forces?[4] A look at the strength, distribution, and appeal of the parties of the day will put them into perspective for testing their influence and importance as a political alternative to sectionalism.

According to many historians, two well-established political parties existed in the United States by the 1840's.[5] The Democratic party had emerged during the previous twenty years, attaining unity and strength under Andrew Jackson and Martin Van Buren.[6] At the same time, the party's policies had led to a reaction against it and the growth, in opposition, of the Whig party.[7] Two parties were obviously present and functioning on the national scene as well as on the state level.[8] Furthermore, presidential election returns between 1836 and 1852 indicate that the two parties were remarkably stable in their vote and that the contests between them were very close:[9]

TABLE 2.1
Percentages of National Presidential Votes, 1836–1852

	Democrats	*Whigs*	*Others**
1836	50.9	49.1	—
1840	46.8	52.9	0.3
1844	49.5	48.1	2.4
1848	42.5	47.3	10.2
1852	50.7	43.9	5.4

* In 1840 and 1844, the Liberty party. In 1848 and 1852, the Free-Soil party.

The extreme closeness of the national returns reflected a growing balance between the two parties, as compared to the previous period. During the Jacksonian era, as Richard McCormick has shown, average differences between the two parties nationally were 11 per cent as compared to only 4.2 per cent in the subsequent period.[10] We can place these figures in perspective by comparing them with similar averages from recent presidential elections. The Democrats won four of five elections. In these the average difference between the two parties was 11.4 per cent and this was after 100 years of party conflict and the emergence of a supposedly mature two-party system. By contrast, in the 1840's the people of the country were divided more closely into two stable parties.

This stability extended below the national level. If we divide the country into the eight regional blocs used by the United States Census Bureau,[11] we find a strong two-party system in every region (Table 2.2). One party's percentage of the total vote cast exceeded 60 per cent only twice. Most of the time, the percentage margin between parties was relatively narrow. Furthermore, if we look at the party percentages broken down into historians' definitions of sections—North, South, and Old Northwest—we find similar results. The Democrats averaged 52.6 per cent of the total popular vote in the South while the Whigs averaged 46.8 per cent. In the Old Northwest, Democrats averaged 48.4 per cent and the Whigs 47.5 per cent. In the North, the Democrats had a 47.1 per cent average and the Whigs had 48.4 per cent (Table 2.3). Obviously, on these lower levels of politics there were stable two-party divisions. We could continue this analysis down to the state level with similar results. The point is that each party had a relatively secure popular following on the presidential level.[12]

We can further demonstrate party presence during the 1840's by examining the results of congressional elections. In every section of

TABLE 2.2
Percentages of Presidential Votes by
Regions, 1836–1852

	1836	*1840*	*1844*	*1848*	*1852*
New England					
Democrats	51.7	44.9	45.6	36.8	44.0
Whigs	48.3	54.5	47.1	43.6	41.7
Others		.6	7.3	19.6	14.3
Middle Atlantic					
Democrats	53.0	48.8	49.5	35.9	50.9
Whigs	47.0	50.8	48.3	49.2	45.5
Others		.4	2.2	14.9	3.6
East North Central					
Democrats	48.0	46.3	49.7	46.6	50.1
Whigs	52.0	53.5	47.6	42.1	42.2
Others		.2	2.7	11.3	6.7
West North Central					
Democrats	60.6	56.8	57.0	53.9	54.4
Whigs	39.4	43.2	43.0	45.0	44.1
Others				1.1	1.5
South Atlantic					
Democrats	51.0	46.0	49.9	48.0	53.9
Whigs	49.0	54.0	50.1	52.0	46.1
East South Central					
Democrats	47.4	44.0	51.2	46.8	52.6
Whigs	52.6	56.0	48.8	53.2	47.3
West South Central					
Democrats	55.5	46.4	55.5	53.7	60.3
Whigs	44.2	53.6	44.5	46.3	39.7

the country substantial numbers of congressmen were elected from
both parties in the Twenty-seventh through Thirty-second Congresses

TABLE 2.3
Percentages of Presidential Votes by
Historians' Definitions of Sections, 1836–1852

	1836	1840	1844	1848	1852
South					
Democrats	49.5	45.1	50.9	48.0	54.8
Whigs	50.5	54.9	49.1	52.0	45.2
Old Northwest					
Democrats	48.7	47.4	51.7	47.4	50.5
Whigs	51.3	52.6	48.3	42.5	42.4
Others				10.1	7.1
North					
Democrats	52.6	47.7	50.1	36.2	48.9
Whigs	47.4	52.3	49.9	47.5	44.4
Others				16.3	6.3

(Table 2.4). In the 1840's, in congressional voting as in presidential,
we do not find the one-party sections we find in later periods of
American history. In several states, although the elected congressmen usually were from only one party, there was always substantial
minority party opposition. If we extended our analysis further, we
could clarify and develop these points. But we can draw the essential
conclusion, that in congressional voting, as in presidential, two strong
parties existed.

In the 1840's, then, each party was national in scope and not confined to particular sections or localities. This was true for both presidential and congressional elections and seems to hold for other elections as well. It is true that in some states and localities one party or
another had a substantial majority but members of the minority party
were also present.[13]

The division of the American people into two large and stable
national parties during elections is only one aspect of our inquiry into
the presence of political parties in the 1840's. It is entirely possible
that these statistics conceal much about politics. It may be true that
there were many Whig and Democratic voters throughout the country,

but does that mean that people voted for the same policies and principles in every part of the country? Or did the party mean something
different in one section from what it meant in another? We must de-

TABLE 2.4
Congressmen by Party and Section,
27th to 32nd Congresses

	27	*28*	*29*	*30*	*31*	*32*
New England						
Democrats	10	16	9	9	11	12
Whigs	27	14	19	20	15	17
Others	—	—	2	2	4	2
Middle Atlantic						
Democrats	29	37	37	19	13	36
Whigs	34	22	20	37	47	23
Others	—	4	6	7	3	1
South Atlantic						
Democrats	31	29	38	25	31	33
Whigs	29	15	9	22	16	12
Others	—	—	—	—	—	5
South West						
Democrats	19	26	31	30	31	26
Whigs	19	11	12	13	13	13
Others	1	—	1	1	—	4
Old Northwest						
Democrats	9	28	32	26	27	26
Whigs	21	13	11	17	15	15
Others	—	—	—	—	1	2

termine, in other words, if each party had a common program which
was acceptable to people everywhere. Only if each party did, could
historians' contentions that national political parties were an important
behavioral influence be valid.

II

Students of current political behavior believe that contemporary
party battles are meaningful contests because each party stands for
different goals and each appeals to different groups in the electorate.
But were the political parties of the 1840's similarly divided? We can

answer this by answering two further questions about party coalitions in post-Jacksonian America: Did different groups and individuals in American politics support one party or the other because their goals and desires differed from the goals and desires of those who supported the other party?[14] And, as a result of this, did the two major parties, in their quest for votes, stand for and publicly espouse different programs?[15]

Although most American historians agree that two parties existed in the 1840's, some have alleged that the contests between the two meant little. Party conflicts, to quote Charles Sydnor's discussion of the South, "had the hollow sound of a stage duel with tin swords."[16] A few historians have even suggested that party members stayed together and fought against their opponents not because of different principles but merely to win offices.[17] Even Glyndon Van Deusen, at the end of an article on the various aspects of Whig party thought, policies, and program, in which he stressed differences from the Democrats, concluded that the "political conflicts of the Jacksonian period were fought more often with a view to gaining control of the government than out of devotion to diametrically opposed political and social ideals."[18]

In contrast to these views, other historians have seen the divisions between the two parties as both real and long standing, and not just a battle for control of patronage.[19] Certainly political leaders of the period were quite concerned because many Americans remained loyal to their parties even after the sectional uproar began. Late in the 1840's as the slavery-expansion crisis deepened, Southern statesmen complained bitterly of the adverse effect party adherence had on sectional unity.[20] Although there may have been splits within each party, apparently people still believed that the parties themselves stood for something and that there were real differences between those called Whigs and those called Democrats.

Obviously the controversy about political parties has created a great deal of confusion. Ante bellum political historians have drawn their interpretations mainly from contemporary personal manuscript data, particularly the letters and other writings of political leaders. But such data do not reflect all aspects of the historical experience and exclusive reliance on such material may lead to confusion and distortion of reality.[21] It may be true, as so many suggest, that most political leaders were fighting for nothing more than patronage and spoils. But was this also true of their followers? These other members of the two political parties are quite often overlooked. We have to know something, in other words, about mass voting behavior before we can understand what parties meant.[22] The leaders could not appeal to the electorate only on the basis of winning the spoils of office. Not everyone among the 2.4 million people who voted in the presidential election of 1840 voted simply to obtain patronage. People vote for a complex of economic, cultural, and psychological factors. As Lee Benson has indicated, these factors fall into three main categories: pursuit of political goals by individuals or groups, individual or group fulfillment of political roles, and negative or positive orientation to reference individuals or groups.[23] Each party has to stand for some combination of these motives in order to attract voters to it.

Individual voting, then, is shaped by various combinations of influences, and political leaders try to win votes by playing on as many of these as possible. In the 1840's the leaders appeared to make their appeals through the two national parties. Each group of leaders identified its party as the one which would win desired legislation. Once the leaders had attracted voters through such appeals they tried to maintain voter identification with their party by legislating those things which the party membership desired.[24] Thus, we begin to see how the presence of strong national parties in the 1830's and 1840's could have played a significant role in the behavior of individual congressmen. Congressmen were the products of the complexities of party identification. They were elected, presumably, by voters who responded to a particular set of social influences expressed through one of the parties. The congressmen would also respond to these influences in order to give to the voters what they wanted, especially if they, the congressmen, wanted to appeal to this same electorate for re-election.[25]

We must know still more about political parties and their relationship to legislation, however. For instance, what kind of issues divided them? Analysts can answer this question when they, to use Lee Benson's word, "saturate" themselves in the pronouncements, appeals and demands of the groups and individuals making up each party. The major source for this saturation is national, state, and local party platforms and resolutions, and petitions from the electorate.[26] Although it has long been fashionable to dismiss much of this material as "buncombe," we should remember that each party was trying to attract as many votes as possible and platforms were one major source of attraction. The voter responded to the platform appeal because he expected party representatives to attempt to carry out their pronouncements.[27] Thus this material seems to be a fruitful source for determining what parties meant to the voters and what was the basis of each party's appeal.

The legislative demands of the people in the 1830's and 1840's reflected their reactions to the era in which they lived, an era of rapid geographic and economic growth.[28] After 1815, the country entered a long period of peace and internal development, characterized by the growth of commercial agriculture, industry, and population.[29] The especially rapid economic growth during the 1830's led to over-investment, culminating in a severe depression between 1837 and 1843. After 1843, however, the American economy entered a new phase of rapid, sustained growth and maturation.[30] In less than a century after breaking their colonial bonds, the American people had started a rise to international economic affluence and leadership.

Along with the country's economic growth there was intensive land settlement and a rapid population increase. In 1815, the American people numbered 8.4 million. By 1850 they numbered 23.2 million, an increase of almost 300 per cent in 35 years. Western growth was particularly marked throughout the period. In 1820 there were only 792,719 people in the Old Northwest, but by 1850 they numbered 5,523,260. In addition, two new Wests had formed—one along the Pacific Coast and one across the Mississippi River.[31]

In concert with the country's rapid expansion and development, articulate leaders expressed great optimism for the future. Since the United States was so fully endowed these leaders concerned themselves with only one major problem. They wanted to stimulate this continual growth as much as possible by utilizing all available resources. They particularly desired that government and private enterprise work together to further the expansion process. They sought to discover what legislation and institutions were needed to allow the American people to quickly and fully reach their "manifest destiny."[32]

Discussions as to the best means of reaching particular goals permeated all levels of the community. The frontier farmer and the urban industrialist were united in their desire for rapid development.

This desire for internal development influenced political parties. In the course of the country's expansion different groups formed and demanded programs that would further their own economic and social development.[33] Their opposition to each other led to political coalitions to push forward common needs. By the late 1830's the American people had organized two parties, each of which presented different policy demands in its platform and in the election of 1840 the electorate's commitment to the party system appeared complete.[34]

Historians have pointed out that even after the parties developed, each of them was badly split, with factional warring often more intense than the interparty disputes. However, we may possibly have exaggerated such factionalism. We know that the Democratic party contained a Van Buren wing and a Calhoun wing which engaged in an especially bitter conflict in the early 1840's.[35] But in emphasizing such struggles we may overlook or play down the possibility that in a strong two-party situation where differences between the parties were real and passionate, the participants in intraparty disputes might put aside their differences when they faced the other party.[36] Factionalism might not be as important as the bonds party members had in common.

We have, then, a situation in the United States in which two well-balanced political parties apparently played a significant role. But what did each party stand for and how did each try to win support? The Democratic party first presented a national party platform in 1840, the Whigs in 1844.[37] But party groups on the local level had issued platforms during the 1830's and early 1840's quite similar in their policy demands and general outlook to the later national platforms of each party.[38] Because of the relative internal unity on local and national platforms, we can see what images the parties projected, what programs they supported, and the guidelines they set for their representatives to follow in public arenas.

Lee Benson, among other historians, has pointed out that in the 1830's and 1840's, the two major political parties generally agreed that the government—federal, state and local—played a major role in the American economic system. Both parties sought legislative enactments which would promote the economic growth of different groups on the American scene.[39] Differences between the parties developed over what specifically the government should do to promote the general welfare.[40] As Oscar Handlin has written, the issues of American economic policy "were not whether the government had or had not a role in the economy, but, what was to be the character of its role, what agencies were to exercise it, who was to control it, and in whose interests it was to operate."[41] Thus the party leaders never engaged in some simple conflict, in the popular sense, between government intervention in the economy on one hand and *laissez faire* on the other. Rather, since each party contained different constituent groups, each group making specific demands, the party leaders contended for different specific benefits from the government. These specific demands were the basis of each party's platform proposals in the period.

The Democrats, during this optimistic age of expansion, wanted the government, in Professor William Appleman Williams' words, "to maintain the basic framework of a system (such as that of money and the rule of law); it had to preserve the competitive situation by acting against monopolies and by helping new or weak entrants into the scramble; and it had to be the agent of expanding and protecting the market place, which was the key to the individual competition producing the general welfare."[42] Democratic rhetoric outlined a program of legislation to protect small economic and social units from the twin monsters of monopoly and special privilege, thereby allowing all enterprises to share in America's future.

To accomplish this, the Democrats wanted some of the governmental aids to special privilege permanently removed. Their program called for no national bank and no protective tariff, and endorsed the idea of a small, well-run, efficient government. Such a program, the Democrats claimed, would allow full development of the country, for it permitted the free play of those natural economic forces which had originally made the country great.

The Democrats thus visualized as the government's positive role the guaranteeing of the free play of natural forces and the prevention of the growth of hampering "unnatural" forces. During the depression of the early forties, Senator George McDuffie of South Carolina introduced a series of resolutions concerning the role of the government during this crisis. He pointed out that here was an "unexampled spectacle," a country with "unbounded resources . . . all of the blessings that a beneficent Providence can confer upon a people," and yet it was involved throughout its area "in one universal scene of distress."[43] To meet this emergency he wanted Congress to adopt measures of governmental retrenchment, to end the public debt, to cut expenditures so they would not exceed income, to reduce the amount of currency in circulation, and to lower the tariff to one designed solely to raise revenue.[44] He thought that when the government did all of this, the natural economic forces within the United States would be freed from restraint and would then be able to bring the country out of its crisis. In general terms, McDuffie's proposals reflected much of what the Jacksonian party had stood for since the late 1820's and early 1830's.

The Whigs, on the other hand, had a quite different conception of the role of the federal government in the 1830's and 1840's. A writer in the *Whig Almanac* warned that the government "need not and should not be an institution of purely negative, repressive influence." Rather, the government "should exert a beneficent, paternal, fostering influence upon the Industry and Prosperity of the People." To accomplish this, all legitimate powers of the federal government should be exercised to the limit through tariffs, banks, and related measures to foster the full development of American society. Lee Benson has characterized the Whig attitude toward the federal government as "thou shalt."[45]

Central to any economic system are, of course, financial institutions which stimulate credit and carry on the myriad of other financial operations necessary in a capitalist system. Such financial institutions were extremely important in a period of rapid economic development where ample surplus venture capital and credit were vital. The two parties, however, had long divided over who should control any such institutions and what kind of institutions they should be.[46] Since the Democrats' successful destruction of the Bank of the United States in the 1830's, there had been no central governmental financial institution.[47] Instead, the Democrats were determined to create a government-controlled independent treasury as America's only central financial institution and to prevent the creation of another central bank.

Alabama Democrats pointed out that no farmer or mechanic had ever needed a bank. Rather, it was "the adventurer who needs a bank."[48] The only financial institution necessary was a limited house-keeping and credit facility free from the control of the money-power in the United States.[49] Although Democrats had differed over financial policy earlier, by 1841 there was a close relationship on the national level between their hatred of central banking and their support of the independent treasury.[50]

The Whigs' major demand in the financial realm was a government-sponsored national bank. They insisted that the country's economic stability depended upon a sound national currency and a strong central bank. They condemned the Democrats' support of hard money and a limited financial collection agency as dangerous and inadequate. After all, the natural workings of the economy could be stimulated and improved by a judicious banking policy. The Whigs intensified their demands for a bank during the crisis period after the Panic of 1837. In their platform in 1841, the Louisiana Whigs called the national bank the most important part of the Whig program. The Whig leadership brought bank legislation forward before anything else as soon as they took power in 1841.[51]

The parties also divided over tariff policy, which to John C. Calhoun was "the most vital of all questions."[52] The Democrats did not want the federal government to use the tariff to favor one branch of the economy at the expense of another. They especially did not want domestic manufacturing products protected against foreign competition. This, they claimed, would be oppressive to the simple mechanics and farmers of the country who needed to buy manufactured goods cheaply. A protective tariff would also oppress the export agricultural interests, which depended on free-flowing trade and unhampered commerce with England and Europe.[53] Most Democrats realized that some tariff duties were necessary for government revenue and therefore they called for a tariff for revenue only.[54] Until 1846 they did not define how high such a tariff should be, however. Before that, some Democrats wanted to maintain the low rates of the compromise tariff of 1833 while others advocated either lower or higher duties than those of 1833. Although the Democrats themselves differed over how high tariff duties should be, almost all of them called for lower rates than did the Whig party.[55]

The Whigs differed from the Democrats on the function of the tariff system. "The Whig doctrine," said the *Whig Almanac*, "affirms that the Government ought to protect and cherish the Industry of the country to the fullest extent, as a matter of legitimate and necessary concern."[56] The *Almanac*'s writer said that the different groups within American society complemented one another, and did not, as the Democrats insisted, conflict with each other. The tariff was one of the instruments of this complementary relationship. When portions of industry and agriculture were protected, they were protected from the competition of cheap European labor, thereby safeguarding the jobs of American labor. Furthermore, with the growth of American industry, thanks to tariff protection, the agricultural entrepreneurs of the United States would be able to sell their products in the new markets of expanding factory towns and urban centers. Thus, while the tariff only protected one section of the economy directly, it helped all of the American people indirectly by stimulating further development, and promoted both the general prosperity and the general welfare. However, the Whigs asserted that the Democratic tariff policy would hamper the development of the country and even lead to stagnation.[57] During the prostration of the American economy after 1837, some Southern Whigs in particular, added a new theme to the case for a higher tariff. They claimed that only with a raise in custom rates would the government receive enough revenue to keep us out of bankruptcy.[58]

Whigs and Democrats also differed during the 1830's and 1840's over how to dispose of revenues from sale of public land. Land sales contributed a substantial amount of money to the federal treasury as the government sold $64\frac{1}{2}$ million acres of public land between 1830 and 1840.[59] During the prosperous 1830's Democratic leaders, who feared a government with too much financial power, worried constantly about too much surplus revenue in the government's coffers and proposed a variety of plans to deal with it. Although the problem disappeared after 1837 when land receipts fell off, the Democrats continued to worry about surplus money and its relation to the tariff. If land receipts dropped off or land were given away as the Whigs proposed, the government would have only tariff duties as a steady source of revenue. Therefore, Democratic leaders were seriously concerned that tariff rates might be raised.[60]

Many Democrats, particularly in the new states, wanted the government to liberalize land policy. They sought lower land prices, easier credit in land sales, and government protection of the "squatters" on unsurveyed land. They particularly demanded legislation to graduate land prices and to permit pre-emption. They said that such policies would bring more money to the government because the government would be able to dispose of previously unsold marginal land. At the same time a liberal land policy would not necessarily lower the prices of better lands.[61]

The Whigs believed that the receipts from land sales performed several functions. Public lands were the common property of all of the states and receipts from their sale should be returned to the states to aid local internal improvement construction programs. Thus, instead of being dissipated as part of the federal treasury, land receipts would be used to insure America's continued progress.[62] In addition, some Whigs tied land policy to the tariff. In a speech before Congress in 1845, Whig representative William Thomason of Kentucky characterized the protective tariff as necessary to American prosperity. Therefore, he was unalterably opposed to "the sales of public lands forming a part of the national revenue." He wanted the government to distribute sales receipts to the states and to discourage further land purchasing by maintaining a conservative sales program. If this were done, the government would have to keep the tariff high in order to have sufficient revenue.[63]

The expressed views of two parties on internal improvements were the last major policy difference between them. In a rapidly developing economic system people in both coastal and interior areas needed an adequate transportation network. But whose responsibility was it to build, operate, and improve the necessary facilities? The Democrats answered the question in their platforms from 1840 onward when they resolved "that the Constitution does not confer upon the general government the power to commence and carry on a general system of internal improvements."[64] As Lee Benson has pointed out, this had been a cardinal tenet of Martin Van Buren's republicanism even before 1820, and the Democrats continued to accept it, despite some dissent, in the 1840's.[65] The Whigs contended that neither cost nor fear of excess government power should be the controlling influence in an internal improvements policy. Rather, they said, if a project benefited all the people the government should finance it. They looked with favor "upon works of Internal Improvement, regarding them as calculated and intended to give employment to Labor, secure a market to produce, and contribute generally and vastly to the physical improvement of the country and its advancement in Art, Civilization, and Morality."[66]

I have discussed only the main aspects of the national programs of the two parties in the 1830's and 1840's. Certainly, the parties fought over other issues, such as foreign affairs, immigration, "moral" legislation, the power of the central government in specific situations, and many local issues. But with one or two exceptions these issues did not play as vital a role in Congress in the early 1840's, in the midst of a depression, as did those already discussed.[67] However, when they did arise later in the decade, as we shall see, the two parties tended to take opposing points of view in these matters too. Furthermore, several new economic issues came before Congress in the early 1840's, primarily in response to immediate economic and social conditions. On these matters the two parties again differed. For instance, when the Whigs came to power in 1841, they advocated a federal bankruptcy law to cover both individuals and corporations, even though traditionally the states had been responsible for such legislation. Many of the Whigs wanted the federal government to assume state debts also.[68] The Democrats opposed both ideas.[69]

During the 1840's, therefore, the parties, reflecting the groups composing their membership, advocated two separate courses of public action to deal with the economic and financial issues before the country. These different courses were made especially meaningful by the depression after 1837. Although it did no more than delay the growth of the American economy, the depression was a severe shock to the American people.[70] As prices of agricultural goods fell drastically there was strong reaction, especially in politics.[71] Recent political behavior studies have shown that depression conditions create a situation in which fundamental and long-lasting political reorientations take place.[72] The reaction to the conditions of 1837–1843 was not as fundamental or continuing as in more recent depressions, partially because the depression did not last very long. But there was an immediate and sharp political impact that affected Congress during the first half of the 1840's.

This impact occurred in two major ways. First, it helped decide contests for election to Congress. Second, it revitalized several public policy differences dormant since the early 1830's. As we have learned from recent periods of economic distress, most people blame the depression's effects on the party in power. In the late 1830's and early 1840's the American people reacted in the same way. The Democrat Martin Van Buren was President when the depression first hit in 1837 and a strongly Democratic Congress followed his lead. The Democrats' response to popular demands for relief was quite limited in scope. At a time when states felt a financial pinch from overenthusiastic internal improvement programs, and individuals felt the burden of increased debts and bank failures, the Democratic administration refused to deal with the demands engendered by the situation. They issued, rather, a long series of warnings against positive federal action to directly bolster the economy. The Whigs eagerly attacked these Democratic policies as the cause of the continued national distress.[73] Several historians have attributed local, statewide, and congressional Democratic defeats to the depression and to these Whig attacks.[74]

In 1837 the Democrats lost seats in Congress, then regained some in 1838 as the economy partially recovered. Finally, the Whigs routed their opponents in the congressional elections of 1840 and 1841. The Whig congressional triumph was coupled with the election in 1840 of the first Whig president, William Henry Harrison.[75] Once in power, the Whigs determined to present a program of positive federal action to overcome the depression. This program included a bank to restore the country's financial structure and a protective tariff to help put the economy back on its feet, two pieces of legislation which were to be their cornerstones for complete recovery.[76] The Whigs were pushing forward policy lines which the Democrats had traditionally opposed. As the Whig-controlled Congress met in 1841 the opposing congressmen squared off for a vigorous and bitter fight.

In this chapter I have attempted to explain the political context within which congressmen acted during the first part of the 1840's. The two parties were at the center of this situation. Both the Whigs and

Democrats had a strong national following and advocated different so-lutions to the country's problems. The divisions between parties appeared to be very real to party members, for the differences reflected real conditions within society. Party identification appears to be an important variable to measure in Congressional voting.

Party membership was not necessarily the only important political influence in the 1840's, however. Historians have indicated that a sectional political framework also existed in the United States in this period, more important, in their view, than party differences. Furthermore, these sectional differences apparently grew more influential as the 1840's passed. Before we turn to Congress, therefore, we should examine the contours of sectionalism as a force in American life during this time of clearly vigorous national political division.

3. SECTIONAL CONFLICT IN AMERICAN POLITICS, 1840–1850

D E S P I T E the tumult of political party activity in the middle of the nineteenth century, most American historians have emphasized the overriding influence of sectionalism in American politics in that period.[1] They have stressed the many geographic, economic, cultural, and psychological differences between the sections which, in their view, permitted sectional leaders to forge a unified sectional viewpoint in national affairs, particularly in periods of conflict between the regions of the United States.[2] Several writers have pinpointed the 1840's as one such period of intense internal strain. Then, the Congressional controversy over expansion allegedly stimulated the disintegration of the national political parties into their sectional components.[3] How this happened has been spelled out in some detail.

The South's basic sectional viewpoint apparently stemmed from the implications of its economic system. To understand the South, Professor Ulrich B. Phillips wrote, one must first consider the weather which was "the chief agency in making the South distinctive. It fostered the cultivation of the staple crops, which promoted the plantation system, which brought the importation of negroes, which not only gave rise to chattel slavery but created a lasting race problem. These led to controversy and regional rivalry for power, which produced apprehensive reactions and culminated in a stroke for independence."[4]

The development of a Southern sectional viewpoint in national affairs thus began when men had utilized the existing weather conditions and resources to develop a Southern economic and social system. Sectional leaders then sought ways to maintain what had been built as well as to develop their section further.

By the 1840's the South was primarily an area of specialized agricultural production. Although there had been a fairly diversified crop system before the 1820's, major Southern production was later concentrated in several staple crops.[5] The leading staple was cotton; tobacco, rice, and sugar were less important. Historians and economists have repeatedly stressed the importance of cotton production because of its major function both in the South and in the nation as a whole. From the 1790's onward, Southerners had devoted more land to the crop and increased their production from 17,500 bales of cotton each year in the 1790's to 1.9 million bales in the 1840's. Several things contributed to this constant expansion: markets, the profitability of cotton investments, the availability of land, the ease of cultivation, and the efficient utilization of a cheap labor force of Negro slaves. Southerners raised cotton on both large plantations and small, nonslave farms.[6] Although many Southerners grew other crops, cotton producing was their most important endeavor. As Paul Gates has pointed out, nothing "was permitted to interfere with producing cotton."[7]

Outside the areas in which cotton could be grown, other farmers also engaged in some form of staple agriculture. Here, too, Negro slaves were the major work force. In the border states commercial farmers produced tobacco; along the Gulf coast they raised sugar; in other areas farmers grew rice and hemp for market. There were, in addition, many varieties of noncommercial agriculture in the South.[8] But in terms of wealth and economic leadership staple agriculture dominated the Southern economy of the 1840's, with cotton production the most important facet of the system. At this time most Southerners showed great antipathy and animosity towards other economic activities, as they exalted their own agricultural way of life.[9] In the South there was an almost complete lack of manufacturing development and only a primitive commercial enterprise. As long as staple agriculture remained profitable, Southern leaders had few incentives or opportunities to break the mold of their section's economic life.

The economic life of the Old Northwest during the same period was both superficially similar to and different from that of the South. The West, like the South, was primarily an agricultural region. Instead of cotton, Northwestern farmers produced mainly wheat, corn, and other provisions. Despite their later development, the various states of the Old Northwest had already outdistanced the leading Eastern centers in wheat and corn production and, in the Ohio Valley, farmers were developing a stock-raising industry.[10] In general, Westerners engaged in a more diversified agriculture than did Southerners, with a work force composed almost exclusively of yeomen farmers. By the 1840's, however, wheat production was becoming predominant in the Ohio Valley. As in the South, moreover, few Westerners engaged in manufacturing and commerce.

Although Western agriculture was more diversified than was Southern, both based their growth on staple crop production. Farmers in both sections shared the idea of producing a marketable surplus and developing a commercial agriculture.[11] Although the farmers needed capital, cheap transportation, and markets for such development, it was their quest for markets which is particularly relevant to the impact of sectional forces on political activity in the 1840's.[12]

At first, in the 1790's, cotton farmers did not have a developed market for their cotton in the United States because of the dearth of textile mills in the country. Their major markets were in England. Although the Northeast had rapidly industrialized in the years after 1790 and had developed a textile manufacturing industry,[13] cotton producers continued to sell most of their raw cotton in England. By the 1840's cotton growers sold 64 per cent of their crop to English manufacturers and only 29 per cent to Northern factories. The English demand for Southern cotton steadily increased, assuring the cotton producer of a large, steady, available market.[14]

The cotton marketing pattern profoundly affected Western development. As Southerners devoted more and more of their energies to cotton production for the expanding English market they had to import foodstuffs from wherever they could. This gave the Western wheat farmers their great opportunity and they supplied the South with the needed provisions. By the 1840's, Western farmers were the main suppliers of food to the South.[15] Western wheat producers thus had a large and expanding home market.

Western wheat production in the Ohio Valley developed so intensively to supply this market that by the 1840's production outstripped consumption. In 1846, Senator Sidney Breese of Illinois called attention to this overproduction when he asserted that ten counties of Illinois could supply the entire home market as it then stood. The West needed and wanted the "market of the world" for its foodstuffs.[16] The Western farmers' needs were especially acute because of the drop in wheat prices during the depression after 1837. Wheat prices fell from an average of $1.92 per bushel in 1838 to $1.05 per bushel in 1840.[17] At the same time, Southern cotton prices fell precipitously, prompting many Southerners to consider growing grain again instead of cotton. Westerners were frightened by their overproduction and their failing markets. Some of them turned towards foreign markets as a means of selling their surplus and keeping domestic prices up.[18] Increasingly, during the 1840's, Westerners, like Southerners, sought markets outside of the United States for their surplus products.

In addition to markets, both Westerners and Southerners were troubled by the lack of adequate and cheap transportation facilities. Americans had always relied upon the country's waterways to meet their transit needs.[19] Whether by the flatboats of the 1820's or the steamboats in their "golden age" in the 1850's, farmers moved their goods primarily on the rivers throughout the ante bellum era. Southern cotton producers were fortunate because their navigable rivers ran to the Atlantic Ocean and the Gulf of Mexico, where their cotton was picked up by waiting sailing ships.[20] In the Old Northwest farmers transported their goods down the Ohio and Mississippi Rivers and their numerous tributaries. Although Americans had tried other means of transportation, rivers and their feeder canals were still the major source of cheap transportation in both the South and the West. These transportation patterns profoundly affected sectional relationships during the first half of the nineteenth century.[21]

Thus far we have discussed briefly how Southerners and Westerners utilized the climate and geographic resources of their sections. However, we have to know more before we can understand sectional influences in American life. The two sections' similarities and differences did not create political sectionalism. Rather, it was how men viewed their section's needs, based on its resources, and thus developed sectional programs, that is important for our purposes.

Because of the way each section formed, both Southerners and Westerners developed a series of attitudes, demands, needs, and desires which their leaders brought into the political arena. The Southern grower's pattern of life, for example, obviously conditioned his attitudes. The Southerner believed that cotton and other staple crops were grown best on large-scale economic units, where he could use the cheap labor of Negro slaves.[22] Southerners practiced extensive rather than intensive agriculture. They had plenty of cheap land available for cotton planting and it was easier for them to move to newer lands when their old land was exhausted than to learn more efficient techniques of cultivating land. It was easier for them to move even if the new lands were beyond the borders of the United States. Thus, the Southern planter was little concerned with the scientific aspects of agriculture, so long as there was cheap labor, available land, and a cotton market.[23]

Whether or not the Southerner's approach was actually the best or most efficient is irrelevant. Most Southerners seemed to accept these ideas, even those Southerners who were unable to practice this type of production.[24] Many Southern leaders wanted to protect their agricultural practices from any criticism or interference, especially from non-Southerners. They wished to remain free to grow cotton wherever possible using the labor force they considered best suited to it. Although there was little interference from either government or voluntary reform groups at this time, Southern feeling on this point can be gauged from their hypersensitive reactions to abolitionist literature and agitation.[25]

Moreover, as we have seen, the South had become a specialized economic area by the 1840's. Southern farmers believed cotton was king and little else was important. This placed Southerners in a particular sectional position. As we have already noted, cotton farmers had to import foodstuffs and manufactured goods from outside in order to live.[26] They wanted to pay as low prices as possible for the things they had to purchase and wanted to buy goods wherever they were cheapest. In the 1840's English manufactured goods were cheaper than Northern. Southerners did not want a tariff which protected the manufacturers of New England by raising the price of English manufactured goods sent to the South. To the Southern leaders, such a tariff was an unfair tax on their section.[27]

Northern-Southern differences on the tariff were sharpened during the early 1840's. In the aftermath of the Panic of 1837, cotton prices fell to their lowest levels since the beginning of the nineteenth century.[28] Southern planters found that they had insufficient capital to purchase necessary goods. Yet at the same time prices of Northern manufactured goods, cushioned by the tariff, did not fall as drastically as had cotton. As a result, Southerners found it more difficult to buy the necessities of life.

The economic situation grew worse when the fixed costs of cotton production and trade did not fall in proportion to cotton prices. Southern cotton growers found themselves increasingly in debt to Northern capitalists who controlled the credit and transportation facilities needed to carry on the cotton trade.[29]

The Southern planters' sale of their marketable crops also affected their tariff position. The Northern textile industry absorbed just under one-quarter of the Southern cotton marketed during the 1840's. Southerners still had to rely on English textile manufacturers to buy most of the available Southern cotton.[30] Although there were promises of a future home market for raw cotton, they were still too unsubstantial for the present needs of Southern planters. Therefore they considered it imperative that nothing should interfere with the disposal of their surplus cotton in foreign markets. They demanded a lower tariff on English imports, thinking that if England could sell her goods in the United States, her manufacturers would be both more likely and more able to purchase Southern cotton. If, on the other hand, the tariff discriminated against English goods, Southern cotton planters would be the sufferers. They would neither be able to buy English goods nor sell their crop to England. Southern farmers therefore advocated a nonprotective, nondiscriminatory tariff.[31]

Southern leaders also wanted to reduce the federal government's need for revenue so that customs duties could be lowered without endangering normal government operations. They warned that the federal government should not undertake excessive responsibilities which would raise expenditures. For instance, the federal government should not build or improve internal transportation facilities. To further bolster its revenue, the government should raise, and keep, as much money as it could from other sources such as the sale of federal lands.[32]

The people of the Old Northwest agreed with much of this program in the late 1830's and early 1840's. They wanted to expand the foreign market for their surplus wheat. And, like the South, the Old Northwest was an economically dependent area. Westerners had to import from the East those manufactured and nonagricultural necessities which they did not produce themselves.[33] Therefore, Western farmers were continually in debt to Eastern manufacturers. They could alleviate this by buying cheaper foreign goods. The idea of a low tariff was thus as appealing to Western wheat producers as it was to Southern cotton growers.[34]

Western policy makers also advocated less government spending as part of their low tariff policy. They were basically satisfied with their river transportation, and did not desire federal expenditures in that area. Although their waterways needed some improvement and maintenance, they were content during the 1830's to let the states undertake this work.[35] They felt that such expenditures would not affect the tariff.

Commercial agriculturalists, whether Southern or Western, agreed on another policy during the 1840's. Economists have characterized the agricultural practices of both sections as wasteful and destructive to the soil. The farmers of the era felt that intensive, scientific farming was unnecessary with so much land available. When older land wore out or farmers wanted to expand their holdings, there was still much useful agricultural land available within the United States.[36] Farmers realized that even when they exhausted the available American land, good, undeveloped land remained on the American continent.[37] Although the expansive urge of the mid-nineteenth century had various sources, many Southern and Western farmers considered the major reason for expansion to be their need for more farm land. Their land desires were to have important consequences as the depression ended and economic expansion began again.

In contrast to the South and Old Northwest, the Northeast was not an export-agriculture area. Rather, the major thrust of that area's economy was in commerce and manufacturing.[38] The manufacturers particularly, according to some historians, were the people who gave the North a different and conflicting sectional outlook from either the South or the West.[39] Since they imported foodstuffs and raw cotton into the region, the New England manufacturers had an interest in keeping the prices of these goods low. More importantly, as we have noted, it was central to their concern to keep foreign manufactured goods out of the United States through the protective tariff.

The slavery-abolition movement also centered in New England in the early 1830's and apparently gained anti-Southern converts during the depression of 1837.[40] Fears of unfair Southern political power directed against the protective tariff also seemed to condition North-eastern minds against territorial expansion in the early 1840's.[41] Sectional psychological factors played a role here as the moral certainty of New England Puritanism gave additional force to the anti-Southern set of mind in the region.[42]

We can infer from all of the above that sectional influences could have shaped public policy demands in the 1840's. We still have to dis-cover, however, how men articulated sectional desires in the political arena. One way could have been through party politics. Sectional leaders may have controlled one of the parties and used it to promote their section's desires. For example, Professor Henry Clyde Hubbart has characterized the Democratic party in this period as responsive to Southern and Western direction.[43] But both parties were strong in each section, an unlikely situation if one party was thought to be the spokes-man for just one section.

Perhaps the best way for political leaders to express sectional de-mands was not through parties but by first unifying their section behind a particular program and then seeking political aid from another section. Southerners and Westerners, it appeared, could operate to-gether due to reciprocal economic interests. The West depended both on Southern markets and Southern waterways and ports for its eco-nomic livelihood.[44] The South needed Western foodstuffs. With such an interrelationship it appears logical that the political leaders of the two sections would forge an alliance to secure legislation.[45] As early as 1820 Spencer Roane of Virginia called upon Southerners and West-erners to work together because their two sections had identical in-terests. Such intersectional cooperation would, he said, make the United States a great nation.[46] Twenty years later S. H. Anderson of Illinois expressed the same idea in a letter to the voters of his Con-gressional district. Anderson emphasized the common interests of the two sections and suggested that what was best for the South was also best for Illinois.[47] Despite such pronouncements, neither Roane nor

Anderson led the movement to forge the two sections together. Most historians have identified John C. Calhoun of South Carolina as the leader of the intersectional movement. Whether his motive was Southern security or personal power, Calhoun's actions during the early 1840's demonstrated his desire to align the policy demands of the two sections.[48]

An astute politician, Calhoun knew that a legislative quid-pro-quo would have to be worked out between the two sections until permanent bonds of friendship were solidified. He noted that occasionally the West and the South differed over public policy. However, he saw several ways to overcome these differences.[49] In the short run, Westerners had to be convinced that they needed a low tariff before all other legislation. At the same time, the South would help the West get certain other legislative needs. In the long run, since the West's transportation dependence upon the South was the best intersectional tie existing, this had to be greatly improved. With this in mind, Calhoun, as the leader of the South, set out to work with the West.

Internal waterways were the main transportation route between South and West, but by the 1840's railroads were a new element in the situation. From the time of the first successful run of the steam locomotive in the United States in the late 1820's over three thousand miles of rails had been laid, most of these in the Eastern states.[50] These rail lines penetrated areas where there were no natural waterways and were built across such barriers as the Appalachian Mountains. Eastern-Western railroads could profoundly affect Southern-Western trade patterns since New York was nearer to Europe than was New Orleans. Southern leaders could counter the East's advantage only if they built their own rail lines, thus strengthening the existing trade routes before the new East-West lines were completed.[51] From the 1830's onward both Southern and Western leaders planned projects to accomplish this aim, including a railroad line between Charleston, South Carolina, and the Mississippi River.[52] Other projects were planned and executed. The most ambitious of these was the Illinois Central Railroad route, which ultimately stretched from Chicago to Mobile, Alabama.[53] Other plans to improve the trade relations between South and West would have connected Cincinnati and Louisville with the South or built North-South lines along rivers.[54]

Southern leaders realized that railroad building and the economic benefits from such lines were long-term undertakings. In the meantime the South and West would be brought closer in other ways. Westerners were concerned about federal land policy. They wanted more liberal legislation to aid Western entrepreneurs. Since the federal government owned the land, only Congress could liberalize land policy. Calhoun, according to both his biographers and historians of land policy, hoped to support Western demands for liberal land laws with Southern votes. Of course, his actions here could bring him into conflict with the Southern tariff position. Many Southerners wanted the public land revenues to be high so that there would be no need to raise customs duties. But Calhoun felt that if the South aided Western land desires, it would gain more than it lost.[55]

Perhaps nothing, however, was potentially more destructive to Southern-Western relations than the issue of internal improvements. As the 1840's opened this matter was taking on new importance. As long as Westerners had settled along navigable rivers, they had had few transportation problems. During the land boom of the 1830's, however, settlers had filled in areas beyond the rivers. By the 1840's these people wanted to send their surplus crops to market but were handicapped by poor transportation facilities. At first, as we have noted, they turned to the state governments for help. Many of the states responded by building canals and improving rivers, but these projects ended with the Panic of 1837 and the chaos of near state bankruptcy.[56] From then on, only the federal government could undertake the needed transportation improvements. The problem was aggravated because even existing river facilities needed improvement for full use.[57]

The Western need for internal improvements embarrassed Southern leaders. Southern cotton planters traditionally had opposed federal expenditures for roads, canals, and rivers. They didn't particularly need internal improvements themselves, and they feared that such federal spending would seriously affect the tariff. Yet Western demands were becoming more insistent in the early 1840's. If the two sections were to maintain relations, the leaders of both would have to work out some sort of accommodation. Spokesmen in both sections called a "commercial convention" of the Southern and Western states to meet at Memphis, Tennessee, in November, 1845. John C. Calhoun presided over the meeting.[58]

The result of this convention was a memorial to Congress calling for the federal government to undertake extensive improvements of the Mississippi River.[59] Unfortunately for the plans and hopes of sectional leaders, however, too many people opposed the memorial and little resulted from it.[60] Nevertheless, despite its ultimate failure, the Memphis Convention was important because of the conscious attempts of leaders to forge permanent Southern-Western sectional ties.

Southerners and Westerners also agreed that the acquisition of new lands by the United States was mutually beneficial.[61] Furthermore, although it was for different reasons, people in both sections feared foreign presence on American soil. Both Southerners and Westerners forcefully asserted their interest in expansion. On the other hand, many Eastern leaders opposed these aggressively acquisitive desires. As a result, when expansion became an important issue after 1843, Southerners and Westerners seemed to have found another area in which they could cooperate.

Southern-Western cooperation was not confined to common economic policy needs. The two sections also united against policies advocated by Eastern political leaders. Frederick Jackson Turner has shown that rivalry between East and West was as old as the country. During the 1830's and 1840's, for example, Western leaders violently reacted to alleged Eastern domination and unfairness to their section in national politics.[62] One major Western complaint was the large size of new states. Eastern states were generally quite small in area. The smallest, Rhode Island, was only 1200 square miles and many of the others were not much larger. In view of this, Westerners objected when the Eastern-dominated Congress made new Western states as large as it could. Westerners charged that their Congressional representation and thus their power in national affairs was deliberately reduced by these Eastern actions.[63]

Western and Eastern leaders also opposed one another over internal improvements. Westerners became angry when so many Easterners opposed Western demands. The East, a well-developed society, had had its share of such improvements when it needed them, but was unwilling to help the West in the same way.[64] Western leaders sharply attacked Easterners for their opposition to Western interests.[65] This enmity between East and West brought the South and West closer together. Western leaders were already quite receptive to Southern overtures, based on their common interests. Eastern hostility towards Western demands increased this receptiveness.[66]

II

During the 1840's there were some changes in the sectional forces operating in American life which may also have affected political behavior. In fact historians have suggested that these changes resulted in a shifting sectional pattern in the United States and a major political revolution.

The Old Northwest was the fastest growing region in the United States during the 1840's. The completion and utilization of the Erie Canal, and the building of a railroad network towards the Mississippi River, had conquered the Appalachian barrier between East and West.[67] Northeastern settlers, as well as many foreign immigrants, filled in the area around the Great Lakes.[68] This large population was settling a new region and demanding legislative aid from the government. Since they could not use the Mississippi River system effectively, they placed major transportation reliance on Lakes shipping and the railroads. Western goods flowed eastward through the new major trade center of Chicago. By the mid-1840's a major reorientation of interior trade relationships was well under way as traffic through the direct Eastern connection challenged and surpassed the movement through New Orleans.[69] Although trade down the Mississippi River remained a vital factor in the Western economy through 1861, the pattern of Western trade grew more complex from the 1840's onward.[70] As Avery O. Craven and Albert Kohlmeier have pointed out, two Wests were developing in the 1840's: the old Ohio Valley West with its Southern roots; and the Lakes area, looking eastward. And the Lakes area was rapidly growing more populous, stronger, and more important than the Ohio Valley.[71]

The growth of two Wests complicated the sectional influences operating during the era. For example, there was an increased need for more efficient transportation connections to the Lakes, as well as railroad building in newly settled areas. As early as the 1830's sectional leaders planned to build several canals into the Great Lakes which would then lead East through the Erie Canal.[72] But the people of the Lakes region needed much more. As we have already noted, most of the state internal improvement projects collapsed in the aftermath of the Panic of 1837.

Since the states had no money to improve transportation routes, the federal government had to build, maintain, and repair the transportation facilities needed by the Lakes' population.[73]

The demands by the people of the Great Lakes for such federal expenditures were not supported by the South or the Ohio Valley West. The river-trade area feared that too much spending would adversely affect the tariff since the government would need additional revenue.[74] As we have seen, the tariff was always the primary policy consideration in the South and the river West. On the other hand, people of the Lakes region were not as vitally concerned about the level of customs duties. The East was rapidly urbanizing and they could sell their grain in that expanding home market. Since the South and the Ohio Valley West differed from the Lakes West in their attitude towards federal expenditures, a potential policy conflict was apparent.

We can see the growing changes in sectional relations in the second of the internal improvements conventions of the 1840's. At the Memphis meeting in 1845 Southerners and Westerners worked together for federal legislation. The convention at Chicago in 1847, however, was Eastern oriented. In fact there was a definite anti-Southern bias to many of the deliberations. Western leaders called this convention after the defeat of the Memphis proposals and the veto of the Rivers and Harbors Bill of 1846 by the Southern President, James K. Polk. The Westerners, who were quite angry at the South, were impatient with constitutional arguments which allegedly limited federal power over internal improvements and pointed out that the Lakes needed aid regardless of any other considerations. In tone and purpose, the Chicago meeting was a long way from the Memphis Convention.[75]

There were other areas of friction between Southerners and people of the Great Lakes. They differed, for example, over the direction of territorial expansion. There were many people in and around the Lakes area who wanted the United States to expand into Canada and to the Pacific, and who militantly advocated such a policy as a means of acquiring more land for Western farmers.[76] However, if the United States expanded into Canada and the Northwest there would be conflict with England which would rupture Southern trade relations. Led by Calhoun, Southern leaders counselled the Western expansionists to follow a more moderate policy.[77]

The disposal of public lands was still another source of potential conflict between the South and the Lakes West. As more and more settlers pressed into new lands they urged the government to lower the price of federal land. They had won a pre-emption policy but they wanted cheap or free land for themselves.[78] The Southern leaders, however, did not want land laws liberalized because it might lead to higher tariffs.[79]

Finally, slavery grew more important as an issue between the South and the Lakes West. Westerners in the Ohio Valley had been tolerant of the institution. But the new Western settlers were not. They condemned slavery on moral grounds. They also realized that Southerners had more national power than they deserved because of the three-fifths clause in the Constitution. An intense political struggle could develop if Southerners used their additional power to thwart Western demands for internal improvements or expansion.[80]

In the 1840's, therefore, it is plain that there were sectional attitudes present in the United States. As a result of these attitudes sectional leaders pressed for certain policies to foster their section's development. But we still have to ascertain whether or not these sectional attitudes and demands led to a strong sectional *influence* on politics, or whether political leaders could ignore purely sectional demands and act in national terms. The two national political parties could have been even more influential than sectional forces if they were able to mute and moderate sectional demands in the interest of achieving a common good. Finally, we should note that sectional influences did not necessarily operate in all matters.

Although many American historians have focused their attention on the idea that sectional influence grew so important during the 1840's that the American people reacted, in their political activity, primarily in sectional terms, however, as we have noted in Chapter One, they have not demonstrated the exact contours of this reaction. In the political situation of the 1840's there were so many different and conflicting factors present that, before we can generalize as to what influenced political behavior, we have to measure and compare the influence of all of the different forces present. To do this, we can begin with the first Congress elected in the decade. It met in May, 1841.

4. THE ANTIPATHIES OF WHIG AND DEMOCRAT, 1841–1845

T H E Twenty-seventh Congress met in special session on May 31, 1841. In his message to the assembled legislators, President John Tyler stressed the country's unhappy financial condition, pointing out that many individuals had been ruined and several state governments financially embarrassed by the persistent depression of the past four years. The President blamed the situation on the previous Democratic administrations which had erected a chaotic national financial structure. Speculators had taken advantage of the weaknesses in that structure to invest carelessly and excessively and their activities had culminated in economic collapse. Tyler concluded by emphasizing Congress' responsibility to enact constructive legislation to bring the country out of its economic collapse.[1]

The President made certain policy recommendations in his message that followed, in the main, the Whigs party's traditional program. Congress, Tyler said, should create a sound and constitutional fiscal agency, controlled by the government. It should pass a law to distribute to the states the revenues from land sales as an economic stimulant. Contrary to traditional Whig policy, however, Tyler hesitated on the tariff. He hoped that there would be no tampering with the existing low tariff, which, if coupled with sound financial practices, would restore the country's economy.[2]

A preponderantly sympathetic audience heard Tyler's message. The Whig party had substantial majorities in both houses of Congress.[3] There were some differences within the party, however, that could hinder the enactment of legislation. For instance, there were some Whigs who would support the President's tariff position, although most Whigs desired a higher tariff.[4] Henry Clay was recognized as the party's legislative leader, if not its national leader. His lieutenants commanded the House of Representatives while he was Chairman of the Senate Finance Committee. Clay believed that he would be able to win the President's support for all of the Whig program and enact it without too much difficulty.[5]

The Whig leadership turned its attention immediately to the country's financial institutions, introducing a bill repealing the Democratic-sponsored Independent Treasury, followed by a measure to create a new Bank of the United States. They then pressed home their advantage and brought forward other parts of the Whig recovery platform. During the emergency session congressmen considered both a distribution bill and a bankruptcy bill to aid individuals and corporations.[6] In addition, under pressure from a large segment of the party, the Whig leaders introduced a higher tariff.[7] Some Whigs went even further and sought federal assumption of state debts.

Historians have traced the course of all of this legislation, its passage, the President's response, and the split between Tyler and Henry Clay. We have many studies of the period focusing on this split and the failure of the Whigs to achieve their legislative goals.[8] This study, however, is not primarily concerned with the details of the intraparty conflict culminating in Tyler's expulsion from the party.[9] Instead of concentrating on this fight, we can more usefully go behind the party history and analyze the impact of the split on the Whig program and how it affected Congressional voting behavior. Since we know little about the behavior of the mass of the members of either party in the face of the Whig leadership split, an analysis of the entire Congress will permit us to understand all levels of national legislative politics.[10]

Congressional voting during the Tyler administration did not take place in a vacuum. Congressmen responded to a whole complex of previously held attitudes as well as to immediate problems. They were also pressured both by Congressional leaders and by their constituencies.[11] This system of attitudes and pressures apparently operated either through the two political parties or through the sections. Certainly, in their debates between 1841 and 1845 different congressmen supported or rejected legislative proposals in both party and sectional terms and seemed to be reacting to both of these major political influences.

Specifically, Whig and Democratic leaders advanced proposals to deal with the country's economic situation. Both parties drew upon their traditional legislative policies and, in the debates and editorial warfare on these proposals, each party's leaders clearly set forth partisan positions and criticized their opponents in partisan terms.[12] Whig newspapers suggested that unless Congress enacted the Whig proposals over Democratic opposition the depression would continue.[13] The Democrats answered in kind, saying that if congressmen enacted Whig tariff, land, or bankruptcy legislation, the country would fall into chaos and the Constitution would be overthrown.[14] Obviously, spokesmen for each party kept the national partisan position before Congress throughout the period.

At the same time, some politicians articulated sectional positions on these issues. They identified a particular policy as either beneficial to, or detrimental to their particular section. The *Mobile Register*, for instance, called the protective tariff a facet "of Southern oppression and source of discord" which no Southerner could support.[15] Various people expressed similar sectional attitudes on most of the legislation presented.[16] However, in contrast to the bitter expressions from the political parties, sectional positions were still confused and unclear. When someone said that a particular policy was good or bad for his section, he was often met with contrary arguments from within that section.[17]

Thus, in the period between 1841 and 1845 congressmen were subjected to both partisan and sectional rhetoric. We can see from a brief survey of the debates and fights of the years 1841–1845 that congressmen could have reacted to either in their voting. However, it is obvious that while there was an intense and clear Whig-Democratic split in the viewpoints expressed, there were so many different spokesmen espousing different sectional points of view as to suggest that sectional influences were not yet as clear-cut as were the partisan influences. The important thing still, however, was the actual voting patterns in Congress during these years.

Congressional Voting

We can divide the legislative activity of the Twenty-seventh and Twenty-eighth Congresses into three major policy areas.[18] The first of these included issues of long-standing partisan dispute. At the beginning of these Congresses the country was primarily concerned with the depression. Congressmen first considered legislative items to relieve those affected by the economic collapse and to reinvigorate the country's economy. These items, over which the parties had differed since the 1830's, included the bank, the tariff, a government bankruptcy bill, and the distribution of land sales revenue. Thus we have a series of proposals brought before Congress which had been previously associated with party conflict. In addition, there was another issue in this group, internal improvements, which although not directly related to the depression, had been another subject of long-standing partisan differences between Whigs and Democrats.

A second policy category included two issues not directly involved in partisan differences heretofore, although they contained elements of such partisanship. The House of Representatives considered a bill to give the federal government the power to apportion seats in Congress. The Senate, at the same time, acted on several foreign policy matters, particularly our relations with Great Britain.

The third and final group of issues in these Congresses were either considered at the time to involve sectional differences, or else historians have characterized them as sectional issues. Since we know that American political life later became sectionalized, the presence of sectional voting as early as the Tyler administration would be of great interest to our study.[19]

There were five scalable issues in the first category of long-standing partisan disputes. The first involved financial matters, specifically the Independent Treasury and the new Bank of the United States.[20] Congressional voting on this issue was not limited to the several votes on chartering a new Bank of the United States and the political maneuvering therein, but also included the repeal of the Independent Treasury and the rechartering of banks in the District of Columbia. From these different votes we can construct for the House of Representatives a pro-to-anti bank scale which included ten separate votes.[21] The most striking thing about this scale was the presence of a large group of congressmen at each end of the scale of attitudes with only a few relatively small blocs scattered in between.[22]

We can observe a very high party correlation on this issue.[23] There was a Whig point of view at one end of the scale where 86.5 per cent of the Whigs voted. Similarly, 94.4 per cent of the Democrats voted at the other end of the scale. Although there were a few dissenters in each party who are interesting and logical subjects for further study, they do not significantly detract from the highly partisan nature of this vote:[24]

TABLE 4.1
Financial Issue, Party Division,
27th Congress, House of Representatives

	Scale Type	Whigs		Democrats	
		No.	%	No.	%
Pro-bank	(0–3)	106	86.5	5	5.6
Moderate	(5–7)	9	7.1	—	—
Anti-bank	(8–10)	8	6.4	85	94.4

The importance of these partisan considerations are highlighted when they are compared with sectional groupings on the same scale.[25] The members of the House of Representatives from each of the major sections—North, South, and Northwest—were scattered over the whole range of attitudinal positions:

TABLE 4.2
Financial Issue, Sectional Division,
27th Congress, House of Representatives

	North		South		Northwest	
	No.	%	No.	%	No.	%
Pro-bank	60	57.1	37	43.5	17	63.0
Moderate	1	1.6	7	7.3	1	3.7
Anti-bank	43	41.3	41	48.2	9	33.3

A similar pattern of voting dispersal existed for a East-West sectional breakdown, and for regional patterns as well.[26]

Senators also voted in a highly partisan manner on the financial issue.[27] There, all twenty Democrats displayed an anti-bank attitude. At the other end of the scale, twenty-one of twenty-four Whigs voted in favor of a national bank. The three Whigs in the moderate position included one Senator each from Massachusetts, Mississippi, and Virginia—a widely scattered trio, geographically.[28] And when we again compare partisan divisions with sectional breakdowns, we find the sections, whether North, South, and Northwest, or East and West, were scattered almost evenly over the whole range of voting positions.[29]

The voting patterns evident on the financial issue indicate the general nature of Congressional voting in this whole policy area. On the next three scales—tariff, land policy, and depression relief measures— Congressional voting behavior was similar to that on the financial scale.[30] That is, most of the men in both parties voted at opposite ends of the scale of attitudes from each other. In the Senate the voting patterns on these three issues were as follows:

TABLE 4.3
Tariff Issue, Party Division,
27th Congress, Senate

		Democrats		Whigs	
	Scale Type	*No.*	*%*	*No.*	*%*
High	(6–8)	2	10	25	83.3
Moderate	(3–5)	—	—	3	10.0
Low	(0–2)	18	90	2	6.7

TABLE 4.4
Distribution Issue, Party Division,
27th Congress, Senate

		Democrats		Whigs	
	Scale Type	*No.*	*%*	*No.*	*%*
Pro	(8–10)	1	4.6	27	96.4
Moderate	(5– 7)	2	9.0	1	3.6
Anti	(0– 3)	19	86.4	—	—

TABLE 4.5
Relief Issue, Party Division,
27th Congress, Senate

		Democrats		Whigs	
	Scale Type	*No.*	*%*	*No.*	*%*
Pro (govt. relief)	(7–9)	—	—	22	76.0
Moderate	(4–6)	—	—	6	24.0
Anti	(0–3)	19	100	—	—

In the House of Representatives there were similar partisan voting patterns:

TABLE 4.6
Tariff Issue, Party Division,
27th Congress, House of Representatives

	Scale Type	Democrats		Whigs	
	Scale Type	No.	%	No.	%
High	(0– 3)	2	2.2	84	70.0
Moderate	(4– 7)	3	3.2	23	19.2
Low	(8–10)	87	94.6	13	10.8

TABLE 4.7
Distribution Issue, Party Division,
27th Congress, House of Representatives

	Scale Type	Democrats		Whigs	
	Scale Type	No.	%	No.	%
Pro	(0–1)	2	2.1	111	88.1
Moderate	(2–3)	—	—	3	2.4
Anti	(4–5)	94	97.9	12	9.5

TABLE 4.8
Relief Issue, Party Division,
27th Congress, House of Representatives

	Scale Type	Democrats		Whigs	
	Scale Type	No.	%	No.	%
Pro (govt. relief)	(0– 5)	8	8.2	89	75.4
Moderate	(6–11)	1	1.1	9	7.6
Anti	(12–17)	88	90.7	20	17.0

As on the bank issue there were congressmen whose behavior on these issues did not follow the general pattern of partisan voting. However, they did not vote in any coherent regional or sectional grouping which would suggest the presence of influential sectional voting determinants. The deviant voters were scattered among different sectional and regional groups, while the bulk of each section's or region's congressmen always voted with their party.[31] Thus, on all of these issues, in both houses of Congress, there was a Whig-oriented end of the voting spectrum and a Democrat-oriented end, with only a few deviant voters within each party, who were from every section of the country.

The only one of the "traditional" issues with a different voting pattern was the question of support for internal improvements. As we noted in Chapter 2, the Whig Party had traditionally advocated federal expenditures for rivers and harbors improvements. The Democrats had opposed such federal expenditures.[32] During the debates on the various bills in the Twenty-eighth Congress these earlier tendencies were somewhat modified. Although congressmen from all sections of the Union asserted their party's traditional position with accustomed vehemence, other congressmen challenged their party's position for both sectional and local reasons.[33] John Wentworth, Democratic congressman from Chicago, affirmed his deep devotion to his party and its principles but also strongly supported rivers and harbors legislation as necessary for his city and section.[34] Other congressmen echoed Wentworth's view, provoking an internal squabble among the Democratic representatives on the floor of Congress.[35]

The internal improvements scale in the House of Representatives contained several legislative proposals, including some projects in every region of the country.[36] Both parties split apart on the issue, with party loyalty replaced by a heightened localism. Just over one-half of the Democrats, thirty-nine in all, disapproved of these measures and voted against federal subsidization of internal improvements. Thirty-four other Democrats broke with their colleagues. Five of six Northwestern Democrats were in the moderate or favorable positions on the scale and were joined by five of the fifteen Southwestern Democratic congressmen, ten of the fourteen Democrats from Pennsylvania, and eleven of the eighteen Democrats from New York State.[37] Obviously, local considerations in several areas were important enough on this particular issue to cause a great many Democrats to break with a previously held party position, certainly an unusual occurrence in these years.

The Whig congressmen also splintered into local and regional blocs on this issue, with substantial numbers of them voting in every position on the attitude scale:

TABLE 4.9
Improvements Issue, Whig Congressmen
27th Congress, House of Representatives

	Total	North	West	South
Pro (govt. intervention)	59	40	13	6
Moderate	36	19	2	15
Anti	23	1	—	22

Clearly, many of the Southern Whigs were uncomfortable about federal internal improvements. On the other hand, other Southerners were not. At the same time, the Northern Whigs also splintered while the Western Whigs were overwhelmingly in favor of federally-financed construction projects. Evidently local and sectional considerations were as important to the Whigs as to the Democrats in this voting area.

In the Senate voting on internal improvements legislation, local influences were as pronounced as in the House of Representatives. The Democratic party was badly divided with a large bloc of Senators voting at both ends of a scale of ten issues.[38] The Whigs were not as badly split as the Democrats but they, too, had Senators voting at opposite ends of the scale:

TABLE 4.10
Internal Improvements Issue, Party Division,
28th Congress, Senate

		Democrats		Whigs	
	Scale Type	No.	%	No.	%
Pro (govt. intervention)	(0– 2)	8	38.0	13	56.6
Moderate	(3– 5)	2	9.7	3	13.0
Anti	(6–7, 9)	11	52.3	7	30.4

Sectional and regional groups were similarly scattered over the whole scale.[39] The closest approach to unified blocs involved the eight senators from the Northwest states, all of whom voted in either the moderate or pro position on the scale, and the seven of nine Southern Democrats who voted against federal aid for internal improvements.[40]

Several different influences, partially regional, partially local, apparently affected Congressional voting on the internal improvements issue. Amid these conflicting differences two things clearly stood out. At a time when such improvements were considered to be vital in some areas of the country, neither party nor sectional ties could bind all congressmen to a particular course of action. Secondly, although congressmen splintered on this issue, their splintering did not affect the voting on other issues in the same Congresses where party differences were the important influence.

We can clearly see the continuing influence of the national parties in two other issues where there had not been major party pronouncements in the past. In the voting on the federal apportionment of Congressional seats, and on foreign affairs, most congressmen clearly formed party blocs:[41]

TABLE 4.11
Apportionment Issue, Party Division,
27th Congress, House of Representatives

		Democrats		Whigs	
	Scale Type	*No.*	*%*	*No.*	*%*
Pro (fed.apportionment)	(0–1)	6	8.1	76	69.1
Moderate	(2–3)	11	14.9	27	24.5
Anti	(4–5)	57	77.0	7	6.4

TABLE 4.12
Foreign Relations Issue, Party Division,
27th Congress, Senate

		Democrats		Whigs	
	Scale Type	*No.*	*%*	*No.*	*%*
Aggressive	(0–1)	9	50.0	—	—
Moderate	(2–4)	7	38.9	5	17.2
Nonaggressive	(5–6)	2	11.1	24	82.8

Although the Democrats were split on the foreign relations scale there was an essentially partisan tone to the total vote in that almost four-fifths of them voted in positions different from most of the Whigs. Democrats may have been internally divided over foreign policy questions but they clearly, as a party, viewed these matters differently from the Whigs.[42]

The final issues considered by Congress during the Tyler administration were of the greatest interest in light of future developments. Questions involving Negro slavery and Western expansion foreshadowed the bitter fights to come in the United States before 1861. But, did Congressional voting on these issues in the early period between 1841 and 1845 anticipate the later, divisive sectional bitterness and thus presage a major change in the usual pattern of Congressional voting?

In the House of Representatives the slavery scale contained fifteen votes in the Twenty-seventh Congress. These votes included several different elements: the gag-rule against antislavery petitions, Negro citizenship, mistreatment of Negro seamen in Southern ports, diplomatic relations with the Negro Republic of Haiti, and the existence of the slave trade in the District of Columbia.[43] Surprisingly, the voting did not reveal clear sectional positions. Rather, partisan considerations apparently modified sectional influences. Several congressmen explained why. Democrats claimed that the Whigs brought up such issues in an attempt to drive a wedge between the Northern and Southern wings of the Democratic party and thus hurt Martin Van Buren's chances in the presidential election of 1844.[44] Some Southern Whigs, in contrast, insisted that they had to vote with their Northern Whig colleagues because part of the issue involved freedom of speech and really not sectional differences.[45] At the same time, the Negro issue did provoke some sectional outcries in Congress. A few congressmen charged that the Liberty party and abolitionists had provoked agitation on this issue for sectional purposes.[46]

As a result of all of the cross pressures on the Negro issue, only the Northern and Western Whigs and the Southern Democrats clearly voted within a sectional context, being respectively, antislavery and proslavery. At the same time only five of thirty-three Northern Democrats were antislavery. The others voted consistently with their fellow Democrats from the South.[47] Three of thirty-one Southern Whigs actually voted on the antislavery side of the scale, and six others voted in a moderate position.[48] Congressmen reacted in several different ways to the Negro issue; sectional influences did not yet override other considerations. Congressmen apparently could still break with their sections if they thought that more important matters of national party cooperation or the enactment of specific programs were at stake.[49]

American expansion into new territories was already becoming an important issue in 1842 and 1843. Here again, we have issues characterized by historians as part of Northern-Southern sectional conflicts.[50] Certainly the later sectional crises of 1850 and 1854 pivoted on questions of territorial expansion. But whether such sectional differences affected the issue in the early and middle 1840's is another question. In their speeches, petitions, and writings, the American people appeared to be concerned about other aspects of expansion besides the extension of slavery.

Citizen's meetings in different parts of the nation supported American expansion and warmly endorsed the acquisition of Oregon and Texas, even if war with England and Mexico resulted. The people at these meetings constantly and aggressively asserted America's right to both territories.[51] At the same time, however, other spokesmen in every section challenged an expansionist course of action. The opponents of expansion saw the acquisitive ambitions of some Americans as a threat to both American civilization and republican institutions. The addition of new territories was not worth that price.[52] Clearly there was nationwide sentiment on both sides of the expansion issue.

In many of the debates on expansion, political leaders did consider the relevance of slavery and sectional power. In his first inaugural address as Governor of Mississippi, for instance, Albert Gallatin Brown happily asserted that the annexation of Texas would allow the South to win all she desired in the political arena. Meanwhile, some Northerners expressed uneasiness about the extension of slavery. Robert Winthrop of Massachusetts went so far as to attach an antislavery rider to an Oregon territorial bill.[53] Generally, however, an expansive American majority brushed aside such sectional sentiments. One Northern newspaper, supporting the admittance of a slave state, placed the expansion issue in perspective when it said that the United States could "better endure the evils of slavery for a season than British domination forever."[54]

When we analyze Congressional voting behavior on the expansionist issue we find that expansion was a party issue in the Twenty-seventh and Twenty-eighth Congresses, since Democrats and Whigs differed in their attitudes towards the acquisition of new territory. In the House of Representatives there were eleven roll-call votes on the territorial expansion scale. These votes included Texas annexation and the Oregon question, as well as the admission of two new states.[55] Of the Democratic congressmen in the House, 75 per cent voted in favor of American expansion, while 88 per cent of the Whigs opposed it. Only a few congressmen deviated from their party's position, 10 of 123 Democrats opposing expansion, and 4 of the 72 Whigs favoring it.[56] At the same time, the major sectional blocs were scattered over the whole range of responses.

Expansion during the years 1843 through 1845 was neither a Western nor Southern issue but was, once again, primarily partisan. The Congressional dissenters from their party's position apparently responded to sectional or local influences, but most members from each section did not:

TABLE 4.13
Expansion Issue, Party and Sectional Divisions,
28th Congress, House of Representatives

	Scale Type	Democrats		Whigs	
		No.	%	No.	%
Pro-expansion	(0– 3)	93	75.6	4	5.5
Moderate	(4– 6)	20	16.3	5	7.0
Anti-expansion	(7–10)	10	8.1	63	87.5

	North		South		West	
	No.	%	No.	%	No.	%
Pro-expansion	21	27.0	51	64.6	25	62.5
Moderate	13	16.6	10	12.6	2	5.0
Anti-expansion	44	56.4	18	22.8	13	32.5

	East		West	
	No.	%	No.	%
Pro-expansion	45	37.8	66	66.7
Moderate	18	15.1	8	8.9
Anti-expansion	56	47.1	24	24.4

The partisan patterns on the expansion issue also prevailed in the Senate. Twenty-two of twenty-three Democrats were grouped together in favor of expansion while the other one voted in a moderate position.[57] Over 90 per cent of the Whigs voted together in opposition. Sectional voting blocs were splintered over the whole scale of attitudes:

TABLE 4.14
Expansion Issue, Party and Sectional Divisions,
28th Congress, Senate

		Democrats		Whigs	
	Scale Type	No.	%	No.	%
Pro-expansion	(0– 3)	22	95.7	—	—
Moderate	(4– 7)	1	4.3	2	6.9
Anti-expansion	(8–11)	—	—	27	93.1

	North		West		South	
	No.	%	No.	%	No.	%
Pro-expansion	7	38.9	5	62.2	10	38.5
Moderate	—	—	—	—	3	11.5
Anti-expansion	11	61.1	3	37.8	13	50.0

	East		West	
	No.	%	No.	%
Pro-expansion	10	33	12	57.1
Moderate	2	7	1	6.7
Anti-expansion	18	60	8	36.2

This high degree of party cohesion in expansion matters suggests that the divisions over expansion were not affected by questions of slavery or other sectional differences. Rather, what seemed important to a congressman was the position his party took on the issue. The voting on expansion reflected and summed up the prevailing voting pattern of the Twenty-seventh and Twenty-eighth Congresses, a pattern of strong and tenacious national political party groupings.

The Nature of Congressional Voting

As American congressmen acted on a great mass of legislation in the early 1840's, their voting indicated the nature of the influences operating upon them at the beginning of this decade. Whether it was policies congressmen had divided over for a generation, such as finance, land, or tariff, or the newer issue of western expansion, Congressional voting reflected the intense party divisions of the era. Each political party appealed to the voting electorate in different terms, and each party meant something different to the people of the United States. As we have seen, this led to strong party loyalty and, in Congress, a high degree of party discipline. In six major areas of Congressional voting, party unity dominated the voting:

TABLE 4.15
Highest Party-Unity Percentages,
27th and 28th Congresses, House of Representatives

	Democrats	Whigs
Finance	94.4	86.5
Tariff	94.6	70.0
Distribution	97.9	88.1
Relief	90.7	75.4
Apportionment	77.0	69.1
Expansion	75.6	87.5
Average	88.4	79.4

TABLE 4.16
Party-Unity Percentages,
27th and 28th Congresses, Senate

	Democrats	Whigs
Finance	100.0	87.5
Tariff	90.0	83.3
Distribution	86.4	96.4
Relief	100.0	76.0
Foreign affairs	50.0	82.8
Expansion	95.7	93.1
Average	87.0	86.5

The party unity averages are even more impressive when compared to the amount of sectional unity on the same issues (Tables 4.17, 4.18).[58] Sectional representatives generally voted in party blocs at different points on the scales so that, with only occasional deviations, sectional-unity percentages approximated party divisions within each section. Parties were united; therefore, sections were split.[59]

On the two issues of internal improvements and Negro slavery, Congressional voting was not as influenced by party discipline as on other issues. Instead, sectional and local considerations played important roles. Still, despite the fact that voting on this legislation did not follow the prevailing partisan pattern seen in other matters, some congressmen reacted, even here, in terms of their party membership. Finally, what is most important perhaps, was that any sectional or local forces operating in Congress on these two issues were limited in scope and influence and did not affect Congressional voting on other matters.

On all of the issues in these two Congresses there were some congressmen who bolted from the positions taken by their parties. If these dissenting congressmen were members of some coherent local or regional group we would have to acknowledge the existence of some secondary but important voting influences. However, such was not the case. Bolting congressmen did not constitute an identifiable bloc of any kind. Rather, the members of the dissenting blocs changed from issue to issue without any internal coherence to the groups or any relationship between the dissenters on one issue and those on the next. Whenever a sectional group, for instance, bolted its party, any sectional significance was vitiated by the fact that a majority of the members

TABLE 4.17
Sectional-Unity Percentages,
27th and 28th Congresses, House of Representatives

	North	South	Northwest
Finance	57.1	48.2	63.0
Tariff	51.1	60.2	57.1
Distribution	58.6	59.1	61.5
Relief	60.0	67.9	62.5
Apportionment	52.7	34.7	50.0
Expansion	56.4	64.6	62.5
Average	56.0	55.8	59.3

	North	South	East	West
Finance	58.8	48.2	50.6	56.7
Tariff	52.5	60.2	48.0	63.5
Distribution	59.2	59.1	52.9	67.3
Relief	60.4	67.9	48.4	58.6
Apportionment	52.2	34.7	47.7	35.1
Expansion	48.2	64.6	47.1	66.7
Average	55.2	55.8	49.1	58.0

from the same section did not bolt their party.[60] We also cannot identify particular individuals as those most likely to put aside party discipline. Individuals who left their party on one matter rejoined it on succeeding issues.[61] The dissenting voting suggests, of course, that from time to time, local, personal, and regional considerations influenced particular congressmen but that these influences were transitory. More importantly, whatever was the nature of these other determinants, they did not change the main pattern of Congressional voting between 1841 and 1845.

At the beginning of the 1840's, then, congressmen still reacted to the political influences of an earlier era. The two political parties that had developed during the 1820's and 1830's were still meaningful both on traditional issues as well as on newer issues brought before Congress. On other issues where congressmen did not respond to partisan programs and discipline, the considerations affecting them were of limited power and duration. The men in Congress responded generally

TABLE 4.18
Highest Sectional-Unity Percentages,
27th and 28th Congresses, Senate

	North	South	Northwest
Finance	53.9	46.0	57.0
Tariff	72.2	45.8	50.0
Distribution	64.7	52.0	57.1
Relief	55.6	40.9	50.0
Foreign affairs	61.5	52.7	42.9
Expansion	61.1	50.0	62.5
Average	61.8	47.9	53.3

	North	South	East	West
Finance	50.0	46.0	64.0	68.4
Tariff	65.4	45.8	63.3	55.0
Distribution	58.4	52.0	70.0	68.4
Relief	50.0	40.9	51.7	57.9
Foreign affairs	56.0	52.7	65.5	44.4
Expansion	53.8	50.0	60.0	57.1
Average	55.6	47.9	62.5	58.5

to the political institutions most meaningful to them, the national parties. They did not primarily react to those influences which they considered to be less important, and it appears that sectional factors fell into the second category.[62] By 1845, there was little sign in Congress of an impending period in which sectional considerations would strongly affect voting behavior.[63]

5. DEMOCRATIC POLICIES
AND PROBLEMS, 1846

THE first session of the Twenty-ninth Congress was pivotal in the politics of the 1840's. With safe majorities in both houses, the Democratic Congressional leaders, as well as President James K. Polk, were determined to erase the Whig legislative successes of the previous four years.[1] They also would consider new matters vitally important both to the country's future development as well as to the politics of the period. American historians have repeatedly stressed the importance of this particular session of Congress. They see it as the focal point of a decade of change in which the representatives and senators began to shift their allegiance from the two national parties and adopt, instead, sectional patterns of behavior in most legislative matters.[2]

This characterization of the first session of the Twenty-ninth Congress is a useful one in examining the political processes of the time. Congressmen generally had voted along party lines in the years before 1846. Sectional influences, while present, had not been strong enough to have an important impact on voting behavior. Now, however, new issues allegedly shifted the balance from nationalism to sectionalism. But the basic element in this concept remains to be tested: Did, in fact, a new political structure, rooted in conflict between the North and the South, begin to emerge in the Twenty-ninth Congress? The national parties had been quite strong through the preceding period. Were they strong enough to resist the new pressures released by territorial expansion and war with Mexico?

In his message to Congress, President Polk advocated a return to the financial policies of earlier Democratic administrations and attacked both the Whig tariff of 1842 and the repeal of the Independent Treasury.[3] He asserted that the tariff of 1842 was discriminatory and unfair to most of the country, and in violation of the purpose for which tariffs were levied—the raising of government revenue. Furthermore, government monies should not be deposited in banks because they would not be used there in the public interest. What was needed, he concluded was a separation of banks from government and an Independent Treasury under government control.[4]

In this message President Polk reasserted traditional Democratic principles recently reaffirmed by the party in its national platform.[5] The party's position on these matters and Polk's action in bringing them before Congress pointed up the first policy area with which Congress would be concerned. Similar issues had produced bitter partisanship during the Tyler administration. Now, with Democratic majorities in both Houses, Polk's suggestions had an excellent chance of approval, unless new behavioral influences emerged and destroyed party discipline among the Congressional Democrats.

Polk also devoted a large part of his message to foreign affairs. Our external relations had deteriorated as America's expansive push into Oregon and Texas had provoked an uneasy militancy in England and Mexico. Polk suggested that both nations were unfriendly and unwilling to negotiate concerning American interests in these territories. Furthermore, he felt that England's presence on our continent was a definite threat to the United States. He wanted Congress to consider these matters preparatory to asserting our territorial rights.[6]

Although the President did not mention the question of federally financed internal improvements, Congress would have to consider that subject also.[7] Over the previous decade Westerners had constantly pointed out their need for federal aid to finance improvements. They had been relatively quiet during the depression after 1837, but with the economic upturn of the early 1840's, they quite forcefully reasserted their earlier demands.[8] In response to this growing pressure Congress took up the subject early in the new session.[9]

Thus, the Twenty-ninth Congress dealt both with traditional legislative problems and with new issues related to the growth of the United States. The parties were united in their viewpoints concerning the older issues of tariff and Independent Treasury, and with Democratic majorities in both houses it seemed that they could dispose of these issues quickly. However foreign affairs was a different matter. The Democrats, as we have seen, were in favor of American expansion.[10] But the issue of expansion had now become a question of tactics rather than simply one of ideological commitment. As the President indicated, two foreign nations opposed any further American growth in the West. Democratic leaders had to decide, then, how militantly they were going to push for territorial acquisition. They had to decide whether the country should go to the point of war with Great Britain and Mexico to achieve its ends or whether it should negotiate and accept the best settlement it could get.[11] Although most Democrats agreed on an expansionist policy, they differed in their speeches and writings on these tactical matters.

Another factor present in the expansion situation also could influence Congressional behavior. The United States had already peacefully annexed Texas. Some Western leaders feared that with Texas already in the Union, those political leaders who valued Texas more than Oregon might now be less militant on the expansion question and more willing to negotiate.[12] If there were such tendencies and consequent differences over tactics, the favorable Congressional attitude towards expansion could be divided and weakened.

The question of internal improvements was also potentially divisive to the Democratic Congressional majority. In previous Congresses local and sectional, as well as national, political pressures had influenced Congressional voting on this matter. Earlier, however, because of the depression and the fights over financial and economic legislation, internal improvements had not been an important issue. Therefore, individual differences over internal improvements had not affected voting in other legislative areas. But as the Twenty-ninth Congress began, the situation changed. Although President Polk had not mentioned the subject, many Democratic areas of the country were now demanding national internal improvements legislation.[13] Democratic congressmen had to respond to these demands from their constituents. Once again, John Wentworth, the Chicago Democrat, while attesting to his party loyalty, asserted his deep concern for his city's needs. He was determined to push for improvements legislation despite his party's traditional opposition to federal activity in the matter.[14]

The Western Democrats had high hopes of enacting the needed in-

ternal improvements legislation for several reasons. In 1845 the
Memphis Convention had strongly endorsed such legislation and John
C. Calhoun, previously an opponent of internal improvements, had
led the Memphis deliberations.[15] Because they expected that Calhoun
would influence many Southern congressmen to vote with them, Westerners were confident of success in 1846 and determined not to permit
anything to stand in their way.[16]

The Westerners' optimism on internal improvements was not entirely justified, however. Calhoun's acquiescence to federal aid was
repudiated by other Southern Democrats, even in South Carolina.
Many of these Democrats had traditionally opposed such federal expenditures and looked upon the current Western demands as a threat
to the rest of the party's program. They were therefore determined to
prevent the federal government from becoming involved in any further
internal improvements.[17]

The Democratic party's majority in Congress thus could be dissipated by their internal divisions on several issues. In addition to these
issues, however, the party had just been through a period of intense
fighting over its presidential nomination in 1844. The old Jacksonian
leadership of the party under Martin Van Buren had received a set-
back in 1840, and had been overthrown in 1844 by younger Democrats
behind James K. Polk. Many of the Van Buren men were bitterly dis-
appointed at their displacement and their feelings had not been soothed
since the election. In fact, they had become even more angry because
of Polk's appointments policy which seemed to be a deliberate slap at
Van Buren.[18] Since Van Buren had supporters in all parts of the nation,
there could be local repercussions from the leadership fight which
would affect Congressional behavior.

The Democratic Congressional majority, then, might not be able to
hold together due to four considerations. The party members had different and often conflicting needs and desires. The issues on which
their differences were especially intense were now prominently before
Congress. There was bitterness within the party. And finally, there
were relatively few Whigs in Congress; there was no strong, challenging
opposition to provoke the Democrats to remain united. Historians have
suggested that these conditions led to the breakdown of the Democratic
party and the emergence of permanent sectional groupings in Amer-

ican politics despite the strength of the two national parties before
1846. This, however, remains to be investigated.

Congressional Voting

As noted above, the issues of the Twenty-ninth Congress divided into
three policy areas. The first included the traditionally divisive issues of
tariff and land legislation.[19] In the voting on both of these issues there
was a high degree of party cohesion. The voting pattern apparent in
the Twenty-seventh and Twenty-eighth Congresses, of large party blocs
voting at opposite ends of a scale, was still present in 1846.

In the House of Representatives the tariff scale included seven
separate roll-calls.[20] A tariff bill, drafted by the Democratic majority
on the Ways and Means Committee, reflected the party viewpoint on
the issue.[21] As a result, and despite their previous differences about
the tariff, all but one of the Whigs who voted could agree that the bill's
schedules were much too low for them. On the other hand, just under
70 per cent of the House Democrats voted at the other end of the scale
in favor of accepting the bill. In addition, another 15 per cent of the
Democrats voted in the moderate position. Only one Whig went that
far towards a lower tariff:

TABLE 5.1
Tariff Issue, Party Division,
29th Congress, House of Representatives

		Democrats		Whigs	
	Scale Type	No.	%	No.	%
Low Tariff	(0–2)	91	67.4	—	—
Moderate	(3–5)	21	15.6	1	1.4
High tariff	(6–7)	23	17.0	71	98.6

The voting on the land scale shows similar partisanship. On a scale
of seven issues, sixty-three of sixty-four House Whigs voted against
the Democratic land-graduation bill and cheap land prices.[22] At the
other end of the scale three-quarters of the House Democrats followed
their party's lead (Table 5.2).

There are two particularly suggestive things in these scales. First,
the Whigs were even more united than they had been during the previous Congress.[23] Apparently, they were better able to unite against

TABLE 5.2
Land Issue, Party Division,
29th Congress, House of Representatives

		Democrats		Whigs	
	Scale Type	No.	%	No.	%
Liberal	(0–2)	88	76.5	—	—
Moderate	(3–5)	3	2.6	1	1.6
Conservative	(6–7)	24	20.9	63	98.4

something offered by their opponents than they had been on their own legislation. Secondly, the Democratic dissidents on both scales were from the same group. The House Democrats who broke with their party on both tariff and land issues were almost entirely from the Middle-Atlantic states.[24] Here was a case where both regional and local pressures apparently overcame national party influences.[25] However, the Middle-Atlantic Democrats were the only group to break from the party.

In the Senate there was also a high degree of party unity with only small dissenting groups present on these two issues.[26] As in the House, the Whigs were more united than were the Democrats. On the other side of the aisle, some of the Northern Democrats broke away from the bulk of their party colleagues (Tables 5.3, 5.4).[27]

In 1846 there was a particularly bitter debate on the expansion issue in both houses of Congress. To some historians these debates revealed sectional differences due to conflicting sectional territorial desires. The "Southern" expansionist desire was slaveholding Texas, which in 1846 was already in the process of admission to the Union as a state. On the other hand, the "Northern" expansionist goal, Oregon, was still being fought over and it was still uncertain if she would be acquired, let alone admitted as a state.[28] It was clear that slavery would never go into Oregon. In fact, during the maneuvering on the issue Congress enacted a positive slavery prohibition in the territory.[29] Thus, the Southern congressmen possibly might hesitate about supporting the acquisition of Oregon. And in the debates on the issue some sectional pronouncements were made.[30]

In contrast to the importance of sectionalism, however, we have seen that expansion had previously been a party issue, with support and

TABLE 5.3
Tariff Issue, Party Division,
29th Congress, Senate

		Democrats		Whigs	
	Scale Type	No.	%	No.	%
Low tariff	(0–2)	20	80.0	—	—
Moderate	(3–4)	1	4.0	1	4.0
High tariff	(7–8)	4	16.0	24	96.0

TABLE 5.4
Land Issue, Party Division,
29th Congress, Senate

		Democrats		Whigs	
	Scale Type	No.	%	No.	%
Liberal	(0–1)	24	85.7	—	—
Moderate	(2–3)	1	3.6	3	13.0
Conservative	(8–9)	3	10.7	20	87.0

opposition to it present in all sections of the country. The Democrats had favored expansion against Whig opposition.[31] Now, in early 1846, these partisan positions were rearticulated during the Oregon debate.[32] When congressmen voted on the expansion issue they broke into their usual partisan groupings. In both houses most Democrats were more in favor of American expansion into new territory than were any of the Whigs. However, there also were sudden sharp differences within each scale grouping. In the Senate, for instance, the Democrats split bitterly over how militantly the government should press for new territories.

In the House of Representatives there were thirteen roll-calls on the expansion scale.[33] Seventy-five per cent of the Democrats were at the pro-expansion end with only five opposed to the pending measures of territorial acquisition. All but one of the Whigs were either anti-expansionist or moderate on the issue (Table 5.5).

The Democratic anti-expansionists were a few congressmen from Virginia and Alabama who voted in opposition to most of their state and party colleagues. The moderates were more widely scattered.[34] Whatever it was that influenced those dissenters, it was of a local or

TABLE 5.5
Expansion Issue, Party Division,
29th Congress, House of Representatives

		Democrats		Whigs	
	Scale Type	No.	%	No.	%
Pro-expansion	(0– 3)	97	77.6	1	1.7
Moderate	(4– 8)	23	18.4	18	31.0
Anti-expansion	(9–13)	5	4.0	39	67.3

individual character, and not sectional. On the other hand, the Whig moderates on this scale included fourteen of the eighteen Southern Whigs who were willing to go further than their Northern and Western colleagues in favor of the expansionist measures. In relation to the whole scale, however, these Southern Whigs did not go as far as did most Democrats.

In the Senate the Whigs were completely united against expansion. The Democrats were more factionalized (Table 5.6).[35] The pro-

TABLE 5.6
Expansion Issue, Party Division,
29th Congress, Senate

		Democrats		Whigs	
	Scale Type	No.	%	No.	%
Pro-expansion	(0– 3)	13	40.6	—	—
Moderate	(4– 7)	12	37.5	—	—
Anti-expansion	(8–11)	7	21.9	24	100

expansion group in the Senate included six of eight Northern Democrats, one of eighteen Southerners, and all six Western Democrats. The moderate group comprised ten Southern Democrats and the remaining two Northern Democratic Senators. The Democratic anti-expansion group included seven Southern senators.[36] The important thing about these divisions within the Democratic party was that, as we have noted, the splits occurred not over expansion itself but rather over how militantly we should press the question. Obviously, many Democratic Senators feared that the expansionist urge was leading us towards war with England.[37] To prevent this some of them (from the Carolinas, Mississippi and Florida) were willing to vote with the Whigs against the pending expansion measures. Other Democrats took a more moderate voting position, between the Whigs and the most aggressive Democrats. All of which suggests that although there certainly was a partisan element in the expansion issue, the effect of regional influences also has to be considered.

The third area of legislative interest in the Twenty-ninth Congress involved internal improvements legislation. In the past both parties had splintered somewhat on this issue, with the Whigs somewhat better able to maintain party unity than the Democrats.[38] This continued to be true in 1846. The Whigs were very united on the issues brought before them, while the Democrats had some trouble, primarily due to pressures generated by local conditions:[39]

TABLE 5.7
Improvement Issue, Party Division,
29th Congress, House of Representatives

		Democrats		Whigs	
	Scale Type	No.	%	No.	%
Pro (govt. intervention)	(0– 5)	38	27.1	61	87.1
Moderate	(6–12)	10	7.2	2	2.9
Anti	(13–19)	92	65.7	7	10.0

TABLE 5.8
Improvements Issue, Party Division,
29th Congress, Senate

		Democrats		Whigs	
	Scale Type	No.	%	No.	%
Pro (govt. intervention)	(0–2)	3	10.1	17	89.5
Moderate	(3–6)	10	37.0	1	5.2
Anti	(7–9)	14	51.9	1	5.2

The Whig dissenters on internal improvements were a varied group whose distinguishing characteristic was neither sectional nor regional cohesiveness, but an isolation from most of their sectional, regional, and state colleagues.[40] Among the Democrats, on the other hand, there was some regional cohesion. In both House and Senate, Western Democrats tended to break with their party's position on the issue. Many of these dissenters came from the Old Northwest as well as from

several of the Southwestern states.[41] Once again, however, there is a
qualification to this apparently sectional response. In both houses the
Westerners differed among themselves on the issue.[42] Furthermore,
some of the Western Democrats in the House of Representatives were
as much against internal improvements in their voting as the most
strict-constructionist Southern or Eastern Democrat:

TABLE 5.9
Western Democrats and International Improvements,
29th Congress, House of Representatives

	Ill.	Mich.	Ind.	Ohio	Mo.	Ky.
Pro (govt. intervention)	3	2	3	10	2	2
Moderate	—	1	—	1	1	—
Anti	3	—	2	2	2	2

Of the thirty-six representatives from these six Western states, just
over 61 per cent favored federal aid to internal improvements, 30 per
cent voted at the opposite end of the scale, and 8 per cent voted in-
between. Obviously, there was a strong sectional force influencing some
of the Western Democrats to vote for federal internal improvements.
This sectional influence stemmed from the West's need for such improvements for its development. However, we should also note that
Western pressure varied from district to district and depended on the
local need for harbors, river improvements, or canals. Thus, while
there were loud, unhappy cries of recrimination from some of the
Westerners when the President vetoed the internal improvements bill
passed by Congress, other Western Democrats voted to sustain the
President's course.[43] The pro-improvements group was particularly
bitter when it could not override Polk's veto, but the result should not
have been surprising in light of party pronouncements and previous
voting on the issue.[44] Nevertheless, here was a large sectional grouping
of congressmen acting against their party because of overriding sectional desires. Still, their sectionalism was only one part of a larger
picture and it remained to be seen whether they would let sectional
hostility and anti-partyism affect their voting on other issues.[45]

Congress considered one additional legislative area in the first session of the Twenty-ninth Congress: the Mexican War. Our militant

expansionism and Mexico's resistance to it had led to armed conflict. When fighting broke out Congress had to enact a body of war legislation.[46] Although in the final passage of most of these bills congressmen voted almost unanimously in favor of the legislation, the political maneuvering in debate and the votes taken before the final one revealed both prowar and antiwar positions on the issue:

TABLE 5.10
War Issue, Party Division,
29th Congress, Senate

	Scale Type	Democrats		Whigs	
		No.	%	No.	%
Prowar	(0–1)	25	92.6	—	—
Moderate	(2–4)	—	—	3	15.8
Antiwar	(5–6)	2	7.4	16	84.2

In the Senate the war issue was clearly a partisan one. The only two Democrats against the legislation were the South Carolinians, John C. Calhoun and George McDuffie, both of whom first assailed the administration's policy in debate and then voted against the war measures. But none of the other Southern Democrats joined them in their opposition. At the same time, the Whigs were united against the war legislation with only three Whig moderates on this issue from Maryland, Georgia, and Tennessee. The other eight Southern Whig senators were completely opposed to the war. Clearly, then, as the debates and the voting demonstrated, both parties sought to make political capital from the war. The voting indicated that sectional and regional interests were not deeply involved:

TABLE 5.11
War Issue, Party Division
29th Congress, House of Representatives

	Scale Type	Democrats		Whigs	
		No.	%	No.	%
Prowar	(0–1)	61	45.2	15	23.1
Moderate	(2–4)	71	52.6	11	16.9
Antiwar	(5–6)	3	2.2	39	60.0

Voting in the House of Representatives differed from the Senate's on the war issue. Although just under half of the Democrats voted full support of the administration's policies and all but a few of them demonstrated more support for the war than did most Whigs, there was a great deal of party disruption on this issue. The most cohesive group present, in fact, was sectional. The Southern representatives apparently were the most enthusiastic supporters of the administration's war policy since 85 per cent of the Southern Democrats and 61 per cent of the Southern Whigs voted at the most favorable end of the scale.[47] The rest of the Southern Democrats and 22 per cent more of the Southern Whigs were in a moderate position. Whether or not this was a slaveholder's war, the voting of the Southern congressmen reflected a more militant support of the war against Mexico than came from any other part of the nation.

In the North there were party differences on the moderate to anti-war end of the scale. Over 90 per cent of the Northern Democrats were in a moderate position while 80 per cent of the Northern Whigs voted against the war. In the West there were similar partisan differences; all opposition to the war came from the Whigs, all support came from the Democrats:

TABLE 5.12
War Issue, Non-Southern Voting by Party,
29th Congress, House of Representatives

	Democrats		Whigs	
	No.	%	No.	%
Prowar	6	8.7	—	—
Moderate	60	87.0	9	18.4
Antiwar	3	4.3	40	81.6

Outside of the South, then, there was party voting on the war issue. But within the South, congressmen apparently viewed the war as above partisanship and political advantage. Whether it was the alleged militancy of the South or their closer ties to this war, we do have here clear sectional behavior. But such sectionalism was still limited in scope. Although one group of congressmen responded to the war in sectional terms, the rest of the senators and representatives did not.

The Nature of Congressional Voting

In 1846 Congress considered five different legislative areas in which the two national parties continued to be quite influential. However, sectionalism was more important in 1846 than it had been in earlier Congresses. Nevertheless, we must delineate this sectional factor very carefully. There was as yet no general, overall sectional pattern in Congress. Rather, congressmen formed into different sectional groupings in different houses on different issues with no discernible regularity. Furthermore, the major sectional influences present primarily affected the Democratic party. In both houses the Whigs manifested a very high degree of party unity. In fact, in the Senate they were more unified than they had been during the Twenty-seventh and Twenty-eighth Congresses (Table 5.13).[48] In the House of Representatives, on four of the five issues, Whig unity was also greater than it had been in previous Congresses (Table 5.14).[49]

TABLE 5.13
Party-Unity Percentages, Whigs,
29th Congress, Senate

Tariff	96.0
Land	87.0
Expansion	100.0
Improvements	89.5
War	84.2
Average	91.3

TABLE 5.14
Party-Unity Percentages, Whigs,
29th Congress, House of Representatives

Tariff	98.6
Land	98.4
Expansion	67.3
Improvements	87.1
Average	87.9

There were some Whig dissenters on all of these issues. These dissenters did not form any coherent sectional or regional pattern, however, coming instead from all parts of the country, and changing from issue to issue. Apparently local and personal influences occasionally affected the behavior of some congressmen. But other than these few cases, there was as yet no clearly identifiable permanent voting influence challenging the force of party identification. The Whig party remained a strongly united coalition.

The Democratic party was also very united on six issues in the first session of the Twenty-ninth Congress. In the Senate, on the issues of the tariff, land policy, and the Mexican War, the average Democratic percentage of party cohesion was slightly higher than it had been in the previous Congresses. Five Democratic senators broke with their party on the tariff issue and three did so on the question of land legislation. On both issues the dissenters included the two Pennsylvania Democrats and their colleague from Connecticut. In addition, both Mississippi Democratic senators split with their party colleagues on the tariff. As in the case of several of the Whigs, local and personal pressures seemingly affected these men strongly enough to cause them to take the unusual step of breaking with their party. On the war issue, the two South Carolina senators were the only Democratic dissenters.[50] All of the other Southern Democrats voted with the party. Once again local or personal considerations were a strong force, but they affected only a few senators:

TABLE 5.15
Party-Unity Percentages, Democrats,
29th Congress, Senate

Tariff		80.0
War		92.6
Land		89.3
	Average	87.3

In the House, the Democrats were also strongly united on the three issues of land policy, the tariff, and expansion. As in the Senate, the party dissenters were a few representatives from larger groupings. Most of the New York, New Jersey, and Pennsylvania Democrats broke with their party on the land issue, but at the same time other Northern Democrats from New England, New York, and Pennsylvania remained regular. On the tariff it was all of the Pennsylvania Democrats, one-third of the New Yorkers, plus a scattering of others, who particularly refused to vote with the party. On the expansion issue some Democrats from New York, Virginia, South Carolina, and Alabama broke from the party position while the rest of the representatives from these states remained firmly partisan:

TABLE 5.16
Party-Unity Percentages, Democrats,
29th Congress, House of Representatives

Land	76.5
Expansion	77.6
Tariff	67.4
Average	73.8

Party identification remained the most important influence in Congressional voting in 1846 although other pressures occasionally affected different congressmen at different times. But nonparty voting was limited to a few men on a few issues and did not reflect widespread disagreements with traditional party positions.

Sectional considerations did affect Congressional behavior in one group of issues in 1846. However, this sectionalism occurred within a broad party framework. Sectional influences affected some Whigs, for instance, only in the voting on the war issue in the House, where the party voted against the administration's war policy, and an identifiable sectional group, sixteen of the twenty Southern Whigs, voted with the administration in favor of a vigorous prosecution of the war.

Within the Democratic party sectional groups appeared on the internal improvements and war issues in the House and on the expansion and improvements issues in the Senate. The Western Democrats in both houses broke with the rest of their party on the issue of federal aid for internal improvements while the Westerners and Northerners were less militant on the war issue than were their Southern colleagues. On the expansion issue it was the Southern Democrats who dissented. Thus, sectional considerations did play a role of some importance on these issues. On the other hand, on all of these issues, although the Democrats split among themselves, most of them usually voted on the side of the scale away from the Whigs. There were party directions on the scale and it was within these that sectional groupings developed. Although these internal splits were very bitter and caused immediate concern, it was still important in the voting whether one was a Democrat or a Whig.

Because sectional influences appeared in 1846 there was a possibility that they could become important, but, as yet, however, they did not strongly affect the total picture of Congressional behavior. Nevertheless, historians have been correct in stressing the intensity of Western reaction to what had happened during 1846. Western Democrats sharply denounced Southern Democratic congressmen, believing that the Southerners had deserted them on expansion and internal improvements.[51] In line with the actual voting they could as accurately have attacked Northerners and some other Westerners. The trouble was not in the Southern voting but in Western frustration and expectations of Southern support. The Western leaders overrated both their understanding with the South at Memphis and the power and influence of John C. Calhoun. When their hopes were dashed, some Westerners found a convenient scapegoat in the Southern voting. They attacked the South and were lukewarm towards President Polk on the war issue. Although the denunciations were fierce and intense, Western resentment was not accurately aimed in being directed simply against the South.

The very fact of Western bitterness, however, whether or not it was mistaken, was important. If the Westerners reacted vindictively against the South, they could provoke reactions from Southerners which would create a sectional situation. Although the sections were not yet unified it was possible for the agitation of a few men to affect the situation. Congress had to deal with this problem during the next three years as it considered the questions raised by the introduction of the antislavery Wilmot Proviso.

6. THE CONSEQUENCES OF MANIFEST DESTINY, 1846–1849

E A R L Y in 1847, President James K. Polk noted unhappily in his diary that some Democrats were challenging his leadership, factionalizing the party, and thus endangering the Democratic program, because of their own selfish concerns.[1] Superficially, the President had reason to complain. Many Democrats were angry at the administration's actions in compromising the Oregon dispute with Great Britain and in vetoing the Rivers and Harbors Bill.[2] Nor was their anger alleviated by an apparent change in the political environment within the United States. Earlier in the 1840's the major issues of concern to the country had been those of finance, tariff, and land. When Congress had considered such matters, despite some internal party differences over legislative priorities, national party unity had been maintained and had been the most important factor in Congressional voting behavior. Unfortunately for President Polk's peace of mind, however, there had also been a few issues during the early 1840's (internal improvements, for example) on which the party coalitions had broken apart into local and regional voting blocs. These had not previously been very important in the total picture of Congressional voting, but now, in 1847, the issues of intense two-party differences were no longer the primary concern of Congress, while some of the issues threatening party cohesion still awaited solution.[3]

The differences within the Democratic party were particularly bitter after the veto of the Rivers and Harbors Bill of 1846. Some disgruntled Western congressmen had attacked both the President and other leading members of their party. They specifically directed their anger at Southern Democrats who, they thought, controlled the Polk administration's policies.[4] In a definite anti-Southern move in 1846, some Westerners supported an amendment against slavery extension, the Wilmot Proviso, to a war appropriations bill.[5]

Whether or not the Wilmot Proviso was a reaction to alleged Southern intransigence on the internal improvements issue as some historians have claimed,[6] or was the result of a genuine antislavery feeling,[7] many of the Southern congressmen were frightened and angry when the Westerners introduced it. In the ensuing debate several Southerners warned that such a proviso so threatened their rights and endangered their institutions that Congress must not even consider it.[8] Despite these warnings, however, some of the Westerners intensified their attack. The sectional debate became so vehement that President Polk and Congressional leaders from both parties and from both sections attempted to soothe ruffled congressmen by suggesting that the Wilmot Proviso was neither important nor necessary.[9] Although sectional agitators quieted down for the moment, it was clear that Congress had not seen the end of efforts to restrict slavery. Congress would have to deal with many territorial problems for, in addition to the Oregon country, it was apparent that we would also acquire land from Mexico. These new territories could stimulate renewed agitation over the Wilmot Proviso.

In early 1847, Congress moved to consider one of the issues which had made Westerners so unhappy during the previous year, and this further complicated the problem of easing sectional tensions. Polk's veto had not ended Congressional differences over federal support for internal improvements. The Western reaction to the veto made it clear that Western congressmen were going to introduce another rivers and harbors bill and organize and agitate for its passage. In early 1847, ten thousand Westerners attended an internal improvements convention in Chicago.[10] After several days of speeches in favor of certain Western policies, they passed resolutions which demanded federal appropriations to protect Western commerce and lives.[11] There was widespread Western approval for the convention's demands and for its anti-administration and anti-Southern tone. The Chicago convention and the continued pressure for internal improvements fueled the fire of existing sectional bitterness.[12]

During 1846 and 1847, therefore, due to the internal improvements and territorial issues, there was an obvious increase in articulate sectional pronouncements in the United States. The question remained, however, whether these expressions reflected a widespread desire among congressmen to forget traditional party differences in the interest of establishing sectional coalitions. Although there were tensions within the existing parties which might cause their breakdown into sectional blocs, many political leaders still debated issues in partisan terms and still considered the national parties as the primary instrument of political action.[13] Such leaders were not ready as yet to form sectional political groupings.

Congressional Voting

Throughout the second session of the Twenty-ninth Congress (December, 1846 to March, 1847), and the whole of the Thirtieth Congress (December, 1847 to March, 1849), there was a melange of sectional and nationalist rhetoric in the debates on the different issues. Fortunately for those who wanted to continue working through national parties, the Mexican War was the first important problem considered by Congress. While sectional groups argued over internal improvements and the Wilmot Proviso, United States troops had clashed with the Mexican army.[14] In this country, after the first flush of nationalistic support for the war, controversy developed over our Mexican policy and the administration's war aims. The Congressional debates over the causes, conduct, and settlement of the war had definite partisan overtones. Most Democratic congressmen supported the administration and the war; the Whigs articulately opposed the actions of the Polk administration and insisted that the war was both unnecessary and iniquitous.[15] The Whig-controlled Ohio legislature, for example, passed resolutions condemning the war and commending those congressmen who had opposed the administration's "unjust" war policy. Other Whigs followed the Ohio group's lead.[16] The debates on "Mr. Polk's War" were as intensely partisan as any of the arguments over economic issues in earlier years.

Congressional voting on war measures during the second session of the Twenty-ninth Congress and in the Thirtieth Congress further demonstrated that war policy was primarily a partisan issue. In both houses, members of the two national parties consistently voted against one another (Tables 6.1–6.4).[17]

TABLE 6.1
War Issue, Party Division,
29th Congress, House of Representatives

		Democrats		Whigs	
	Scale Type	No.	%	No.	%
Pro (war policy)	(0– 3)	123	87.2	—	—
Moderate	(4– 7)	16	11.3	9	13.2
Anti	(8–11)	2	1.5	59	86.8

TABLE 6.2
War Issue, Party Division,
30th Congress, House of Representatives

		Democrats		Whigs	
	Scale Type	No.	%	No.	%
Pro (war policy)	(0– 3)	91	91.0	—	—
Moderate	(4– 7)	6	6.0	7	6.8
Anti	(8–11)	3	3.0	97	93.2

TABLE 6.3
War Issue, Party Division,
29th Congress, Senate

		Democrats		Whigs	
	Scale Type	No.	%	No.	%
Pro (war policy)	(0– 2)	18	62.1	—	—
Moderate	(3– 7)	11	37.9	2	8.3
Anti	(8–10)	—	—	22	91.7

TABLE 6.4
War Issue, Party Division,
30th Congress, Senate

		Democrats		Whigs	
	Scale Type	No.	%	No.	%
Pro (war policy)	(0–2)	22	64.7	—	—
Moderate	(3–4)	9	26.5	—	—
Anti	(6–7)	3	8.8	17	100.0

Although the Democrats did not support all of the administration's war policies unanimously, most of them favored those policies more strongly than did the majority of the Whigs. We can see further evidence of this party influence when we compare the party blocs with sectional and regional groupings.[18] Despite the Democratic squabbling in previous Congresses, on the major issue at the beginning of these Congressional sessions national party unity continued to be quite strong.[19]

During the years from 1847 through 1849 both houses also considered some of the older issues which had been so important in earlier Congresses. As on the Mexican War issue, there was a high degree of party unity in the voting on all of these issues. For example, the Senate acted upon the land and internal improvements questions once again. The land scale included seven different votes (Table 6.5).[20]

The same partisanship was present on the internal improvements issue as the Democrats and Whigs reacted differently (Table 6.6).[21] Despite the differences within the Democratic party on internal improvements, over 85 per cent of the senators of that party were more opposed to federal construction of internal improvements than all but one Whig.

TABLE 6.5
Land Issue, Party Division,
29th Congress, Senate

		Democrats		Whigs	
	Scale Type	No.	%	No.	%
Liberal	(0–2)	20	74.1	—	—
Moderate	(3–5)	4	14.8	4	17.3
Conservative	(6–7)	3	11.1	19	82.7

TABLE 6.6
Improvements Issue, Party Division,
30th Congress, Senate

		Democrats		Whigs	
	Scale Type	No.	%	No.	%
Pro (govt. intervention)	(0–1)	4	14.3	13	92.9
Moderate	(2–4)	13	46.4	—	—
Anti	(5–6)	11	39.3	1	7.1

In the House of Representatives, the pattern of voting on the two issues of the tariff and internal improvements also indicated continuing party strength and vitality (Tables 6.7, 6.8).[22] In both of these areas the Whig party, in its opposition role, was particularly united. Al-

TABLE 6.7
Tariff Issue, Party Division,
29th Congress, House of Representatives

		Democrats		Whigs	
	Scale Type	No.	%	No.	%
Low tariff	(0–2)	76	63.3	2	3.0
Moderate	(3–5)	42	35.0	—	—
High tariff	(6–7)	2	1.7	65	97.0

TABLE 6.8
Improvements Issue, Party Division,
30th Congress, House of Representatives

		Democrats		Whigs	
	Scale Type	No.	%	No.	%
Pro (govt. intervention)	(0– 2)	27	25.2	90	94.7
Moderate	(3– 6)	13	12.2	4	4.2
Anti	(7–10)	67	62.6	1	1.1

though the House Democrats divided significantly among themselves on the tariff, all but three of them voted against the body of the Whig party. On the internal improvements issue, one-quarter of the Democratic representatives voted with most of the Whigs. On the other hand, the other three-quarters of the Democrats clearly opposed the Whig position. Interestingly enough, the Democrats were less divided on the internal improvements issue than they had been in previous years, despite the bitterness expressed on the question and the organized pressures present. Whatever the reasons for this, it is clear that most Democrats still subscribed to the party's stated position on the issue.

If we stopped our analysis at this point, we could easily suggest that the desire of many of the party leaders to play down sectional issues in favor of national issues had been successful. In Congressional behavior on the war, tariff, land, and improvements issues, there is no doubt that the national parties continued to play an important role in the last years of the 1840's. However, Congress also considered other issues, the most important of which concerned the territorial expansion of the United States. Questions involving California, New Mexico, and Oregon dominated the time and activities of Congress by 1849.

In 1846, due to the Wilmot Proviso agitation, there had been some sectional overtones to the expansion issue. On the other hand, partisan considerations had also played a role. The two parties had repeatedly differed over expansion in the early 1840's, the Democrats supporting American expansion, the Whigs voting against further acquisition of new territories.[23] Party leaders continued to advocate their earlier positions in the debates over territorial indemnity from Mexico. A Democratic newspaper in Athens, Georgia, the *Southern Banner*, declared that the "larger our empire, the more freedom—more justice—more strength."[24] At the same time a Whig congressman, Robert Schenck of Ohio, introduced a bill calling on the President to return to Mexico all seized territories, declaring that he had always resisted the acquisition of new territory.[25] Neither of these were isolated examples in the debates on the issue. If the voting in Congress was a matter of whether or not to acquire territory, then, based on previous votes and present declarations, there would have been strong party cohesion.

In both the Twenty-ninth and Thirtieth Congresses, however, some congressmen reopened the questions of slavery extension and the Wilmot Proviso every time territorial matters were discussed. The resulting debates were prolonged, acrimonious, and constant, since there was a great deal of territorial business before Congress in these years. Whatever partisan differences existed on expansion matters were drowned out by the intensity of the sectional arguments offered in the floor of both houses of Congress. When David Wilmot had first introduced his provision in 1846, Southerners had either been confused or indifferent to it.[26] Many of them, however, quickly recovered and demonstrated their hostility to an antislavery act of this kind. They expressed their anger in increasingly belligerent terms. Some of them even threatened secession in 1847 and 1848.[27] As the month passed the Wilmot Proviso apparently grew into a major issue in Southern politics. In election campaigns during this period Congressional candidates constantly had to assert their opposition to the Proviso.[28] Southern newspapers continually played up the issue and local political meetings as well as several state legislatures formally protested against the Proviso as a threat to Southern rights and institutions.[29]

In the Northern states at the same time there were similarly numerous and pointed discussions of the Wilmot Proviso. In legislative debates, public meetings, and newspaper editorials, Northerners defended Wilmot's proposal and attacked the spread of slavery into new territories. As Southerners reacted to the Proviso, Northerners increased these antislavery attacks until political meetings and state legislatures formally supported the Proviso, and candidates for offices also had to promise to support it.[30]

During the second session of the Twenty-ninth Congress, the House of Representatives considered the issues raised by the Wilmot Proviso, as well as the problem of slavery in the Oregon territory. The voting revealed a clear North-versus-South sectional pattern which overrode previous national party commitments.[31] The Southerners were almost completely united at one end of the scale, with 94 per cent of the Northern congressmen voting differently from them (Table 6.9).

At the same, time, however, there were differences among the Northern congressmen on this issue. And interestingly enough, these differences were partisan. While the non-Southern Democratic congressmen were very splintered on the issue, all of the Northern Whigs voted in the antislavery position (Table 6.10).

Northern Democrats and Northern Whigs apparently saw the slavery issue in different terms during late 1846 and early 1847. While it is true some of the Northern Democrats joined the Whigs and voted

TABLE 6.9
Slavery-Extension Issue, Sectional Division,
29th Congress, House of Representatives

		North		South	
	Scale Type	No.	%	No.	%
Proslavery	(0–2)	8	6.2	86	97.7
Moderate	(3–6)	50	38.8	—	—
Antislavery	(7–8)	71	55.0	2	2.3

TABLE 6.10

Slavery-Extension Issue, Northern and Western Division,
29th Congress, House of Representatives

	Northeast Whigs		Northeast Democrats		Northwest Whigs		Northwest Democrats	
	No.	*%*	*No.*	*%*	*No.*	*%*	*No.*	*%*
Proslavery	—	—	—	—	—	—	6	20.0
Moderate	—	—	33	75	—	—	17	56.7
Antislavery	40	100	11	25	10	100	7	23.3

against slavery, three-quarters of them were more moderate on the issue than all of the Whigs. In the West old ties of background and economic relationships may have led some congressmen to vote as they did.[32] In addition, some Democratic spokesmen partisanly claimed that the whole issue had been raised only to defeat the administration by dividing the Democratic party. Therefore, they said, they would ignore the sectional implications of the issue and preserve party unity.[33] Whatever the reasons for their vote, the Northern Democrats obviously considered the issue more complex than a simple matter of being for or against slavery.

The Northern congressmen's attempted moderation on the slavery question was potentially dangerous to them since many Northerners wanted their representatives to vote against slavery and pressured them to do so. As a result, during the Thirtieth Congress many congressmen tried to allay the existing sectional suspicion and animosity.[34] The Northern Democrats who favored a moderate course were joined by some Whigs who also feared the effects of the sectionalizing of political parties. These Whigs added another element to the discussion by claiming that the way to avoid the slavery issue and preserve the Union was not to acquire any territory from Mexico.[35] It was obvious, however, that Northern moderates had little support in playing down the slavery issue. Americans wanted to expand, and despite hopes to the contrary, the slavery issue came up every time Congress discussed expansion.[36]

Finally, in early 1848, moderate senators managed to refer several proposed solutions to the slavery issue to a select committee to work out a final settlement of all pending matters. The select committee reported the Clayton Compromise in July, 1848, which would have set up territorial governments in Oregon, California, and New Mexico, and left the matter of slavery in those territories to be determined by the Supreme Court.[37] In addition to this proposal, the two houses of Congress also voted on several other territorial bills as well as the Wilmot Proviso in several forms. Moreover, some Northern congressmen challenged the slave trade in the District of Columbia. Congressmen, as a result, were constantly voting on different aspects of the slavery issue, whether they wished to or not.

In each house of Congress a single scale revealed the different attitudes towards all of these slavery matters.[38] As in the House of Representatives in the Twenty-ninth Congress, the voting on these scales was primarily sectional:

TABLE 6.11
Slavery-Extension Issue, Sectional Division,
30th Congress, House of Representatives

		North		South	
	Scale Type	No.	%	No.	%
Proslavery	(0– 3)	10	8.8	86	100
Moderate	(4– 8)	9	7.9	—	—
Antislavery	(9–12)	95	83.3	—	—

TABLE 6.12
Slavery-Extension Issue, Sectional Division,
30th Congress, Senate

		North		South	
	Scale Type	No.	%	No.	%
Proslavery	(0– 3)	—	—	24	80
Moderate	(4– 8)	8	32	6	20
Antislavery	(9–13)	17	68	—	—

It appears that the various domestic pressures on the slavery issue affected the Northern congressmen more in the Thirtieth Congress than previously, since they were much more united than they had been in the Twenty-ninth Congress. Furthermore, Northern voting had shifted from the moderate position toward the antislavery position.[39] As a result of that shift, the voting patterns in the House of Representatives indicate the existence of two extreme blocs on the slavery issue and a moderate group that was much smaller than it had been earlier.

A final significant point in the voting on the slavery issue was that all but one of the Northern moderate and proslavery votes were Democratic. The Northern Whigs were overwhelmingly antislavery in their voting behavior in both houses. The Northern Democrats, on the other hand, were somewhat splintered over the whole scale of attitudes:

TABLE 6.13
Slavery-Extension Issue, Northern and Western Division,
30th Congress, House of Representatives

	Northeast		Northwest	
	Whigs	*Dems.*	*Whigs*	*Dems.*
Proslavery	—	5	—	5
Moderate	1	3	—	5
Antislavery	55	16	14	11

TABLE 6.14
Slavery-Extension Issue, Northern and Western Division,
30th Congress, Senate

	Northeast		Northwest	
	Whigs	*Dems.*	*Whigs*	*Dems.*
Proslavery	—	—	—	—
Moderate	—	3	—	5
Antislavery	10	4	1	2

The Nature of Congressional Voting

As a result of the Mexican War and American expansion into new territories much of the Congressional activity between 1846 and 1849 focussed on problems posed by slavery extension. The constant discussions in Washington and the domestic pressures elsewhere apparently sectionalized Congressional voting on expansion issues. This was not the whole story of these years, however. Congress also considered war policies as well as some traditional legislative issues, including the tariff, land policy, and internal improvements. On these issues a high correlation existed between national party ties and Congressional voting behavior.

The Whig party was especially united on the traditionally partisan issues. In the House of Representatives, Whig party unity averaged 92.9 per cent on these issues.[40] In the Senate, Whig cohesion averaged 94.3 per cent on the four nonterritorial scales.[41] The party had remained highly cohesive between 1841 and 1849, since the percentage of Whigs voting together was not remarkably different after the appearance of the slavery-extension controversy from what it had been in the earlier Congresses of the decade.[42]

The failure of other pressures to influence Whig voting on partisan issues can be further seen by looking at the Whig dissenters on these scales who were not a coherent sectional or regional group but, rather, a few random individuals. Although in the first session of the Twenty-ninth Congress Southern Whigs had been more prowar than their party colleagues, this no longer was true.[43] On this issue as well as on the others, those Whigs who dissented from their party seemed to do so for local or personal reasons rather than in reaction to any larger coherent pressure.

Although the Democratic party's cohesion was not as high as the Whigs's on the older issues, most of the Democratic congressmen seemed to follow party direction. In the House of Representatives the Democrats were 76 per cent united on these issues.[44] In the Senate they averaged 61.8 per cent.[45] In both Houses they were somewhat less unified than they had been earlier in the decade.[46] Of course, the Democrats had been bickering among themselves since the Polk administration had come to power, and the decline in party unity from the 1841–1845 period may have reflected this fact.[47] Although the Democrats did split somewhat, usually they did not vote in every position on the scale of attitudes. Most Democrats voted together on the part of the scale away from where most of the Whigs voted. In other words, despite the internal Democratic differences, few of them adopted the Whig position on these matters. Furthermore, the few Democrats who did vote with the Whigs were not a sectional or regional bloc but rather, as in the case of the Whig dissenters, random individuals. It seems that Democrat dissenters, too, responded to local and personal pressures when they broke with their party.

The continued partisan quality of Congressional voting is further evident when party blocs are compared with sectional groupings on the same issues. Since the congressmen for each section generally split along party lines, sectional percentages reflected only the partisan composition of each section:

TABLE 6.15
Sectional Breakdown,
29th and 30th Congresses, Senate

	North	South	West		North	South	West
		War (29)				War (30)	
Prowar	33.3%	32.1%	57.1%		31.3%	46.2%	62.5%
Moderate	5.6	39.3	14.3		12.4	15.4	25.0
Antiwar	61.1	28.6	28.6		56.3	38.4	12.5
		Land (29)			Improvements (30)		
Liberal	23.5%	42.3%	71.5%	Pro	72.7%	33.3%	14.3%
Moderate	17.6	19.2	—	Moderate	—	29.2	85.7
Conservative	58.9	38.5	28.5	Anti	27.3	37.5	—

TABLE 6.16
Sectional Breakdown,
29th and 30th Congresses, House of Representatives

	North	South	West		North	South	West
		War (29)				War (30)	
Prowar	44.3%	67.0%	67.5%		26.5%	54.1%	55.0%
Moderate	10.2	12.8	7.5		2.4	10.6	5.0
Antiwar	45.5	20.2	25.0		71.1	35.3	40.0
		Tariff (29)			Improvements (30)		
Low tariff	32.9%	63.2%	50.0%	Pro	78.8%	40.0%	57.5%
Moderate	13.9	9.2	26.3	Moderate	8.3	1.0	22.5
High tariff	53.2	27.6	23.7	Anti	12.9	59.0	20.0

Despite the high degree of partisanship and the relative lack of sectional cohesion on most issues considered in the Twenty-ninth and Thirtieth Congresses, there was one area where political party coalitions collapsed and sectional blocs formed in their place. When Congress considered the issue of slavery extension into the Mexican Cession, Northern and Southern congressmen voted with their sectional colleagues regardless of party affiliation. So that, although expansion had been a partisan issue in the early 1840's, its increasing involvement with the slavery issue seemed to have changed the nature of voting divisions.

There were subtle differences within the framework of sectional cohesion on the slavery-territorial issue. Southern congressmen were much more united than were the Northern representatives. On the three slavery scales the Southern congressmen were 92.6 per cent united whereas, on the same issue, only 68.8 per cent of the Northern congressmen voted together.[48] However, the more moderate stand of the Northerners was qualified by two factors. First, all but a few of the Northerners voted against most Southerners. That is, there were differences of degree among Northern congressmen but these differences did not cause many of them to join Southern voting blocs. And second, as Congress continued to vote on the issue, the Northerners became more united, suggesting that they were reacting to sectional influences more and more.[49] We can see how important sectional pressures were when we compare sectional voting with partisan voting on the slavery issue. Members of each party voted all over the scale of attitudes:

TABLE 6.17

Slavery Issue, Party Division,
29th and 30th Congresses, House and Senate

	House (29)		House (30)		Senate (30)	
	Dems.	*Whigs*	*Dems.*	*Whigs*	*Dems.*	*Whigs*
Proslavery	51.1%	28.8%	63.5%	33.6%	51.5%	31.8%
Moderate	35.9	—	8.4	1.0	30.3	18.2
Antislavery	13.0	71.2	28.1	65.4	18.2	50.0

There were several dissenting voters in each section. In the South they were random individuals, which suggests that they reacted to local and personal considerations. Although most of the Northern dissenters were also random individuals,[50] there were specific influences at work as well. While some Northern Democrats showed a moderate or even a proslavery attitude, Northern Whigs uniformly voted against slavery. Partisanship could, it seems, still partially influence the voting on a sectional issue. Nevertheless the partisan influences now operated within a sectional framework.

In the second session of the Twenty-ninth Congress and in both sessions of the Thirtieth, partisanship and sectionalism existed side by side and influenced congressmen. The relative importance of each depended upon the issue considered. And, although the newer element of sectionalism had become important, congressmen did not see everything in sectional terms. The one issue of slavery extension, however, was beginning to dominate Congressional activity. Although some congressmen wanted to ignore it, they were unable to, due to the pressure of events and the conscious desire of a few leaders to fight on the question.[51] Since Congress had not settled the slavery issue in the Thirtieth Congress these leaders worked to unify their section's representatives so they could settle the matter favorably during the Thirty-first Congress.

7. THE MOVEMENT FOR SECTIONAL UNITY, 1841–1850

E A R L Y in 1848 the editor of South Carolina's leading newspaper, the *Charleston Mercury*, urged all Southern political leaders, whether Democrat or Whig, to "forget all petty animosities, bury recollections of past differences, and unite. . . . firmly and truly in the defense of . . .[Southern] rights."[1] A call for sectional unity was not unusual for the *Mercury*'s editor,[2] but his request ran contrary to the nature of much of American political life in the 1840's. In the politics of the day, sectional coalitions were generally not as important as national partisan alignments. This being so, most political leaders did not readily respond to appeals for sectional unity. There was little indication in Congress in the early and mid-forties, for example, that there existed much of a sympathetic audience for any demand to desert either of the two national parties in favor of sectional political groupings.

On the other hand, despite the traditional political habits of most Americans, there were a few individuals in both the North and the South, who, like the editor of the *Mercury*, advocated sectional political coalitions in place of the existing national parties. In the South, John C. Calhoun, warning his sectional colleagues that they were threatened by Northern antislavery sentiment, was among the first to suggest that Southerners should forget all party differences and unite to protect their section.[3] Calhoun had received little support for his earlier warnings but by the mid-1840's some other political leaders in the South expressed agreement with him. Several state legislatures passed resolutions against Southern division in the face of the danger to their way of life.[4] A group of Southerners attempted in 1847 to establish a Southern newspaper at Washington, D. C., which would, they hoped, counteract the antisectional nature of the existing party press and promote unity of the South.[5]

A similar sectional unity movement existed in the North in the same period. Since the late 1830's, several Northern groups, particularly the Liberty party, had called for Northern political unity to end the South's power in national affairs.[6] These Northerners ran sectional candidates in the presidential elections of 1840 and 1844. Although there was very little support for such candidates in those years,[7] anti-Southern sentiment in the North continued to increase, particularly when Southerners opposed Northern legislative proposals.[8]

The continued pronouncements in favor of sectional unity emanating from spokesmen in both North and South indicated a potentially vital political movement.[9] Despite the apparent vitality, however, there were still a great many Northerners and Southerners who strongly opposed sectional political behavior as unnecessary and dangerous. Such people did not respond to alleged sectional dangers with the same degree of concern as John C. Calhoun or James G. Birney. They wanted national political parties to continue and therefore attacked leaders of the sectional-unity movements. Southern antisectionalists, for instance, pointed out that both of the national party coalitions benefited the Southern people, for only through the Democratic and Whig parties could the economic, political, or social programs of different groups of Southerners be achieved.[10] They insisted, furthermore, that if the South had to be defended from outside pressures, sectional unity was not the best answer. Southerners, they pointed out, were a numerical minority nationally, and their best defense was to maintain close ties with Northerners within the traditional party coalitions. Northerners who were not committed against slavery would work with Southerners on other, more vital issues.[11]

Many Southerners also distrusted the leaders of the Southern unity movement, particularly John C. Calhoun. Since the nullification controversy of 1832 there had been Calhoun and anti-Calhoun factions within the Democratic party in many Southern states.[12] Furthermore, Calhoun's attitudes and actions against the Polk administration generally, and the Mexican War particularly, angered the many Southern Democrats who supported the policies of the national Democratic administration.[13] The Southern Whigs also suspected Calhoun to be an untrustworthy and ambitious political renegade since his break with their party in the late thirties. Several of them suggested that he was probably calling for sectional unity in order to promote his own interests.[14] The Whigs, therefore, along with the anti-Calhoun Democrats, refused to join the sectional-unity movement even after the rise of the slavery controversy in 1846. As late as 1848, Calhoun and his associates lamented the Southern failure to unify in the face of the great danger to their section.[15]

In the North, many people were also suspicious of the proponents of sectional policies and strongly opposed them. As in the South, spokesmen in both parties vehemently asserted the necessity of maintaining national party ties and denounced the abolitionist agitation as a threat to the passage of needed legislation.[16] They pointed out that unless the Southern congressmen supported them, Northerners could not get their bills through Congress.[17]

In the middle of the 1840's, therefore, both Northern and Southern politicians were noticeably reluctant to join sectional-unity movements. In both halves of the nation it was obvious that traditional national ties limited sectional activity. By 1848, the sectional unifiers were two frustrated and unhappy groups, each fearing the ruin of its section due to the short-sightedness of those political leaders who refused to give up traditional political ties.[18]

Beginning in 1848, however, the sectionalists thought their chances of overcoming opposition to sectional unity were improving. For two years Congress had considered territorial expansion issues raised by the Mexican War and the Oregon treaty. But nothing had been done due to the injection of the movement to limit slavery expansion.[19] The debates on the issue had grown heated as spokesmen outdid each other in bellicosity.[20] By 1848–1849, it was apparent that Congress could not legislate in other areas until it solved the territorial problems of the Mexican Cession.

As a result of this intensification of the slavery-extension issue in the middle 1840's, the movement for sectional unity changed somewhat. Several individuals in each section made more systematic and intensive efforts to bring all political leaders behind a sectional program. During the national elections of 1848 and the Congressional sessions of 1848–

1849, the sectional unifiers once more pressured their colleagues to forget old party ties and work together. Although the sectionalists had not been successful before, their increased activity coupled with continued bitterness over the territorial issue could materially affect political behavior in the country.

During the presidential election campaign of 1848, although some political leaders continued to stress the importance of the traditional national party divisions, they were vigorously countered by sectional politicians who talked only in terms of the North versus the South. For example, in the South during 1848, sectional leaders asked the Southern people not to automatically accept the presidential nominees of either party. Rather, Southerners should first receive guarantees of their rights in the territories before supporting either candidate.[21] The sectionalists believed that the South would not receive these guarantees because Northern politicians could no longer support Southern rights without risking political oblivion from a Northern electorate aroused by abolitionist propaganda.[22] Since the national parties would inevitably fail the South, the sectional leaders called for specific Southern activity to protect their section.

The greatest stimulant for the Southern unifiers was the Wilmot Proviso. They saw Northern support of the Proviso as a clear demonstration of Northern hostility to Southern institutions. As Northern congressmen repeatedly brought up the Proviso during 1847, more and more Southerners declared themselves against it and demanded that Northern leaders also oppose it to prove their adherence to the Constitution's guarantees of slavery.[23] Finally, in their State Convention, Alabama Democrats resolved not to support any presidential candidate who did not both oppose the Wilmot Proviso and assure Southerners that they could take any and all of their property into the new territories.[24] Other Southerners quickly avowed their sympathy with this platform.[25]

Northern political leaders, because of the opposition to slavery extension, found it very difficult to make the public declaration demanded by the Alabama platform. Although the eventual Democratic nominee, Lewis Cass of Michigan, publicly attacked the Wilmot Proviso and sought to reassure the South,[26] many of the Alabama platform group did not believe that Cass or any Northerner would effectively oppose the Proviso.[27] Some of them concluded that Cass's candidacy was as dangerous to Southern institutions as that of any Provisoist because of the former's susceptibility to the demands of Northern public opinion. They therefore broke with the Democratic party and refused to support Cass.

Several Whig leaders also contributed to the growth of Southern sectional unity through the way they attempted to win the Presidency. Although the movement to nominate Zachary Taylor of Louisana was national in scope,[28] a few Whigs played upon his background as slave-owner and Southerner in order to win the support of volatile Southern Democrats.[29] The Whig leaders perceived a great opportunity for victory if they could break the Democrats into sectional blocs while they held their own party together in both North and South.[30] Although he himself was not consciously a party to this movement, Taylor's candidacy thus became part of the sectional-unity movement in 1848.

The North had an even better-organized sectional political movement in 1848. During the presidential campaign an amalgamation of abolitionists, Liberty party men, "Conscience Whigs," and disgruntled Northern Democrats formed the Free-Soil party.[31] They drafted an antislavery platform and ran a frankly sectional candidate.[32] The Free-Soilers hoped to unite the North in a potent coalition of former political enemies by stressing the issue of slavery in the territories and ignoring those policy areas where the parties had traditionally divided.[33] The Free-Soilers campaigned in every Northern state and won substantial support.[34]

In both sections, then, there was an intensive sectional movement in 1848. This activity, taken by itself, indicated the apparent beginning of a revolutionary change in American politics from a national system to sectional coalitions.[35] Sectional movements, however, were not the only political activity during the presidential campaign. Political leaders in both sections worked very hard to maintain traditional party ties, to assert the continuing importance of other issues besides slavery, and to suggest that national politics could only function effectively through national political parties.

In the South, a substantial number of Democrats spoke out in support of the national Democratic ticket and against any sectional candidates.[36] They stressed that adherence to the Democratic party and the candidacies of Cass and Butler would benefit the South more than Taylor and the Whigs would, since the Northern Democrats were much more friendly to Southern institutions and desires than were the Northern Whigs.[37] Cass's position on the slavery question, for example, was close to that of most Southerners.[38] The Alabama platform was therefore unnecessary, "poor, miserable, [and] disorganizing."[39]

Similarly, in the North, political leaders appealed to the long tradition of party adherence to prevent both Northern Whigs and Northern Democrats from supporting the Free-Soilers. These leaders stressed the importance of maintaining national ties in order to enact party programs.[40] And as in the South, the appeal seemed to work. Some of the leading Northern antislavery activists in both parties decided not to join the new party.[41] The leading party newspapers also refused to quit their party and castigated anyone who did.[42]

In the elections of 1848 the advocates of the two political tendencies of national partisanship and sectional unity conflicted. Although no one has yet ascertained the exact extent and influence of either tendency, it appeared that national partisanship was still more important to most voters.[43] On the other hand, spokesmen voiced sectional demands more frequently than ever before and exerted systematic and intense sectional pressures. In the South some Democrats thought that they had lost votes because Zachary Taylor was Southern and Lewis Cass was not.[44]

The sectional factors present during 1848 and the attempts to counter them revealed two important things about the course of American politics. First, political leaders in both sections were determined to organize politics on a sectional basis. And second, the continuing fight over the territories had helped these sectionalists. Of course the national political parties still functioned and held the allegiance of most voters in 1848. The presence of sectional movements, however, and the disaffection expressed in some quarters because of Taylor's alleged sectional vote, suggest how tenuous the continuation of normal political divisions might be in the future. Congress had not yet resolved the slavery issue in the territories. Further fighting over slavery could give new life to the sectional unifiers and lead frightened and desperate men to believe that sectional coalitions were the best protection for their particular interests.[45]

During the year following the election of 1848, American political leaders did not solve the question of slavery in the territories. The issue remained at the center of increasingly harsh political debates. As a result, the sectionalists were encouraged to continue their drive towards unity. Their efforts, for the first time, now reached directly into the halls of Congress as the representatives discussed the territorial issue.

Throughout 1849, meetings in every section of the country vigorously demanded that Congress do something to organize California and the rest of the Mexican Cession.[46] But congressmen, reacting to the Wilmot Proviso and increased sectional pressures, did little except denounce one another.[47] This stalemate persisted until Representative Daniel Gott of New York introduced in December, 1848, a resolution to abolish the slave trade in the District of Columbia.[48] In the bitter atmosphere in Congress enough Northern votes were rounded up to pass the resolution.[49] Southern leaders were stunned and badly frightened because, for the first time in this era, one of the houses of Congress had moved against slavery, not in a new area, but where it already existed. And there were signs that the Northern success had emboldened some leaders to continue attacking the South's institutions wherever and whenever they could.[50]

Southern sectionalists saw in the Northern success an opportunity to bring Southerners together. Under the leadership of Senator Calhoun, they called a caucus of all Southern congressmen to consider their course of action on the Gott Resolution.[51] The Southern leaders hoped this meeting would strongly reassert Southern rights and show the North that Southerners would act together when endangered.[52]

Despite a great deal of editorial support for the meeting,[53] the sectionalists were once more frustrated by the refusal of most Southerners to either accept the leadership of Calhoun or to break with their traditional political customs. Only 69 Southern congressmen and senators, out of a total of 121, attended the first meeting.[54] Then the sectional unifiers could not control the gathering. The assembled congressmen elected a moderate, Thomas Metcalfe of Kentucky, as chairman, and as he afterwards pointed out, Metcalfe had come to the meeting to prevent any rash sectional action.[55] Many avowed Southern moderates joined Metcalfe with a similar purpose.[56] They insisted that there was no real reason for holding such a meeting and reiterated their previous arguments against sectional political divisions.[57] They particularly and severely castigated John C. Calhoun, whose personal ambitions, they said, were leading the country towards disunion and political chaos.[58]

Political motives also played a role in quieting sectional-unity tendencies at the Southern caucus. With a new Whig President, Zachary Taylor, about to enter the White House, many Southern Whigs apparently felt that he should be allowed to deal with the territorial issue without the South forcing his hand.[59] Among the Democrats, at the same time, President Polk persuasively intervened to warn his fellow Southern Democrats against being a party to the movement. He deplored agitation on the slavery question and called the sectional-unity attempt "ill-advised."[60]

Because of all the opposition to Southern unity the Southern caucus did not achieve the purpose of those who had called it together. Calhoun prepared an address listing the South's grievances against the North but many of those attending considered the document too strong. After intense debate and attempts to substitute a more conciliatory message, they considerably modified the original draft.[61] Even then, of the 121 Southern congressmen, only 48 signed the published address.[62] Several of the most prominent Democrats refused to sign and only 2 Southern Whigs of the 34 in Congress signed the message.[63]

Thus, despite some support in the South, the Southern sectionalists saw their hopes smashed in early 1849. For many reasons Southerners were split among themselves and traditional political enemies would not work together.[64] The Milledgeville, Georgia, *Federal Union* complained that the South's moral power had been "sacrificed at the shrine of the party."[65] Whether the *Union* understood the full complex of individual and group motives behind the fact, it was true that once again most congressmen had chosen to work through national political institutions to get what they wanted. Because of this, in 1849, as in 1848 and before, there was no revolution in the American political process, despite apparent sectional danger.

At several points during the 1840's, some politicians sought to replace national political parties with sectional coalitions. Before 1848, their attempts were spotty and limited. But, due to increased bitterness on the slavery extension issue, the movement for sectional unity intensified during 1848 and 1849. Sectional advocates were then able to gain some ground in their campaign by playing on the differences between Northerners and Southerners, and asserting that national political ties no longer had substantive meaning, that the major issues between parties had disappeared and only sectional matters were now important politically. Despite their vigorous advocacy and activities, the sectional unifiers had to face the fact that most congressmen and politically interested people could not easily "forget all petty animosities" and would not respond to sectional-unity movements. Apparently, most Americans still wanted to remain tied to their national party and therefore resisted the warnings of the sectional leaders as to the necessity for sectional protection.

Nevertheless, the sectional unity movement had some importance in American politics since many men in both sections obviously were working to overthrow traditional political patterns. Most congressmen acted in national terms because they did not view the slavery issue as more important than the other issues they had to consider. Would this remain true, however, if Congress could not settle the slavery issue and the sectionalists kept up their pressure? The sectional unifiers, despite their failures, had presented an alternative course of action which might grow more appealing as Americans grew tired of the territorial stalemate. The Thirty-first Congress, meeting in December, 1849, would have to face the territorial issue once again and there was sure to be further activity on the part of the sectionalists.

8. CRISIS AND COMPROMISE, 1850

T H E major legislative issues confronting the Thirty-first Congress when it met in December, 1849, were those of territorial organization and slavery extension. Despite the efforts of national political leaders since 1846 to stress other issues and to play down slavery, the territorial issue was still alive, still bitterly debated, and still potentially sectionally divisive. Furthermore, with the constant airing of the issue and the vitriolic attacks made by politicians in each section against the other section, there was no time for a cooling-off process or for the consideration of other issues.[1]

The result of the continuing animosity was readily apparent. At the end of 1849 Southern sectionalists renewed their drive for political unity. They called for a convention of all Southern states to consider, once again, joint action on their part against the dangers threatening their section.[2] Although many Southerners opposed such a meeting and others had only limited enthusiasm for it,[3] the calling of the convention itself and the favorable response to the call on the part of some Southerners suggested that as long as the slavery issue remained in politics sectional agitation would continue. Such agitation, aided by pressures building up within both sections, might ultimately force political leaders to adopt irreconcilable positions on the slavery question whether they wanted to or not.[4]

When the month-long fight over the House Speakership in December, 1849, added to sectional tensions,[5] several antisectionalist leaders from North and South in both Houses decided to take the initiative, settle the disruptive territorial problems, and end sectional bitterness once and for all.[6] In the Senate men like Henry Clay, Lewis Cass, and Stephen A. Douglas were convinced that they could work out territorial compromise proposals which the many moderates in Congress, desirous of getting rid of disorganizing sectional tendencies, would support.[7] These leaders were encouraged by the growing support for compromise articulated by spokesmen in all parts of the country, obviously frightened by the vindictiveness of the debates in Congress.[8] The leaders knew that in both North and South, politicians with the inflexibility on the slavery issue of John C. Calhoun would fight against any compromise offered. Such men would label any settlement as a sellout to the other section and would try to chip away at Congressional compromise support by pressing for sectional unity. Despite this, the moderate leaders determined to push ahead.

Their estimates of the sectionalist reaction were correct. Extremists in both sections denied the possibility of compromise. The Southern sectionalists fought against the admission of California as a free state and threatened to leave the Union if Congress admitted her.[9] On the other side, Northern groups wanted first and foremost to admit the free state of California without delay and without tieing it in with any other proposals.[10] They also wanted to pass the Wilmot Proviso.[11] Despite the sentiment for compromise it was apparent that there were irreconcilable differences between the two blocs in Congress. But, while both of these extreme groups opposed each other, they might, at the same time, stand togther against any compromise proposals which did not give either section an advantage.[12]

Throughout the Thirty-first Congress, then, men supported either one of two positions on the territorial business confronting them: nationalist and compromising, or sectionalist and noncompromising. With so much conflict in the situation, it was uncertain whether Congress could do anything at all. And until it resolved the territorial issue all other legislative matters appeared to be submerged.

Congressional Voting

When congressmen acted on issues rising out of the territorial question in 1850 they actually considered and voted on two distinct matters. On one set of issues the emphasis was frankly sectional, a continuation of the hostility of the previous few years and an attempt by sectional leaders to win sectional goals and sectional advantage. In various proposals sectionalists in both North and South either attacked the insti-

tutions of the other section, such as in a motion to outlaw slavery in
the District of Columbia, or sought some particular advantage for their
own section, as in the attempt to pass a stronger fugitive slave bill or to
admit California as a free state, without tieing these demands to other
proposals as the compromisers thought necessary.[13] On the second set
of issues however, compromise, not sectional advantage, was at the
heart of the proposals. As the antisectionalists around Clay and Douglas pushed forward the compromise "package" opposed by Calhoun
and others like him, the question became not one of direct sectional
advantage, but whether or not one was willing to forego such advantage, forget differences, and unite to settle the question on the terms
proposed.[14]

On the first set of issues, that involving sectional differences, the
congressmen split principally into Northern and Southern blocs (Table

TABLE 8.1
Sectional Issue, Sectional Division,
31st Congress, Senate

		North		South	
	Scale Type	No.	%	No.	%
Pro-North	(0– 5)	16	55.2		
Moderate	(6–12)	10	34.5	4	14.2
Pro-South	(13–18)	3	10.3	24	85.8

8.1). Since most of the Northern and Southern Senators voted in different halves of the scale, sectional pressures were apparently strong
enough on these questions to split the national parties and to raise in
their place sectional coalitions which ignored the former partisan
differences within sections.

Upon further investigation of the scale, however, we can see some
important differences in the voting, indicating that other influences
were still present within the sectional framework. Southern senators
were much more united than were the Northerners. Most of what little
Southern dissent there was, however, came from the Whig party—
three of the ten Southern Whig senators refused to go along with the
sectional position.[15] At the same time, only one of nineteen Southern
Democratic senators, Benton of Missouri, moved away from the extreme sectional position (Table 8.2).

TABLE 8.2
Sectional Issue, Southern Voting by Party,
31st Congress, Senate

	Democrats		Whigs	
	No.	*%*	*No.*	*%*
Pro-North	—	—	—	—
Moderate	1	5.6	3	30.0
Pro-South	17	94.4	7	70.0

In the North the moderating influences on sectionalism came from the Democratics as many of them refused to become extremists on the slavery issue. In contrast, eleven of the thirteen Northern Whigs were sectionalist in their voting:

TABLE 8.3
Sectional Issue, Northern Voting by Party
31st Congress, Senate

	Democrats		Whigs	
	No.	*%*	*No.*	*%*
Pro-North	4	26.7	11	84.6
Moderate	8	53.3	2	15.4
Pro-South	3	20.0	—	—

The surprising fact here, in terms of a sectional interpretation of American politics, is that three Northern Democrats, from Michigan, New York, and Pennsylvania, voted in the pro-Southern position on the scale.[16]

Although the voting on these territorial questions tended to be sectional in nature, partisanship did have some role. Northern Democrats and Southern Whigs were more moderate in their voting than Northern Whigs and Southern Democrats. This same pattern had also appeared in the voting on slavery in previous Congresses.[17] Whether or not that fact reflected basic fears of disunity among some Congressmen or the greater acceptance of sectional pressures by Northern Whigs and Southern Democrats, it is clear that Whig and Democratic differences still existed, albeit within a sectional voting pattern.[18]

Similar differences also appeared when the House of Representatives considered slavery-extension and related issues in 1850. In that House, on a scale of thirteen issues, most Northern and Southern representatives opposed each other:[19]

TABLE 8.4
Sectional Issue, Sectional Division,
31st Congress, House of Representatives

	Scale Type	North		South	
		No.	%	No.	%
Pro-North	(0– 4)	82	62.9	—	—
Moderate	(5– 9)	42	37.1	6	7.5
Pro-South	(10–13)	—	—	75	92.5

Southerners in the House, as in the Senate, were more united than were Northerners. A major difference between the voting of Southern representatives and Southern senators appeared, however. The South was a great deal more unified in the House than it had been in the Senate. There were only six dissenters from the sectional position, less than 10 per cent of all Southern representatives.[20] Apparently, the sectional pressures operating in this Congress more readily influenced representatives than they did senators.[21]

Unlike their Southern colleagues, the Northern members of the House of Representatives voted much as had the Northern senators:

TABLE 8.5
Sectional Issue, Northern Voting by Party,
31st Congress, House of Representatives

	Democrats		Whigs	
	No.	%	No.	%
Pro-North	20	44.4	55	79.7
Moderate	25	55.6	14	20.3
Pro-South	—	—	—	—

The same moderate tendencies on sectional matters appeared among Northern Democratic representatives as had among the senators from that group, even while the Northern Whigs in both houses reacted in somewhat more sectional terms. The desire to play down sectional issues and to cooperate with their Southern allies on national issues apparently continued to influence the Northern Democrats even when they had to cope with sectional problems.[22] On the other hand, their desire for intersectional cooperation could not and did not lead them to vote with the South. Their moderation existed within a sectional framework thanks, it seems, to the rising pressures on these issues throughout the country.[23]

The compromise scale in the Thirty-first Congress also revealed significant voting differences between the two houses of Congress and between the two political parties. In the Senate, the voting divisions were predominantly sectional although some partisan undertones were present.[24] In a scale ranging from pro-compromise to anti-compromise attitudes, Northern Senators generally voted against compromise, Southerners generally for it (Table 8.6).

In addition to the dominant sectional pattern, some partisan qualities also were present in the voting, particularly in the case of the Northern Whigs and the Southern Democrats. The former were united, with one exception, in the anti-compromise position.[25] The Southern Democrats also clustered, but at the opposite end of the scale in favor of compromise on the slavery-extension issue.[26] On the other hand, partisan conditions seemingly did not affect either the Northern Democrats or the Southern Whigs, both of whom fragmented, in their voting, over the whole range of scale positions (Table 8.7).[27]

The voting patterns in the House of Representatives on the compromise scale, were somewhat different from those of the Senate since in a scale of thirteen separate roll-calls neither party nor sectional groupings remained (Tables 8.8, 8.9).[28]

In addition to the breaking apart of the parties and sections, with few exceptions, the various subgroups were more splintered than they

TABLE 8.6
Compromise Issue, Sectional Division,
31st Congress, Senate

		North		South	
	Scale Type	No.	%	No.	%
Pro-compromise	(0– 3)	6	21.4	19	68.0
Moderate	(4– 6)	4	14.3	6	21.4
Anti-compromise	(7–10)	18	64.3	3	10.6

TABLE 8.7

Compromise Issue, Sectional Voting by Party,
31st Congress, Senate

	Northern Whigs		Northern Democrats		Southern Whigs		Southern Democrats	
	No.	%	No.	%	No.	%	No.	%
Pro-compromise	1	7.7	5	35.7	5	50	14	77.8
Moderate	—	—	4	28.6	3	30	3	16.7
Anti-compromise	12	92.3	5	35.7	2	20	1	5.5

TABLE 8.8

Compromise Issue, Sectional Division,
31st Congress, House of Representatives

	Scale Type	North*		South	
		No.	%	No.	%
Pro-compromise	(0– 4)	54	43.9	51	63.0
Moderate	(5– 7)	32	26.0	7	8.6
Anti-compromise	(8–13)	37	30.1	23	28.4

*Includes six Free-Soilers, Americans, and Independents

TABLE 8.9

Compromise Issue, Party Division,
31st Congress, House of Representatives

	Whigs		Democrats	
	No.	%	No.	%
Pro-compromise	48	50	55	55
Moderate	24	25	15	15
Anti-compromise	24	25	30	30

had been earlier. The Southern Whigs, all of whom favored the compromise proposals were clearly a coherent bloc on the compromise issue. At the same time a large majority of the Northern Democrats also favored compromise. But their position was muddied by the presence of many of their members in other positions the scale than that of the majority. Both the Northern Whigs and the Southern Democrats were almost completely fragmented between the different scale positions (Table 8.10).

TABLE 8.10

Compromise Issue, Sectional Voting by Party,
31st Congress, House of Representatives

	Northern Democrats		Northern Whigs		Southern Whigs		Southern Democrats	
	No.	%	No.	%	No.	%	No.	%
Pro-compromise	32	68.1	22	31.4	27	100	24	44.4
Moderate	8	17.0	24	34.3	—	—	7	12.8
Anti-compromise	7	14.9	24	34.3	—	—	23	42.8

Most members of the House of Representatives reacted in individual and local terms to the compromise proposals. The divisions within the Southern Democrats, Northern Democrats, and Northern Whigs occurred within, as well as between different regions and states, reflecting the differences present most of the time in every voting bloc since the sectional issue arose.[29] Congressmen apparently reacted differently due to a variety of local and individual pressures on the issue rather than to the pressures of large sectional or partisan coalitions. The result was a more confused pattern of Congressional voting than had been the case in earlier Congresses. Although the major issues were sectional in nature, and with the growth of sectional pressures Congressional behavior was more sectionalized than ever before, there were at the same time, other reactions to these issues. Regional, local, and individual pressures also affected Congressional voting and produced conflicting and chaotic patterns of behavior.

In addition to territorial matters in 1850, the House of Representatives also considered the issues of land policy and internal improvements legislation.[30] In light of the pattern in previous Congresses where differences over slavery had not affected other legislative areas,[31] the voting on these two matters is particularly interesting and important, coming as it did during a period of heightened sectionalism. The first of these, land policy, involved the extension of the military bounty provisions enacted during the Mexican War.[32] When the representatives voted on this issue they did not divide into clear-cut partisan or sectional blocs in opposition to one another (Tables 8.11, 8.12).[33]

TABLE 8.11
Land Issue, Party Division,
31st Congress, House of Representatives

	Scale Type	Democrats		Whigs	
		No.	%	No.	%
Liberal	(0–1)	41	44.6	47	54.7
Moderate	(2–3)	39	42.4	17	19.7
Conservative	(4–5)	12	13.0	22	25.6

TABLE 8.12
Land Issue, Sectional Division,
31st Congress, House of Representatives

	North		South	
	No.	%	No.	%
Liberal	77	63.6	15	23.8
Moderate	24	19.8	32	50.8
Conservative	20	16.6	16	25.4

TABLE 8.13
Land Issue, Northern Voting by Party,
31st Congress, House of Representatives

	Whigs		Democrats	
	No.	%	No.	%
Liberal	44	64.6	28	62.6
Moderate	8	10.8	16	35.4
Conservative	17	24.6	1	2.0

TABLE 8.14
Land Issue, Southern Voting by Party,
31st Congress, House of Representatives

	Whigs		Democrats	
	No.	%	No.	%
Liberal	3	17.7	12	26.1
Moderate	9	52.1	23	50.0
Conservative	5	30.2	11	23.9

Sectional party groupings similarly fragmented with a general moderate to liberal bias among all of the blocs (Tables 8.13, 8.14). In the North more Whigs than Democrats opposed the land legislation, but in the South, the parties were equally scattered over the whole range of voting attitudes. Regional and state blocs also fragmented.[34] The land issue apparently was another legislative area where congressmen reacted differently because of local, constituency, or statewide pressures. Although the national parties had not held together on this issue, other large-scale groupings did not replace them.

In earlier Congresses local and regional pressures were important on the internal improvements issue.[35] This continued to be true during the Thirty-first Congress as the voting blocs splintered over the whole range of attitudes (Tables 8.15, 8.16).[36]

TABLE 8.15

Improvements Issue, Sectional Division,
31st Congress, House of Representatives

		North		South	
	Scale Type	No.	%	No.	%
Pro (govt. intervention)	(0–2)	45	36.3	34	44.2
Moderate	(3–6)	29	23.4	9	11.6
Anti	(7–9)	50	40.3	34	44.2

TABLE 8.16

Improvements Issue, Party Division,
31st Congress, House of Representatives

	Democrats		Whigs	
	No.	%	No.	%
Pro (govt. intervention)	47	45.6	29	31.9
Moderate	5	4.9	32	35.1
Anti	51	49.5	30	33.0

Both the Democratic and the Whig voting, neither of which revealed a particular tendency on this issue, reflected the lack of national partisan influences. In the Whig party all of the regional groups also divided quite evenly among themselves (Table 8.17). Within these groupings there were, occasionally, some statewide Whig pressures as well as different local pressures. The Whig congressmen's response to the internal improvements legislation of this Congress varied on an individual basis, from state to state and from locality to locality.[37]

Democratic voting on the improvements issue was somewhat more coherent than was the Whig (Table 8.18). The Northeastern Demo-

TABLE 8.17
Improvements Issue, Whig Congressmen,
31st Congress, House of Representatives

	Northeast	Northwest	South
Pro (govt. intervention)	15	4	10
Moderate	24	2	6
Anti	19	5	6

TABLE 8.18
Improvements Issue, Democratic Congressmen,
31st Congress, House of Representatives

	Northeast	Northwest	South
Pro (govt. intervention)	1	22	24
Moderate	1	1	3
Anti	17	5	28

crats continued to vote, as they had in earlier Congresses, against federal expenditures for internal improvements. At the same time, the Western Democrats continued to support such legislation. The dissenters within these groups voted in both bloc and random patterns. All of the dissenters from the Western Democratic position, for instance, came from Ohio. Yet other Ohio Democrats voted with the rest of the Northwest.[38]

The Southern Democratic voting on this legislation was surprising considering their record in earlier Congresses. They no longer opposed internal improvements legislation as a group, dividing instead along regional lines.[39] Democratic representatives from South Atlantic states voted against the legislation, while the Southwesterners tended to favor the improvements. There were a few local variations in this pattern, but it held in essential respects.[40] In the early 1840's the Southern Democrats had opposed internal improvements expenditures largely out of fear of raising the tariff. Now, however, since Congress was considering North-South railroad lines (the Illinois Central Railroad in particular), as well as Southern lines, some of the Southerners apparently responded to local and regional desires in this area and overcame their previous objections.

The Nature of Congressional Voting

Congressional voting behavior during the pivotal Thirty-first Congress revealed a basic change from the voting of the previous decade. Since the Twenty-seventh Congress, there had been a very high degree of party unity on most issues considered. However, during the first session of the Thirty-first Congress, the parties had fragmented quite dramatically compared to earlier patterns. Distinct Northern and Southern sectional groupings had appeared as a major pattern on some issues. There were also regional voting blocs as well as local and anarchic patterns. Occasionally, there were small-scale partisan groupings. These voting patterns varied according to the issue considered, and sometimes according to the particular house of Congress.

The Senate voted on two sets of issues in 1850. Party unity averaged only 55.1 per cent on these two scales:

TABLE 8.19
Party-Unity,
31st Congress, Senate

	Democrats	*Whigs*
Sectional issue	57.1%	43.0%
Compromise issue	59.4	60.9

In the House, the party unity average was 50 per cent, which is no unity at all:

TABLE 8.20
Party-Unity,
31st Congress, House of Representatives

	Democrats	*Whigs*
Sectional issue	53.5%	58.5%
Compromise issue	55.0	50.0
Improvements issue	49.5	35.2
Land issue	44.6	54.7

Sectional cohesion was more apparent than at any time in the preceding decade. In the Senate, Northern and Southern senators voted on opposite sides of the two issues considered. The same sectionalism was present in the House's vote on the sectional issue. On these three issues Southern unity averaged 79.0 per cent, Northern 60.8 per cent. Obviously, however, although sectional influences had become important in 1850, they did not dominate Congressional voting as completely as had the national parties in earlier periods. Within each section there were conflicting attitudes about sectional unity, and partisan divisions still had some meaning. Depending on the issue involved, Southern Whigs and Southern Democrats voted against one another as did Northern Whigs and Democrats. However, although such partisanship was important as a modifying element, it should be noted that these partisan differences occurred strictly within sectional boundaries. There was no voting relationship apparent between the members of a party in one section and the members of that party in the other section. Nor was such sectional partisanship a regular thing. Different groups coalesced on some issues but not on others.[41]

Occasionally, in this Congress, as when the House voted on the issues of land, internal improvements, and the territorial compromise, neither national nor sectional coalitions, nor sectional partisan groupings, had much meaning. Instead, other voting influences, localism for example, appeared to be more important. Of course local and regional pressures had always operated on congressmen. During the 1840's, however, these had been either part of the national party pressures or had been modified by national partisanship. With the apparent disappearance of the parties in 1850, however, these local and regional pressures operated more effectively. In some cases, as with the Southern Democrats on the internal improvements issue, there were regional voting blocs since Southwesterners and Southeasterners diverged in their attitudes. Sometimes, state voting blocs were present as another type of regional group. In addition to these cohesive blocs there was also a great deal of random dissent from sectional, partisan, or local blocs. These votes probably reflected constituency pressures which varied in nature and meaning from one constituency to the next. Thus, it is clear that there were several different and changing interest groups operating during this Congress.

Congressmen had been a relatively well-disciplined group throughout the 1840's. But the source of their earlier discipline weakened in 1850 and was partially replaced by the new discipline of sectionalism. However, sectional influences were not as stable or as widely influential as had been national political ties. Whereas, in the latter, there had been random dissent from the main party position, here whole blocs modified the sectional positions, suggesting that cross-currents and pressures operated within the sections. Congressional voting behavior in 1850 was both more complex and more chaotic than ever before.

Congress had achieved one major triumph in 1850, however. Enough of the different blocs were able to vote together and pass the legislation necessary to settle finally the question of slavery in the territories acquired from Mexico. As a result, as 1850 ended there were no questions involving slavery extension before Congress, for the first time since mid-1846. But, this issue, which had had such an impact upon the traditional course of politics, had left behind a heritage of bitterness and chaos. Congressmen had sniped at one another in sectional terms for a long period and sectional pressures had built up on the outside and affected Congressional voting. In the face of all that had happened, especially the weakening of traditional voting patterns, questions about the nature of future political divisions in the United States remained to be answered.

9. TO ATTEND TO THE BUSINESS OF THE NATION, 1851–1852

T H E second session of the Thirty-first Congress convened in December, 1850. In the months before the reassembly of the nation's representatives, however, a sharp debate had erupted as to the future shape of American political life. Some obserevrs believed that even with the slavery-extension crisis now settled, the controversy, with its accompanying drive for sectional unity, had permanently weakened national party coalitions. Since nothing appeared strong enough to replace those coalitions, it was feared that political life would become fragmented and chaotic.[1] On the other hand, a few leaders hoped that the disappearance of the slavery issue meant they could now reconstitute the national parties on the same basis as before.[2] Such rebuilding, of course, would not be easy. No one could foresee completely what issues Congress would have to deal with and what type of voting blocs would emerge on these matters, considering the present state of relative political disorganization. Traditional partisan positions and prejudices were still being voiced, however, and a presidential election loomed on the horizon with all of the opportunity it presented for the re-establishment of national parties if still possible.[3] And in Congress there were a number of important nonterritorial issues to be considered which had been deferred due to the slavery-extension controversy.

In addition to those calling for the re-emergence of national partisanship, sectional spokesmen were also present in Congress and the country. The forces which had promoted sectionalism during the late 1840's were neither dead nor quiescent. Rather, their spokesmen seemed determined to destroy the Congressional settlement so laboriously worked out. They realized that if either the North or the South rejected the Compromise of 1850, the slavery problem would probably erupt all over again. Therefore they worked to secure such rejection.[4] In the South, for example, sectional agitators charged that the legislation of 1850 was not a compromise but, rather, a complete Northern victory. As far as these Southerners were concerned, all the compromises had come from the South while the North received all the rewards, especially the new territory acquired from Mexico. Further, these men believed that even the Fugitive Slave Bill, an obvious sop to the South, would not last and would be repealed under Northern pressure.[5]

At the same time, Northern spokesmen also attacked the Congressional settlement of the territorial issue. Their primary target was the Fugitive Slave Law, characterized by one Northern editor as both "damnable and wicked."[6] They denounced those Northern congressmen who had voted for the bill and determined to replace such moderates with others.[7] But they did not stop there. At the same time they called upon the Northern people to assist any slave who escaped to the North instead of helping the authorities recapture him as required under the Fugitive Slave Law.[8] Some Northerners followed this suggestion, and clashes between citizens and the federal officials attempting to carry out the law ensued.[9] Riots and protests against the Fugitive Slave Law were often effective, and the apprehension of runaway slaves became difficult and expensive.[10]

Even as sectional animosity continued in both the North and the South after 1850, national political leaders pushed hard to restore American politics to more traditional channels. They denounced continued agitation on sectional matters; there had been enough of it. The American people were tired of fighting over slavery. Too many other problems remained to be considered and solved. Congress, these leaders suggested, would have enough to do just "to attend to the business of the nation."[11] Northern nationalists demanded compliance with the Fugitive Slave Law as the only means of solving all sectional problems and bringing peace to the country.[12] They sought to defeat public office holders who agitated against the law and they played up the dangers of nonadherence to the law. They tried, also, to have public leaders express support for the whole Compromise including the fugitive slave provision.[13]

In the South, the nationalists opposed the Nashville Convention and any threat of secession. Since they faced a more immediate sectional danger than did the Northerners, Southern nationalists organized themselves politically to fight against the sectional movement. Pointing out that most of the Northern people accepted the Compromise measures, including the Fugitive Slave Law, they warned that Southern secession would destroy not only the Union but the South as well. In state after state there were political contests between these Unionists and their Southern-Rights opponents. At public meetings the nationalists pushed through resolutions acquiescing in the compromise measures and attempted to tone down the force of the Nashville Convention.[14]

Nationalists in both North and South believed that if Congress declared the Compromise measures to be its final legislative action on the slavery issue, they would then have a firm basis to press for peaceful reconciliation between the sections.[15] Senator Henry Foote of Mississippi and Representative William Polk of Tennessee introduced a formal resolution into Congress saying that the Compromise of 1850 was Congress's final declaration on the subject.[16] As was to be expected, the sectionalists in both North and South argued against the finality resolutions as a betrayal of their section's rights and privileges.[17] In response, the nationalists vigorously defended the resolution as the only sure and permanent way to achieve peace on the vexing slavery issue.[18] The nationalists went another step and urged the adoption of the finality idea in the platforms of the two major parties during the presidential campaign of 1852.[19]

Clearly, the sectional crisis did not end with the passage of the Compromise of 1850. One group of political leaders continued to argue in favor of sectional rights and sectional coalitions to win those rights. When a second group of leaders challenged them and demanded a return to national political differences, there was a prolonged and bitter fight. In the South the moderates finally triumphed when they won the elections for delegates to the Nashville Convention, for congressmen, and for state officials,[20] in contests where the issues between the sectionalists and the nationalists were clearly drawn.[21]

In the North the moderates also were victorious as Free-Soil and fire-eating legislators lost elections for office or found it necessary to withdraw from the political arena. It was obvious that in both sections, although some degree of animosity remained, most people wanted to stop agitation on the slavery issue.[22] This was not a steady sentiment for there were times when sectional passion increased in response to some provocation, but there was a definite quieting of the issue and a reopening of national channels of political communication. This was best seen in the growing force of the movements to resurrect the national parties. Opinion leaders in both sections wanted the Democrats and the Whigs to reform their ranks and challenge the other party on some of the older issues of American politics.[23]

Congressional Voting

While political maneuvering, sectional cross-currents, and controversies beset the country, Congress met and considered the questions raised by the sectional agitation and the finality movements.[24] In the House of Representatives there were eight separate roll-calls on the sectional issue.[25] The resultant scale of attitudes ranged from positions favoring further agitation on the sectional theme to those for ending all such controversy forever. In this scale there were no clear-cut party or sectional voting groups, but only small, coherent subgroups:

TABLE 9.1

Sectional Issue, Party Division,
32nd Congress, House of Representatives

		Democrats		Whigs	
	Scale Type	No.	%	No.	%
Pro-agitation	(0–1)	35	33.0	29	46.0
Moderate	(3–5)	6	5.8	3	4.8
Anti-agitation	(6–7)	65	61.2	31	49.2

TABLE 9.2

*Sectional Issue, Sectional Division,**
32nd Congress, House of Representatives

	North		South		West	
	No.	%	No.	%	No.	%
Pro-agitation	38	58.5	10	13.7	20	52.6
Moderate	3	4.6	5	6.8	2	5.3
Anti-agitation	24	36.9	58	79.5	16	42.1

* Includes three Free-Soilers, three Unionists and two others.

	North		South		East		West	
	No.	%	No.	%	No.	%	No.	%
Pro-agitation	58	56.3	10	13.7	48	47.1	20	26.7
Moderate	5	4.9	5	6.8	8	7.8	2	2.6
Anti-agitation	40	38.8	58	79.5	46	45.1	53	70.7

Clearly, the North and the West were internally divided on the issue. Although the South was more united, and more opposed to agitation, it too contained a group which voted all the way on the opposite side from the main sectional group. A further breakdown of voting blocs indicates similar divisions on the regional level:

TABLE 9.3
Sectional Issue, Sectional-Party and Regional Divisions,
32nd Congress, House of Representatives

	Whigs			Democrats		
	North	South	West	North	South	West
Pro-agitation	19	—	10	17	10	8
Moderate	2	—	1	—	5	1
Anti-agitation	8	23	—	16	33	16

	New England	Middle Atlantic	South Atlantic	South Central	North Central
Pro-agitation	16	23	9	—	20
Moderate	—	3	5	—	2
Anti-agitation	7	17	22	37	16

Although each group manifested some particular attitudes in their voting, only the Western Whigs, the Southern Whigs, and the Congressmen from the South-Central States, held unequivocal positions. The Western Whigs wanted continued agitation on sectional matters, the other two groups wanted such agitation to cease. Except for these three groups, the congressmen apparently reacted to local and individual pressures in casting their votes.

The Senate's voting on the sectional issue was somewhat different from the House of Representatives'. Senators formed definite large-scale blocs, the most significant of which were the parties, although Whigs and Democrats did not vote on opposite sides of the issue. The sectional scale in the Senate contained five separate votes, all concerned with the Fugitive Slave Law:[26]

TABLE 9.4
Sectional Issue, Party Division,
32nd Congress, Senate

		Democrats		Whigs		Free-Soil	
	Scale Type	*No.*	*%*	*No.*	*%*	*No.*	*%*
Pro-agitation	(0–1)	2	6.7	1	5.5	3	100.0
Moderate	(2–3)	2	6.7	3	16.7	—	—
Anti-agitation	(4–5)	26	86.6	14	77.8	—	—

There was little disagreement in the Senate on this issue, a large majority of the senators being against any further slavery agitation. The dissenters from this position, however, were all Northerners:

TABLE 9.5
Sectional Issue, Sectional Division,
32nd Congress, Senate

	North		South	
	No.	*%*	*No.*	*%*
Pro-agitation	6	21.4	—	—
Moderate	5	18.0	—	—
Anti-agitation	17	60.6	23	100.0

The three Free-Soilers from the North and West (Chase of Ohio, Hale of New Hampshire, and Sumner of Massachusetts), clearly wanted further activity against the Fugitive Slave Bill. One Whig, Seward of New York, and two Democrats, Dodge of Wisconsin and Wade of Ohio, joined them.[27] The five Northern moderates included three Whigs, Upham and Foote of Vermont and Davis of Massachusetts, and two Democrats, Hamlin of Maine and Shields of Illinois. Except for these men, all of the Whigs and Democrats in the Senate voted for peace on the issue.

The Expansion of the United States

At the opening of the second session of the Thirty-first Congress, the long-time antislavery advocate, Joshua Giddings of Ohio, angrily attacked the Fugitive Slave Law.[28] He was immediately answered by two

Western Democrats, William J. Brown of Indiana and John Wentworth of Illinois, both of whom called upon the House to stop discussing such irrelevant topics.[29] They pointed out that there was a great deal of legislation before Congress, passage of which was essential for the future development of the United States, and which had been too long delayed by the slavery controversy.[30]

Underlying this colloquy was the American people's renewed interest in their country's growth. The 1840's had been a time of great expansion and internal development in the United States.[31] Despite the long slavery controversy this growth had continued. Many people, inside Congress and out, were unhappy because the government had not enacted legislation to stimulate this growth.[32] Expressions of this unhappiness had been generally muted during the years of sectional controversy,[33] but, as the exchange between Giddings and the others in the House indicated, many Americans impatiently awaited Congressional action. They wanted federal rivers and harbors legislation to improve commerce on navigable waters,[34] changes in the tariff, and reforms in financial institutions.[35] Some also made new demands for railroad land grants, and for improved federal services in newly settled areas.[36] Finally, there were resurgent and constant demands for land reform.[37]

During its two sessions immediately following the crisis of 1850, Congress, responding to the demand for federal promotion of American development, considered a variety of legislative proposals. These matters involved four different scales, two relating to government financing of transportation improvement and expansion, one pertaining to land legislation, and one concerning the expansion and cheapening of postal services. The internal improvements scales in both houses contained votes on rivers and harbors bills and on railroad land grant proposals.[38] In the Senate there were ten roll-calls on the internal improvements scale in the Thirty-first Congress and twelve in the Thirty-second.[39] On these scales some congressmen coalesced into party groups, others did not. At the same time, smaller, nonpartisan subgroups also formed on the issue (Tables 9.6, 9.7).

Whig senators exhibited a high degree of unity as most of them supported federal aid for internal improvements. There were only a few dissenters from the party majority on each of the two scales and this group moved only to a moderate voting position. Furthermore, al-

TABLE 9.6
Improvements Issue, Party Division,
31st Congress, Senate

		Democrats		Whigs	
	Scale Type	No.	%	No.	%
Pro (govt. intervention)	(0– 2)	9	27.7	18	90.0
Moderate	(4– 7)	6	17.8	2	10.0
Anti	(8–10)	18	54.5	—	—

TABLE 9.7
Improvements Issue, Party Division,
32nd Congress, Senate

		Democrats		Whigs	
	Scale Type	No.	%	No.	%
Pro (govt. intervention)	(0– 2)	3	10.7	10	71.4
Moderate	(3– 6)	13	42.9	4	28.6
Anti	(7, 10–12)	12	46.4	—	—

though there was a slight sectional quality to the dissent in the Thirty-second Congress, the overwhelming number of Northern, Southern and Western Whigs continued to follow the traditional Whig party line on internal improvements legislation.[40]

Unlike their adversaries, the Democratic senators split apart on the internal improvements issue with substantial numbers voting in every position on the subject. Furthermore, the sectional groups within the Democratic party were similarly scattered (Tables 9.8, 9.9).

As in previous situations,[41] the Democrats apparently split because of conflicts between local needs and national financial attitudes. On the other hand, the Whigs must have found their local needs compatible with their partisan attitude toward government expenditures for such improvements.[42]

In the House of Representatives the two internal improvements scales included nine and nineteen roll-calls respectively.[43] The voting in the House, however, differed between the two Congresses. In the Thirty-first Congress both parties were generally united, although a number of congressmen sharply dissented from the majority positions. Most representatives of both parties took traditional positions in these

TABLE 9.8
Improvements Issue, Democratic Party,
31st Congress, Senate

	Northern	Southern	Western
Pro (govt. intervention)	2	1	6
Moderate	1	2	3
Anti	3	14	1

TABLE 9.9
Improvements Issue, Democratic Party,
32nd Congress, Senate

	Northern	Southern	Western
Pro (govt. intervention)	1	1	1
Moderate	—	5	8
Anti	2	9	2

TABLE 9.10
Improvements Issue, Party Division,
31st Congress, House of Representatives

		Democrats		Whigs	
	Scale Type	No.	%	No.	%
Pro (govt. intervention)	(0–2)	14	17.3	76	86.4
Moderate	(3–6)	5	6.2	5	5.6
Anti	(7–9)	62	76.5	7	8.0

TABLE 9.11
Improvements Issue, Party Division,
32nd Congress, House of Representatives

		Democrats		Whigs	
	Scale Type	No.	%	No.	%
Pro (govt. intervention)	(0–5)	40	33.1	43	57.3
Moderate	(6–8, 10–13)	13	10.7	21	28.0
Anti	(14–19)	68	56.2	11	14.7

votes. And, although there were dissenters within each party, they did not form into regional blocs, coming as they did from different parts of the country (Table 9.10).

In the Thirty-second Congress, however, party cohesion disappeared and congressmen scattered all over the scale of attitudes (Table 9.11). Neither sectional nor subregional voting groups replaced the parties in this scale. Such groups were generally scattered over the whole range of attitudes. Although there was a Western tendency in favor of the legislation, Westerners voted in every position on the scale.[44] In the Thirty-second Congress the representatives apparently reacted once more primarily to local considerations.[45]

The irregular patterns present on the internal improvements scales carried over into the remaining issues dealt with by Congress in these two sessions. On two other issues involving national development— government operations and land policy—partisan and sectional tendencies occasionally appeared. But both patterns were spasmodic in their appearances and limited in their effect, giving little indication of clear-cut, concrete, and all-encompassing voting influences, comparable in strength to those of earlier Congresses. The Senate, for example, considered a bill to improve and cheapen mail service throughout the country. In voting on six roll-calls senators scattered over the whole range of scale positions without reference to party groupings (Table 9.12).[46] Northern senators were scattered in every voting position. Southern and Western legislators, while not concentrating their votes

TABLE 9.12
Postage Issue, Party Division,
31st Congress, Senate

		Democrats		Whigs	
	Scale Type	No.	%	No.	%
Expansive	(0–1)	6	20.7	6	28.6
Moderate	(2–4)	11	37.9	7	33.3
Limited	(5–6)	12	41.4	8	38.1

TABLE 9.13
Postage Issue, Sectional Division,
31st Congress, Senate

	North		South		West	
	No.	%	No.	%	No.	%
Expansive	6	40.0	—	—	7	63.7
Moderate	6	40.0	8	32.0	4	36.3
Limited	3	20.0	17	68.0	—	—

in one position on the scale, did reveal some definite tendencies on this legislation: the Westerners favored the expansion and development of postal operations, the Southerners opposed such expansion. These were only tendencies, however, since there was a great deal of internal division within both sections (Table 9.13).[47]

A partisan voting tendency appeared in the Democratic column when the House of Representatives considered legislation designed to expand and improve government operations and services. The Whigs were more scattered:[48]

TABLE 9.14
Government Operations Issue, Party Division,
31st Congress, House of Representatives

		Democrats		Whigs	
	Scale Type	No.	%	No.	%
Expansive	(0–1)	13	14.1	47	51.1
Moderate	(2–4)	16	17.4	34	37.0
Limited	(5–7)	63	68.5	11	11.9

Sectional and regional groupings, as well as smaller partisan blocs within the sections, split apart with one exception—the Southern Democrats, who were overwhelmingly opposed to the suggested development of government services. Their unity also heavily contributed to the Democratic tendency noted above. Democratic representatives from other areas of the country were badly split. Since Whig groups were similarly scattered, the unity of the Southern Democrats was the one exception to a pattern of individualistic and localized voting.[49]

On the land issue considered in the Thirty-first Congress the prevailing pattern of occasional alignment amidst general breakdown of voting blocs continued. In the Senate, on a scale of four roll-calls involving military bounty lands and homestead legislation, the Democrats broke apart, the Whigs united in opposition to a liberal land policy, and Southern senators, regardless of party, demonstrated a high degree of cohesiveness unlike the senators from other sections (Table 9.15).[50] There was a general Northwestern moderate-to-liberal tendency on this legislation. But a group of Northwestern Democrats were the only vigorous supporters of it. And they were just under one-half of their total group.[51]

TABLE 9.15
Land Issue, Party and Sectional Divisions,
32nd Congress, Senate

	Scale Type	Democrats		Whigs	
		No.	%	No.	%
Liberal	(0–1)	5	16.1	1	5.0
Moderate	(2–3)	7	22.6	2	10.0
Conservative	(4)	19	61.3	17	85.0

	North		South		West	
	No.	%	No.	%	No.	%
Liberal	2	11.8	—	—	5	41.7
Moderate	5	29.4	1	3.8	5	41.7
Conservative	9	58.8	25	96.2	2	16.6

Again, in the House voting on the land issue, both national parties split apart. Sectional blocs also broke down with only the Northwestern representatives showing a clear tendency one way or the other:[52]

TABLE 9.16
Land Issue, Party and Sectional Divisions,
32nd Congress, House of Representatives

	Scale Type	Democrats		Whigs	
		No.	%	No.	%
Liberal	(0–2)	39	36.5	14	23.9
Moderate	(3–5)	29	27.0	20	34.5
Conservative	(6–7)	39	36.5	24	41.6

	North		South		West	
	No.	%	No.	%	No.	%
Liberal	9	15.0	18	25.3	27	65.9
Moderate	27	45.0	20	28.2	7	17.05
Conservative	24	40.0	33	46.5	7	17.05

There was a partially partisan quality to the Northwestern representatives' votes on the land issue. Although the Western Whigs divided almost evenly at opposite ends of the spectrum, the Western Democrats were united in support of the legislation.[53] In the other sections, in contrast, there were no party differences in the voting. Once again, as so often in these years, some blocs formed, most splintered, and local and individual pressures operated with an occasional challenge from either national parties or sectional groupings.

Both houses of Congress dealt with one other issue in 1851–1852, that of foreign affairs. During the 1840's the national parties had disagreed about the two foreign relations issues of that period, expansion and war.[54] The Democrats had been more assertive and expansive than the Whigs.[55] Congress had settled these earlier issues; but now, a new subject arose which contained some of the same elements of American aggressiveness in world affairs—the European revolutions of 1848 and particularly Louis Kossuth, the Hungarian revolutionary leader.

After his defeat by the Austrian Army, Kossuth went from country to country seeking support for his cause.[56] He came to the United States in 1851 apparently hoping to induce the American government to intervene directly against Austria.[57] The American people had been quite sympathetic towards the revolutions of 1848, and, to many Americans, Kossuth and his fellow revolutionaries were martyrs to the cause of republican liberty.[58] Many political leaders were in favor of some American action to relieve the Hungarians of their suffering.[59]

Other Americans were frightened by the sympathy for Kossuth's cause. They feared that the United States would be carried by interventionist enthusiasm into some sort of provocative and dangerous foreign adventure against Austria or Russia, in the name of Hungarian liberty.[60] A full-scale debate erupted over the Hungarian situation, with Kossuth's defenders arguing that American foreign policy should be aggressively assertive in favor of liberty anywhere in the world,[61] and their opponents insisting that the United States ought to pursue a peaceful, noninterventionist policy. [62]

Some historians have suggested that the debate over Kossuth had sectional overtones. Allegedly, Northerners supported Kossuth and republican liberty, while Southerners did not.[63] When Congress considered the question of Kossuth's reception in the United States, however, there was no North-South sectional breakdown in the voting. Rather, the different positions on foreign relations produced an interventionist-noninterventionist scale, with some apparent partisan and regional overtones.

In the Senate, in a scale of eight roll-calls, neither party nor sectional influences clearly dominated the voting.[64] But partisan tendencies were present to some degree, as most Democrats voted differently from the overwhelming majority of the Whigs:

TABLE 9.17
Foreign Relations Issue, Party Division,
32nd Congress, Senate

		Democrats		Whigs	
	Scale Type	No.	%	No.	%
Aggressive	(0–2)	17	51.6	1	7.2
Moderate	(3–5)	4	25.8	5	35.7
Nonaggressive	(6–8)	5	22.6	6	57.1

Sectional groupings did not appear on the scale in any significant quality.[65] All of the nonagressive Democrats were Southern to be sure, but all of the aggressive senators from that region were Democrats also.[66] Apparently, something of the partisan quality of foreign relations issues in the forties carried over into 1852, although with more splintering than before, more cautiousness among some Southern Democrats than before, and consequently, somewhat weaker partisan coalitions than before.

In the House of Representatives the foreign relations scale included five votes and involved more than just the Kossuth affair.[67] As in the Senate, some partisan tendencies were apparent in the voting patterns while nonpartisan sectional and regional groupings were not present:

TABLE 9.18
Foreign Relations Issue, Party Division,
32nd Congress, House of Representatives

		Democrats		Whigs	
	Scale Type	No.	%	No.	%
Aggressive	(0–1)	66	59.5	4	5.9
Moderate	(2–3)	39	35.1	40	58.8
Nonaggressive	(4–5)	6	5.4	24	35.3

Most members of each party voted on opposite sides of the scale of attitudes on the foreign relations issue. Moreover, few party dissenters voted at the opposite end of the scale from the majority of their party.

Southerners were the dissenters in both parties: the aggressive Whigs were Southerners, although the bulk of the Southern Whigs were in the moderate and nonaggressive positions; the nonaggressive Democrats also were Southerners, although the overwhelming majority of Southern Democrats were as aggressive as any of their colleagues from the other sections.[68] Apparently, local and individual pressures influenced these dissenters somewhat. Party cohesion was not what it had been; the positions of the two parties were closer to each other than they had been earlier. But there was a Whig-Democrat dichotomy on this issue. Perhaps in a time of chaotic voting blocs and the relative absence of national cohesion, the limited party differences on the foreign relations issue were as much as could be achieved.

The Nature of Congressional Voting

During the two sessions of Congress immediately following the crisis year of 1850, congressmen continued to deal with the sectional problems of the previous few years as well as to renew their interest in some of the same types of issues so important in the early forties. The most significant fact in the legislative voting in 1851 and 1852 was that large-scale cohesive forces no longer influenced Congressional behavior to the degree they once had. Rather, the voting suggested that different factors influenced congressmen at different times. Voting influences important on one issue were not necessarily so in any subsequent legislative area. Congressional voting had broken down, more than ever before, into a multiplicity of factional groupings, behavioral factors, and individual decision-making, with only occasional alignments of these patterns into large-scale partisan or sectional groupings.

National parties did coalesce in the votes on the internal improvements issue in the Thirty-first Congress and, to some degree, on the foreign relations scale, but such partisan cohesion appeared only sporadically in the other issues considered. Party commitments, while still present to an extent, obviously were not as important and dominant as in the early 1840's.

Occasionally during these two sessions of Congress there was sectional voting. For instance, the South was completely united against any further agitation on the slavery issue. Once in a while other sectional tendencies on the part of the West or the South appeared; but sectional unity was never a widespread, influential factor in the voting. Rather, when sectional cohesion occasionally did appear, it did not affect all sections, and its importance varied from issue to issue. Similarly, local and subregional pressures also operated in these Congresses, but in no systematic pattern. Congressional voting behavior during the 1840's had responded to broad nationally cohesive patterns. Then there had been, in addition, a brief and limited response to sectional influences. But the latter had not replaced the former. Apparently, however, the fight over slavery extension had weakened the forces producing the national patterns. This, coupled with less concern for most of the issues in which partisan divisions were important, had greatly affected Congressional behavior. Whether the national parties were weaker than before or not, they were still present and occasionally influential. The glue which had held them together may have lost much of its effectiveness but, in a few spots, it still held.

10. A FOOTNOTE ON THE SOUTHERN–WESTERN ALLIANCE

IN most analyses of the sectional process in the United States there has been persistent identification of a special relationship between the slave states and the Old Northwest in the pre-Civil War period. Apparently this relationship led, at different times, to a close intersectional political alliance. Professor Frank Lawrence Owsley, for example, described such an alliance as "the normal thing until the end of the first half of the nineteenth century" due to the threads binding the regions together.[1] Other analysts have detailed the story of how and why this special relationship developed to the point of an operative political alliance.[2] The relationship stemmed, it seems, from three particular situations. First, there were the common population ties: Southern farmers were the first settlers of the Old Northwest and dominated the life of that region for a long time.[3] Second, geographic influences tied Southerners and Westerners together. The enormous trade Westerners carried on through the port of New Orleans was the key to their prosperity.[4] Finally, Southerners relied on Western wheat for their food, and this Southern market financed Western development.[5] Because of these cultural, geographic, and economic ties, and the resulting common ideas and needs, political leaders like John C. Calhoun allegedly worked to forge a political connection between Southerners and Westerners.[6]

Most histories of the 1840's pay a great deal of attention to Calhoun's activities as the architect of the Southern-Western alliance; Frederick Jackson Turner, Avery O. Craven, and Charles Wiltse, the biographer of Calhoun, all include in their discussions analyses of the South Carolinian's attempts to bring together and manipulate the groups involved in this political alliance.[7] Other historians have also contributed pieces to the story of the forging of this intersectional connection, either by accepting and incorporating into their own work the outlines of the process, or by expanding and developing different aspects of the relationship. Such examinations range in breadth and depth from Frank Owsley's strong affirmation, already quoted, that such a political alliance not only was "natural" but also actually existed throughout the first half of the nineteenth century, to the occasional, peripheral, and fairly general background remarks of several writers who are involved in understanding the sectional process as an underpinning for their own particular concerns.[8] Writing in 1910, Clark Persinger of the University of Nebraska could even discover an actual case where the leaders of the two sections negotiated a political bargain—each pledging to support the other's major territorial ambitions.[9] Persinger, knowingly or otherwise, was developing the history of this alliance to a point visualized by Frederick Jackson Turner as a logical outgrowth of sectional differences within the United States, wherein the dealings between the sections approximated the treaty-making conferences carried on between European nations.[10]

In addition to identifying and discussing the Southern-Western alliance in general economic and political terms, students of the 1840's have also keyed much of their analysis of the breakdown of American politics in the mid-1840's to the failure of the Southern-Western relationship to survive either the changing economic and trade pattern of the country or the strains of conflict over Texas, Oregon, and the Rivers and Harbors Bill of 1846.[11] In Professor Ray Billington's words, "one by one the ties that bound South and West together were severing, as those two sections developed antagonistic economic interests."[12] The significance of what happened was noted by Avery Craven, who characterized the breakdown of this relationship between South and West as "the most alarming feature of developments in the 1840's."[13]

There is, of course, a great deal of impressionistic evidence that some nineteenth century politicians were consciously seeking a sectional accommodation between Southerners and Westerners. Such evidence includes, for example, Spencer Roane's assertion, in an 1820 letter to James Monroe, that the South should "cherish . . . the western people, they have an identity of interests with us. . . . If driven to it, we can yet form with them a great union."[14] Twenty-five years later Senator Edward Hannegan of Indiana allegedly declared, as repeated by Duff Green in a letter to Calhoun (a letter quoted by many of the historians noted here), that "the West will be united and will demand funds for the improvement of their harbors, rivers, and Cumberland road, and the graduation of the price of public lands, and that if the South will give these to the West the West will go with the South on the tariff."[15] And finally, in the same year, James Gadsden of South Carolina wrote to John C. Calhoun that "I look to this meeting [of the Memphis Convention] as calculated to begin to bind the bonds of Union between the South and West."[16]

Despite such thoughts, quotes, activities, and dreams of political leaders, how successful was the move for a sectional alliance in the 1840's? Most recent historians have agreed that Calhoun's attempt to bring the West and the South together failed. The movement foundered on the twin rocks of Southern opposition to federally-financed improvements of river and harbors, and Southern hesitancy about acquiring all of Oregon. As a result the West moved into an alliance with the Northeast in the years after 1846.[17] The patterns of roll-call voting in Congress in the 1840's confirm the fact that the alliance never became a reality. But the reasoning that underlies most historians' descriptions of why the attempts were made, why they failed, and the consequences of the failure, is not an accurate rendition of the basic nature of American politics in the period. We have seen repeatedly that sectional blocs were neither natural nor dominant factors in Congressional politics then. If one is talking about, as many historians apparently have been, whole sections,[18] then there were no sectional coalitions in the Twenty-seventh and Twenty-eighth Congresses (1841–1845). Congressmen did not generally unite in sectional blocs during these four years and, in fact, the congressmen from each section split along party lines on economic matters and foreign affairs. Even on the rare issue where sectional considerations apparently did influence some congressmen and therefore one section was united in the voting, the congressmen from its supposed sectional ally continued to split along party lines.[19]

In the allegedly pivotal first session of the Twenty-ninth Congress in 1846, the two sections also did not vote together. In the Senate there was never enough unity in Southern voting to suggest that a Southern sectional position existed on any of the issues considered. In the House the Southern representatives did unite on the war question but most of the Western congressmen voted on the end of the scale opposite to the position taken by the Southerners.[20] Sectional positions and sectional cooperation in the broad sense were no more present here than they had been in previous Congresses.

A perhaps more widely accepted conception of the nature of the Southern-Western alliance confines that special political relationship primarily to the Democratic party. Party unity dominated Congress, however, with little dissent from party positions by sectional blocs within the parties. Thus, when Southern and Western Democrats voted together, they were joined by the Northern Democrats.[21] It is true that some Northern Democrats broke with their party on the tariff and land issues in 1846, but as we have seen, most Northern congressmen remained with their cohorts from the South and West as the national party coalitions held together.[22]

Several historians have claimed that whatever the operative state of the Southern-Western alliance was—fully formed, almost consummated, a strong possibility, a faint hope—it irrevocably split apart in 1846 on the expansion and internal improvements issues. It was true that within the Democratic party-framework there were differences on these issues between Westerners and Southerners. There were also differences between Westerners and other Westerners, and Southerners and other Southerners.[23] There was little sectional cohesion in the Twenty-ninth Congress. Therefore there could be no meaningful Southern-Western alliance. Nor could there have been any break in such a sectional coalition.

Western Democrats, however, bitterly denounced Southern congressmen because they believed that the Southerners had deserted them on the expansion and improvements issues.[24] As far as the actual voting went, they could as accurately have attacked Northerners and some of their fellow Westerners. The trouble was not that Southern attitudes and voting changed, but that the West had had over-optimistic expectations of Southern support which were frustrated. The Western leaders over-rated both their understanding with the South at Memphis and the power and influence of John C. Calhoun. When their hopes were dashed by the Oregon compromise and Polk's veto, some Westerners found a convenient scapegoat in Southern Congressional voting. They attacked the South and were lukewarm towards President Polk on the war issue. Although their denunciations were fierce, their resentment obscured too much of what had actually happened in the voting. Many Southerners did not live up to Western expectations, but actually, sectional voting was not yet that important in Congress. Western bitterness was not justified; the South and the West had not been operating together.

Finally, in the years between 1846 and 1850, when Congress incessantly argued over slavery in the territories, no separate intersectional alliance appeared. Neither the West nor the South were united entities in the voting on traditional issues. Instead they continued to split along party lines. True, Southern and Western Democrats, or Southern and Western Whigs, voted together; but they also voted with their Northeastern party colleagues. Even on the issues where Western and Southern Democrats had been somewhat more sympathetic to one another, tariff and land policy, their votes were not materially different from those of the Northern Democrats. Moreover, the Southern-Western alliance did not exist on the slavery issue either. When there was sectional unity on this issue, Western and Southern congressmen tended to vote on opposite sides of the issue.[25] Although some of the Western Democrats were more moderate on the slavery issue than most Northerners, only a few of them voted a proslavery and pro-Southern line, and they were joined in their moderation by a few Northeastern congressmen.[26] As in the case of other issues, there appeared to be local or personal influences which made some Westerners sympathetic to the South on the slavery issue. This was not a general Western position, however, and it did not mean that there was a functioning Southern-Western political alliance.

In other words, although there was some maneuvering by different sectional leaders to win the support of groups in the other section on specific policy proposals, as well as much articulate sentiment in favor of such a "natural" alliance, the results of all of this activity, given the prevailing political situation, were very small indeed. Certainly any statement affirming the existence of a coherent, operating Congressional sectional alliance in Congress during the 1840's, either between the South and the West generally, or within the confines of one party specifically, has to be so rigorously qualified as to make the idea all but meaningless.

11. THE SHRINE OF PARTY

BETWEEN 1841 and 1852 the Representatives and Senators sent to Washington by the American people grappled with a wide variety of national problems. When these congressmen dealt with the issues confronting them, each brought to his deliberations and votes a set of preconceptions, ideals, and institutional loyalties which helped shape his attitude and action on each matter. Among such a heterogeneous collection of individuals representing, as they did, the many interests in the United States, inevitably there would be many points of view expressed, many different influences at work, and many different determinants of action. Although this was true, in the actual roll-call voting the heterogeneity was compressed, with only a few dissenters, within a stable, wide-ranging, and large-scale system of national parties. The United States in the 1840's had an essentially national political culture and most involved people, despite their local differences and viewpoints, operated within the basic institutions of that culture—the Whig and Democratic parties. The forties, in fact, apparently were a high point of national party unity behind coherent national party programs supported in all sections of the country. Such party strength stemmed from both the divergent needs and the divergent values of the American people on every level of the community. In a period of rapid development when different groups visualized their needs in a variety of ways, each group fought in the political arena to win the things it wanted. Since the issues of major conflict—tariff, finance, and land policies—were national in scope, they had to be resolved on the national level, specifically in Congress, where local and regional groups joined together during the 1830's, forming national coalitions to fight for particular legislation.

142

In the years between 1841 and 1846, the divisive issues of the previous decade were still at the center of national political activity. As a result, Congressional voting in this period reflected the two-party division of political life. Although small groups and random individuals occasionally broke with either one of the national coalitions, they were not then of great significance in the total picture of Congressional action. Since a majority of Americans obviously thought that the best means of achieving their legislative goals was through one or the other of the two national coalitions, both the Democrats and the Whigs were stable, powerful political groups in the middle of the 1840's.

Nothing reflects the strength of national party ties more perhaps than the first reactions of American congressmen to the rise of one aspect of the slavery issue. When abolitionist petitions and treatment of free Negroes became matters of concern in this period of two-party stability, congressmen tried to deal with them within the existing partisan framework. Although some sectional voting occurred, many of the congressmen reacted in terms of partisan commitment. This party voting is particularly significant because so many historians have considered the appearance of the slavery issue in the halls of Congress as a signal for the beginning of the relatively complete sectionalizing of American politics despite the continued presence of other issues. In the period between 1841 and 1846 this was not true. The traditionally divisive issues of banks, tariffs, land, and internal improvements remained primarily important to congressmen and they ignored or subordinated the slavery issue. And when the Wilmot Proviso appeared in 1846 it did not profoundly change American politics either. Although some leading spokesmen presented sectional arguments in response to the Proviso, most political leaders apparently viewed even this issue in partisan terms, while other matters, war policy, finance, and internal development, still remained more important to a majority of the members of both parties. Party lines continued to hold, in general, on these issues.

It is true that in the three years following the introduction of the Proviso and the question of slavery in the territories into Congress, some leaders actively tried to change the political context in which Congress specifically and politicians generally operated. And they had a high degree of success. The constant propaganda on the question of slavery extension and the failure to solve the issues raised by the Wilmot Proviso did lead many people to react sectionally, and their congressmen, in response, did also. But, at the same time, national party leaders forcefully resisted the sectionalizing of American politics and managed to keep parties as the most effective influence operating on issues not connected with slavery. Furthermore, when sectional sensitivity grew among some elements, other groups and leaders moved to end the slavery-extension dispute and thus remove the one possible destructive force countering the Democratic and Whig parties. The moderate leaders were, in large part, successful. During 1850 Congress passed a series of measures designed to solve the outstanding sectional disputes.

The success of the moderate compromisers of 1850 was not as complete as they wished. Although sectional voting disappeared along with the sectional issue, as an important influence in Congress, national party coalitions did not immediately reappear during 1851–1852. Regional and local groupings were the major blocs in Congressional voting immediately after the crisis of 1850. Moreover the individuals within these groups moved around from issue to issue, with little large-scale stability to voting coalitions.

Despite their limited success in restoring national party voting in Congress in 1851–1852, the national leaders continued their efforts to restore the primacy of their point of view in American politics. And as the United States moved further into the fifties the party leaders apparently became more successful. The sectionalists, although revived and strengthened by the resurgency of the slavery issue after 1854, had a great deal of difficulty through much of the fifties. As early as 1852, as we have noted, both parties ran national candidates in the presidential election. And during that campaign, many of the sectional advocates of the previous few years returned to the party fold.[1] Furthermore, as late as 1860, Robert Barnwell Rhett of South Carolina, that state's leading sectionalist fire-eater, complained that Southern politicians were "too much of partizans and aspirants, afraid of failure and party proscriptions . . . to hazard anything to direct and shape . . . Southern sentiment."[2]

There are, in addition, other indications that a great many people continued to think in national terms and act through national institutions. In the South, throughout the fifties, there were the politicians of whom Rhett complained, who fought to maintain the national parties, preserve good relations with their allies in the North, and to play down anything likely to disrupt the national politics they believed in.[3] There is also some evidence that in Congress national party discipline was restored and maintained on a variety of issues during these years. In the voting on the Kansas-Nebraska bill in 1854, for instance, there was a degree of party unity within both parties despite the intense sectional rhetoric in Congress.[4] Even in 1860, sectional influences apparently did not determine how every Southern congressman would vote—even on issues dealing directly with slavery in the territories.[5] In the presidential election of that year, also, some Northern groups apparently voted without regard to the sectional influences present.[6]

Such examples drawn from the 1850's are, of course, only guide lines to that decade and are not necessarily completely revealing as to the patterns of politics then. But the story of Congress in the 1840's is more complete. As indicated earlier, most American historians have accepted with varying degrees of intensity, as the central point of political analyses of the pre-Civil war period, that sectional differences, whether superficial and transient, or deeprooted and tenacious, were the predominant factors in shaping and influencing political decisions and actions in this country, particularly between 1846 and 1861. Although most of these writers have paid varying degrees of attention to nonsectional forces as well, they have tended to express the conviction that the latter were destroyed by the overwhelming power of sectional attitudes and actions. When we closely examine a part of the political process, however, we quickly discover that this generalization does not stand up well and, in fact, seems to distort historical reality.

The tenacity with which American congressmen clung to the national political divisions in the 1840's suggests the need for a deeper understanding of how people actually act in politics and how they react to new behavioral influences and changes in the context of political activity. Our comprehension of antebellum political processes has perhaps been wrongly shaped by what I have elsewhere referred to as "the Civil War synthesis" in our historiography.[7] It is obvious, it seems to me, that more detailed study of all levels of American politics, without preconceived notions about the period and without primary reliance on potentially contradictory and misleading evidence, are necessary before we can fully comprehend the antebellum political scene.[8] And, lest we repeat earlier mistakes and misplace emphases such studies should utilize, as has been done here, recent advances in statistical methodology and in our knowledge of how and why human beings act as they do.[9] The first step in this process, at least in most areas of political history is to count—to find out "who the guys were," to quote Sir Lewis Namier.[10] Until such studies are completed we cannot readily accept either unqualified or partially qualified generalizations about the depths of sectional differences or the impact of such differences on American political behavior. Certainly from the work herein it seems clear that although there was a Civil War between the sections in 1861, and many vigorously-presented sectional points of view in the 1840's, there was also something else which, however contemptously referred to as "the shrine of party,"[11] had real meaning, a devoted following, and great importance in American political life—even after 1846.

Appendices

Appendix I
SCALOGRAM OF THE
FOREIGN RELATIONS ISSUE
Twenty-Seventh Congress, Senate

This scale is the one discussed in Chapter 4. Originally there were sixteen roll-call votes on foreign relations matters in this Congress, ranging in content from various aspects of the Webster-Ashburton treaty and our relations with England in Oregon to the question of sending a commercial mission to China. All of them were placed on the chart, but only five of them defined new voting blocs. The others, with one exception, were removed from the final scale since they added no new information to it. Occasionally, however, as in the case of roll-call number three here, as well as several times in other issues discussed in this monograph, extra roll-calls were included for their content or their revelation of some particular individual vote. The fifty-four separate scales constructed for the analysis contained in this work are not reproduced here but may be found on pp. 360–585 of my doctoral dissertation at the University of Iowa, 1963.

I have not discussed here some of the problems of, and recent advances in, the use of the scalogram in roll-call analysis, since there is an extensive literature on the method in political science journals, books, collections of articles, etc., as well as in some works of history. Some of these are referred to in Chapter 1.

Scalogram of the Foreign Relations Issue
27th Congress, Senate

Senator	Scale Score	Aggressive Roll-call						Nonaggressive Roll-call					
		1	2	3	4	5	6	1	2	3	4	5	6
Allen	0	+	+	+	+	+	+						
Bagby	0	+	+	+	+	+							+
Linn	0	+	+	+	+	+	+						
Smith	0	+	+	+	+	+	+						
Sturgeon	0	+	+	+	+	+	+						
William	0	+	+	+		o	+				+		
Benton	1		+	+	+	+	+	+					
Buchanan	1		+	+	+	o	+	+					
Tappan	3				+	+	+	+	+	+			
Cuthbert	3				+	+	o	+	+	+			
Sevier	3				+	+	+	o	+	+			
Woodbury	3				+	o	+	+	+	+			
Wright	3				+	+	+	o	+	+			
Bayard	4				+			+	+	+	+		+
Fulton	4	+			+	+			+	+	+		
Henderson	4				+	+		+	+	+	+		
King	4				+	+		o	+	+	+		
Mangum	4				+	+		+	+	+	+		
Miller	4				+			+	+	+	+		+
Porter	4				+			+	+	+	+		+
White	4				+	+		+	+	+	+		
Clayton	5						+	+	+	+	+	+	
Merrick	5						+	o	+	+	+	o	
Phelps	5						+	o	+	+	+		
Smith, O.	5						+	+	+	+	+	+	
Young	5			+			+	+	o		+	o	
Archer	6							+	+	+	+	+	+
Barrow	6							+	+	+	+	+	+
Bates	6							+	+	+	+	+	+

Senator	Scale Score	Aggressive Roll-call						Nonaggressive Roll-call					
		1	2	3	4	5	6	1	2	3	4	5	6
Berrien	6							o	+	+	+	+	+
Calhoun	6							+	+	+	+	o	+
Choate	6							+	+	+	+	+	+
Conrad	6		+					+		+	+	+	+
Crafts	6							+	+	+	+	+	+
Crittenden	6							+	+	+	+	+	o
Dayton	6							+	+	+	+	+	+
Evans	6							o	+	+	+	+	+
Graham	6							+	+	+	+	+	+
Huntington	6							+	+	+	+	+	+
Kerr	6							+	+	+	+	+	o
Morehead	6							+	+	+	+	+	o
Preston	6							+	+	+	+	o	o
Rives	6							+	+	+	+	+	+
Simmons	6							o	+	+	+	+	+
Sprague	6							o	+	+	+	+	+
Tallmadge	6							+	+	+	+	+	+
Woodbridge	6							+	+	+	+	+	+

Vote Key

The issues and the voting response deemed "aggressive" are as follows (0 indicates an absence on the roll-call):

Roll-call 1. "Aye" on a motion to recommit the Webster-Ashburton treaty and report instead, a resolution directing the President to take immediate possession of the disputed territory; defeated 8–31, August 19, 1842 (*Senate Journal*, 27 Cong., 2 Sess., 696).

Roll-call 2. "Nay" on consenting to the ratification of the Webster-Ashburton treaty; ratified 39–9, August 20, 1842 (*Senate Journal*, ibid., 699).

Roll-call 3. "Nay" on motion to keep in the treaty the definition of the boundry line between Maine and Canada; agreed to 38–11, August 20, 1842 (*Senate Journal*, ibid., 697).

Roll-call 4. "Nay" on motion to keep the Eighth Article in the treaty; agreed to 37–12, August 20, 1842 (*Senate Journal*, ibid., 697).

Roll-call 5. "Aye" on motion to remove from the treaty between the United States and China certain financial restrictions on the President; defeated 19–24, March 3, 1843 (*Senate Journal*, 27 Cong., 3 Sess., 291).

Roll-call 6. "Nay" on motion to refer to the Foreign Relations Committee the bill authorizing the adoption of measures to occupy and settle Oregon and to extend the laws of the United States over the territory; defeated 22–24, February 3, 1843 (*Senate Journal,* ibid., 147).

Explanatory Note

In constructing any scale, certain refinements have to be made in order to place men correctly with their voting group, deal with absences, and test for the validity of the scale. There are relatively well-defined rules in scalogram literature governing these situations which can be best observed by noting some of the refinements made in this particular scale.

The first problem was that of absences. An occasional absence on a vote does not necessarily affect a man's scale position, but an excessive number of them causes enough concern about placing him correctly that he is removed from the final scale. In this case, Senators Wilcox of New Hampshire, McRoberts of Illinois, and McDuffie of South Carolina were so removed. Wilcox was absent three times on the six roll-calls included, while McRoberts and McDuffie each did not vote four times. On the other hand, many senators were absent once or twice but were not removed since their missed votes did not hinder placing them on the scale.

A more serious problem in refining the scale occurs when a congressman does not vote as expected, considering his scale position. Such votes are "errors" in the language of scaling. A perfect scale of roll-call votes theoretically would have all responses as predicted—if a man votes in the position defined as the most extreme he should also vote in all of the less extreme positions on the same subject. But, of course, the expected voting pattern does not always occur. Special circumstances, personal pique, cross pressures of some kind may and do intervene to change a man's voting pattern. For example, on roll-call six, by definition the most moderate of the roll-calls, Senator Bagby voted "incorrectly" on the basis of his votes up to that point. Whatever the reasons for that vote, and they can be well worth investigating, it was his only "error" and does not affect his position on the scale. Similarly, in other cases, an isolated deviation does not change the thrust of the individual's voting record. The occasional congressmen who have these erratic votes are placed in that scale position that gives them the fewest errors. For instance, Senator Conrad's vote on roll-call two seemed to indicate that he would be placed in the aggressive group, but subsequent votes forced us to move him to the least aggressive group on the scale. Sometimes, however, the error occurs at a more ambiguous point, as is the case with Senators Bayard, Miller, and Porter, all of whom started to vote with a particular group but then voted contrary to that group on the next roll-call. The usual rule here is to keep the offenders in the first group since they had begun to establish its pattern and the number of errors will be the same if they are moved to a more moderate group.

Finally, there are occasions when there are so many errors that an individual's position is quite uncertain, indicating perhaps that he is reacting to cross pressures of many different kinds besides his attitude on foreign relations. Senator Robert Walker of Mississippi, for example, had the following voting pattern:

	Aggressive							*Nonaggressive*				
	1	2	3	4	5	6		1	2	3	4	5	6
Walker	+		+	o	+				+		+	

Since his voting here is so confused as to not accurately indicate his position, he was removed from the scale. He was the only one, incidentally, in this area with an ambiguous voting pattern. (The theory and practice of fitting errors into a scale is discussed in Andrew F. Henry, "A Method of Classifying Non-Scale Response Patterns in a Guttman Scale," *Public Opinion Qtly.*, xvi (Spring 1952), 94–106.).

When corrections and refinements have been completed we assign each bloc of voters an identifying score which indicates its position on the scale in relation to all other blocs. (In Appendix II the identifying score for every senator and representative on every scale discussed here is included).

There is one final step—a quantitative test to determine whether the scale, with its errors and absences, falls within the realm of statistical acceptibility. Scalogram analysts have developed several formulae to test the scale. The first used, the coefficient of reproducibility, will be shown here to demonstrate such tests. The other one, the coefficient of scalability, is discussed in Herbert Menzel, "A New Coefficient for Scalogram Analysis," *Public Opinion Qtly.*, xvii (Summer 1953), 268–80.

The Coefficient of reproducibility is defined as:

$$CR = 1 - \frac{\text{no. of responses} - \text{no. of errors}}{\text{no. of responses}}$$

If the result of this computation is higher than .90, a valid scale is said to exist. In the case of the foreign relations scale in the Senate of the Twenty-seventh Congress, the CR was

$$1 - \frac{282 - 8}{282} = .972$$

Therefore, there was a common universe of response on matters of foreign affairs. Once this has been determined we may then proceed to the most important aspect of the whole undertaking, the analysis of the scale itself.

CONGRESSMEN'S SCALE POSITIONS ON ALL ISSUES 1841–1852

In the following appendix are listed all of the representatives and senators who served from the beginning of the Twenty-seventh Congress through the first session of the Thirty-second Congress, along with their scale positions on all issues considered during that period. By comparing the scale score listed on any issue for any particular individual with the appropriate chart in the text the group with which that congressman voted may be determined. Occasionally no number is listed next to some individual on some issue. On that issue that individual either was not present, did not vote enough for his position to be determined, or, in rare instances, he was "unscalable"—his votes being so conflicting as to make it impossible to place him on the scale accurately. Since there were so few unscalable congressmen in these years, I have not singled out such instances any further. When all of the members of one house have no scale score listed on an issue, that issue was not considered in their house. Finally, there are occasionally more senators or representatives listed from a state than were present at any one time due to replacement, resignation, or death during a particular session of Congress.

Key to Party Identification

Party membership is drawn from the *Biographical Directory of the American Congress,* and other standard sources. The explanation of the abbreviations used are as follows:

D — Democrat		W — Whig	
SR — States Rights		Ind — Independent	
R — Republican		A — American	
FS — Free-Soil		FSW — Free-Soil Whig	
U — Unionist		UW — Union Whig	

TWENTY-SEVENTH CONGRESS

Name and Party	*Finance*	*Tariff*	*Land*	*Relief*	*Improvements*	*Apportionment*	*For. Relations*	*Slavery*
ALABAMA								
House								
Chapman D	10	10	5	16	9	5	—	—
Houston D	10	10	5	17	9	5	—	—
Lewis D	10	10	5	17	9	5	—	—
Payne D	10	10	—	16	9	5	—	—
Shields D	10	10	5	16	7	5	—	—
Senate								
Bagby D	—	1	—	2	—	—	0	—
Clay D	0	—	0	—	—	—	—	—
King D	0	1	0	1	—	—	4	—
ARKANSAS								
House								
Cross W	—	10	—	17	2	3	—	—
Senate								
Fulton D	0	1	0	1	—	—	4	—
Sevier D	0	1	0	1	—	—	3	—
CONNECTICUT								
House								
Boardman W	1	5	0	4	4	0	—	0
Brockway W	0	0	0	4	3	1	—	0
Osborne W	2	1	0	1	3	1	—	0
Trumbull W	2	5	0	1	3	—	—	0
Williams W	0	0	0	0	0	4	—	0
Senate								
Huntington W	8	7	10	7	—	—	6	—
Smith D	0	2	9	0	—	—	0	—
DELAWARE								
House								
Rodney W	1	—	0	0	—	—	—	6
Senate								
Bayard W	8	8	10	5	—	—	4	—
Clayton W	9	6	10	9	—	—	5	—

Name and Party	*Fin.*	*Tar.*	*Land*	*Rlf.*	*Imp.*	*App.*	*F. R.*	*Slav.*
GEORGIA								
House								
Alford W	—	—	5	—	—	—	—	—
Black D	—	—	5	—	9	—	—	—
Colquitt D	—	—	—	—	—	—	—	—
Cooper SR	—	—	—	—	—	5	—	—
Crawford W	—	—	—	—	—	0	—	—
Dawson W	8	7	5	—	7	—	—	—
Foster W	9	10	5	—	7	2	—	—
Gamble D	1	8	5	9	7	3	—	15
Habersham D	0	7	5	4	7	—	—	—
King W	2	7	5	0	6	0	—	—
Meriwether W	5	—	5	7	7	0	—	15
Nisbet W	7	—	—	—	—	—	—	—
Warren W	1	9	5	0	7	—	—	15
Senate								
Berrien W	7	3	9	9	—	—	6	—
Cuthbert D	1	0	2	—	—	—	3	—
ILLINOIS								
House								
Casey D	—	8	—	16	0	3	—	7
Reynolds D	—	10	—	17	2	5	—	—
Stuart W	1	5	—	4	0	1	—	7
Senate								
McRoberts D	1	1	0	0	—	—	—	—
Young D	0	1	0	1	—	—	5	—
INDIANA								
House								
Cravens W	2	1	1	0	2	0	—	0
Kennedy D	10	10	5	17	0	—	—	—
Lane W	2	0	1	2	—	3	—	7
Profitt W	8	—	2	14	3	—	—	—
Thompson W	0	1	0	0	0	—	—	7
Wallace W	0	2	0	—	1	3	—	4
White W	2	—	1	0	—	0	—	0
Senate								
Smith W	9	7	—	6	—	—	5	—

Name and Party	*Fin.*	*Tar.*	*Land*	*Rlf.*	*Imp.*	*App.*	*F. R.*	*Slav.*
A. White W	9	7	10	9	—	—	4	—
KENTUCKY								
House								
Andrews W	1	4	0	12	0	2	—	15
Boyd D	10	10	5	17	3	4	—	—
Butler D	10	10	5	17	3	4	—	—
Davis W	0	1	3	12	0	1	—	15
Green W	2	1	0	17	9	0	—	—
Marshall W	0	—	0	12	4	—	—	11
Owsley W	1	1	0	17	8	0	—	15
Pope D	1	1	0	17	4	2	—	15
Sprigg Ind.	—	9	0	17	4	—	—	—
Thompson W	0	—	1	11	8	2	—	15
Triplett W	—	1	0	15	0	1	—	15
Underwood W	1	1	0	13	8	0	—	1
White W	Speaker of the House							
Senate								
Clay W	8	8	10	—	—	—	—	—
Crittenden W	—	—	—	7	—	—	6	—
Morehead W	8	7	10	7	—	—	6	—
LOUISIANA								
House								
Dawson D	—	10	5	1	4	—	—	—
Moore W	0	1	0	2	3	3	—	14
White W	0	1	0	0	4	3	—	—
Senate								
Barrow W	—	8	10	9	—	—	6	—
Conrad W	—	8	—	—	—	—	6	—
Mouton D	2	—	0	—	—	—	—	—
MAINE								
House								
Allen W	0	0	0	0	6	0	—	0
Bronson W	2	—	1	4	—	0	—	0
Clifford D	10	10	5	17	6	—	—	15
Fessenden W	1	6	0	0	2	0	—	1
Littlefield D	10	10	5	17	6	4	—	12
Lowell D	10	—	5	17	6	4	—	12

Name and Party	*Fin.*	*Tar.*	*Land*	*Rlf.*	*Imp.*	*App.*	*F. R.*	*Slav.*
Marshall D	10	10	5	17	9	0	—	12
Randall W	0	0	0	0	2	0	—	0
Senate								
Evans W	—	7	9	9	—	—	6	—
Williams D	—	1	3	0	—	—	0	—
MARYLAND								
House								
Johnson W	7	—	0	0	—	—	—	—
Jones W	—	4	0	6	3	2	—	15
Kennedy W	1	5	0	2	2	0	—	7
Mason W	10	10	5	—	—	—	—	—
Pearce W	5	—	0	0	1	—	—	—
Randall W	1	5	0	—	3	0	—	5
Sewell W	—	10	—	—	—	—	—	—
Sollers W	—	—	0	7	—	—	—	—
Williams D	10	10	5	17	9	—	—	—
Senate								
Kerr W	9	8	10	9	—	—	6	—
Merrick W	9	8	10	8	—	—	5	—
MASSACHUSETTS								
House								
Adams W	1	0	0	0	0	0	—	0
Baker W	1	0	0	0	0	1	—	0
Borden W	3	0	0	0	2	3	—	0
Briggs W	2	1	1	0	1	0	—	0
Burnell W	3	3	0	0	3	0	—	1
Calhoun W	1	0	0	0	2	—	—	1
Cushing W	8	0	1	0	2	4	—	1
Hastings W	0	1	1	—	—	—	—	1
Hudson W	0	5	0	2	0	1	—	0
Parmenter D	10	0	5	12	7	3	—	2
Saltonstall W	0	0	0	0	0	1	—	0
Winthrop W	0	4	1	0	0	0	—	0
Senate								
Bates W	—	7	9	9	—	—	6	—
Choate W	6	7	9	9	—	—	6	—

Name and Party	*Fin.*	*Tar.*	*Land*	*Rlf.*	*Imp.*	*App.*	*F. R.*	*Slav.*
MICHIGAN								
House								
Howard W	0	1	—	0	1	2	—	1
Senate								
Porter W	9	7	8	9	—	—	4	—
Woodbridge W	9	7	10	9	—	—	6	—
MISSISSIPPI								
House								
Gwin D	—	—	—	17	—	—	—	5
Thompson D	—	—	—	—	—	5	—	—
Senate								
Henderson W	6	5	8	9	—	—	4	—
Walker D	0	0	0	0	—	—	5	—
MISSOURI								
House								
Edwards D	10	10	5	16	—	5	—	—
Miller D	10	10	5	17	3	—	—	15
Senate								
Benton D	0	0	0	2	—	—	1	—
Linn D	2	0	0	0	—	—	0	—
NEW HAMPSHIRE								
House								
Atherton D	10	10	5	17	—	5	—	—
Burke D	10	10	5	17	9	5	—	15
Eastman D	10	10	5	17	9	—	—	15
Reding D	10	10	5	17	9	5	—	15
Shaw D	10	10	5	17	9	5	—	15
Senate								
Pierce D	—	—	1	0	—	—	—	—
Wilcox D	—	2	—	—	—	—	—	—
Woodbury D	0	0	0	0	—	—	3	—
NEW JERSEY								
House								
Aycrigg W	1	3	0	0	5	1	—	2
Halstead W	1	1	0	2	5	—	—	0
Maxwell W	1	0	0	0	5	1	—	0

Name and Party	*Fin.*	*Tar.*	*Land*	*Rlf.*	*Imp.*	*App.*	*F. R.*	*Slav.*
Randolph W	2	0	0	0	5	1	—	0
Stratton W	1	0	0	0	1	0	—	3
Yorke W	0	4	0	0	5	—	—	0
Senate								
Dayton W	—	—	—	8	—	—	6	—
Miller W	9	7	10	9	—	—	4	—
Southard W	9	8	10	—	—	—	—	—
NEW YORK								
House								
Babcock W	1	0	0	0	5	0	—	1
Barnard W	1	1	0	0	0	0	—	0
Birdseye W	2	5	0	11	6	0	—	0
Blair W	1	3	0	—	0	0	—	0
Bowne D	10	10	5	16	4	—	—	15
Brewster D	—	—	5	4	1	5	—	8
Childs W	—	0	—	0	0	2	—	0
Chittenden W	1	—	1	4	1	0	—	0
Clark W	0	0	0	0	0	0	—	2
Clarke W	2	—	2	0	0	0	—	0
Clinton D	10	10	5	17	—	5	—	12
Davis D	10	10	5	16	8	5	—	0
Doig D	10	—	5	17	8	5	—	9
Egbert D	10	10	5	17	6	5	—	12
Ferriss D	10	6	5	17	1	5	—	1
Fillmore W	0	1	0	0	0	0	—	0
C. Floyd D	10	10	5	16	6	—	—	13
J. Floyd D	10	10	5	16	9	5	—	1
Foster W	0	3	1	4	1	—	—	1
Gates W	—	—	—	0	1	—	—	0
Gordon D	10	10	5	16	5	—	—	10
Granger W	—	—	—	0	0	0	—	1
Greig W	2	1	—	—	—	—	—	—
Houck D	10	10	5	17	5	5	—	14
Hunt W	0	6	1	0	1	0	—	0
Linn W	1	7	0	0	5	0	—	0
McClellan D	—	10	5	16	6	5	—	12

Name and Party	*Fin.*	*Tar.*	*Land*	*Rlf.*	*Imp.*	*App.*	*F. R.*	*Slav.*
McKeon D	—	10	5	4	—	5	—	—
Maynard W	0	3	0	0	5	1	—	0
Morgan W	0	3	0	0	5	1	—	1
Oliver D	10	—	5	—	9	5	—	1
Partridge D	10	10	—	17	—	5	—	—
Roosevelt D	10	—	5	4	3	5	—	—
Riggs D	10	10	5	17	9	5	—	—
Sanford D	10	—	5	16	3	5	—	0
Tomlinson W	2	3	0	0	0	1	—	0
Van Buren D	10	10	5	16	8	5	—	12
Van Rensaleer W	0	—	0	0	0	3	—	1
Ward D	10	10	5	12	2	—	—	—
Wood D	10	10	5	4	9	5	—	15
Young W	1	—	1	0	0	—	—	1
Senate								
Tallmadge W	9	7	8	9	—	—	6	—
Wright D	0	0	0	0	—	—	3	—
NORTH CAROLINA								
House								
Arrington D	10	10	5	17	9	—	—	—
Caldwell D	10	10	5	17	9	—	—	—
Daniel D	10	10	5	17	9	5	—	—
Deberry W	0	9	0	6	9	0	—	15
Graham W	0	1	0	16	9	1	—	—
McKay D	10	10	5	17	9	—	—	—
Mitchell W	—	—	—	—	—	—	—	—
Rayner W	5	7	0	4	—	0	—	—
Rencher D	3	9	5	—	—	3	—	—
Saunders D	10	10	5	17	9	4	—	—
Shepperd W	0	8	0	17	9	0	—	15
Stanly W	0	5	0	2	4	—	—	—
Washington W	0	—	0	3	9	1	—	5
Williams D	0	7	1	4	—	—	—	15
Senate								
Graham W	9	3	10	7	—	—	6	—
Mangum W	9	6	10	6	—	—	4	—

Name and Party	Fin.	Tar.	Land	Rlf.	Imp.	App.	F. R.	Slav.
OHIO								
House								
Andrews W	1	0	0	0	0	1	—	0
Cowen W	1	1	0	1	—	4	—	0
Dean W	10	10	5	17	—	5	—	15
Doan D	10	10	5	17	—	4	—	—
Giddings W	1	0	0	—	—	1	—	1
Goode W	0	2	0	1	0	0	—	—
Hastings D	10	10	5	17	—	5	—	—
Mason D	10	10	5	—	—	—	—	—
Mathews D	10	10	5	17	—	5	—	15
Mathiot W	1	0	0	0	0	0	—	0
Medill D	10	10	5	17	4	—	—	—
Morris W	1	1	0	9	0	0	—	0
Morrow W	—	1	0	0	0	0	—	1
Pendleton W	2	1	1	0	0	—	—	1
Ridgeway W	0	0	0	0	0	0	—	0
Russell W	0	1	0	2	4	1	—	3
Stokeley W	0	3	1	3	0	3	—	0
Sweeney D	10	10	5	17	9	—	—	—
Weller D	10	10	5	17	2	1	—	15
Senate								
Allen D	0	0	0	1	—	—	0	—
Tappan D	0	0	0	0	—	—	3	—
PENNSYLVANIA								
House								
Beeson D	10	10	5	16	3	—	—	—
Bidlack D	10	—	5	16	5	—	—	15
Black W	2	1	1	—	—	—	—	—
C. Brown D	10	10	—	17	2	4	—	12
J. Brown W	0	3	0	0	0	0	—	0
Cooper W	—	—	0	—	0	0	—	3
Dimmock D	—	—	5	—	—	—	—	—
Edwards W	1	5	0	0	0	0	—	0
Fornance D	10	10	5	17	3	—	—	15
Gerry D	—	10	—	—	9	4	—	—
Gustine D	10	10	5	16	8	4	—	—

Name and Party	*Fin.*	*Tar.*	*Land*	*Rlf.*	*Imp.*	*App.*	*F. R.*	*Slav.*
Henry W	0	1	1	0	0	0	—	0
C. Ingersoll D	10	—	—	16	2	3	—	12
J. Ingersoll W	—	—	—	0	—	1	—	—
Irvin W	0	2	0	0	0	0	—	5
Irwin W	9	0	1	0	1	1	—	2
Jack D	10	10	5	16	3	4	—	15
James W	0	0	1	0	0	0	—	0
Keim D	10	10	5	17	9	4	—	—
Lawrence W	0	1	1	4	—	—	—	1
McKennan W	—	—	—	—	—	0	—	—
Marchand D	10	10	5	17	3	—	—	12
Newhard D	10	10	5	16	3	4	—	—
Plumer D	10	10	5	16	1	4	—	11
Ramsey W	2	0	0	8	5	0	—	3
Read D	—	10	—	—	—	3	—	—
Russell W	—	2	—	0	1	0	—	0
Sergeant W	0	—	1	—	—	—	—	—
Simonton W	0	1	0	4	—	—	—	1
Snider D	10	10	5	17	8	5	—	12
Toland W	0	0	0	0	0	1	—	0
Westbrook D	10	10	5	16	3	4	—	15
Senate								
Buchanan D	1	7	7	0	—	—	1	—
Sturgeon D	1	7	6	0	—	—	0	—
RHODE ISLAND								
House								
Cranston W	2	1	0	0	2	3	—	0
Tillinghast W	1	1	0	4	0	3	—	0
Senate								
Dixon W	8	7	10	—	—	—	—	—
Simmons W	9	7	10	9	—	—	6	—
Sprague W	—	—	—	7	—	—	6	—
SOUTH CAROLINA								
House								
S. Butler D	—	—	5	—	—	—	—	—
W. Butler W	5	7	5	15	7	3	—	15
Caldwell D	10	10	5	17	9	—	—	—

Name and Party	*Fin.*	*Tar.*	*Land*	*Rlf.*	*Imp.*	*App.*	*F. R.*	*Slav.*
Campbell D	9	10	5	17	9	3	—	—
Holmes D	10	10	5	16	—	5	—	—
Pickens D	10	—	5	16	9	—	—	—
Rhett D	10	10	5	17	9	5	—	—
Rogers D	10	10	5	17	9	—	—	—
Sumter D	—	10	5	17	9	5	—	—
Trottie D	—	10	—	—	—	—	—	—
Senate								
Calhoun D	0	0	0	3	—	—	6	—
Preston W	9	2	5	5	—	—	6	—
TENNESSEE								
House								
Arnold W	0	1	1	0	8	3	—	6
A. Brown D	10	10	5	17	9	5	—	—
M. Brown W	1	1	0	2	6	0	—	15
T. Campbell W	0	2	0	9	8	3	—	15
W. Campbell W	2	9	5	17	7	4	—	15
Caruthers W	1	1	0	9	7	2	—	—
Gentry W	5	10	0	12	7	3	—	15
Johnson D	10	10	5	17	9	0	—	—
McClellan D	—	10	5	17	9	2	—	—
Turney D	10	10	5	17	9	0	—	—
Watterson D	10	10	5	17	9	3	—	—
C. Williams W	5	9	—	—	7	5	—	—
J. Williams W	3	4	0	0	9	1	—	9
Senate								
Nicholson D	0	—	1	—	—	—	—	—
vacancy								
VERMONT								
House								
Everett W	1	0	0	2	1	3	—	0
Hall W	2	1	0	4	7	2	—	0
Mattocks W	2	0	0	12	5	0	—	0
Slade W	6	5	0	2	4	—	—	0
Young W	0	1	0	1	2	1	—	0
Senate								
Phelps W	9	7	10	8	—	—	5	—

Name and Party	*Fin.*	*Tar.*	*Land*	*Rlf.*	*Imp.*	*App.*	*F. R.*	*Slav.*
Prentiss W	—	7	10	5	—	—	—	—
VIRGINIA								
House								
Banks D	10	10	5	—	—	—	—	—
Barton W	0	5	—	12	3	3	—	15
Botts W	0	9	0	11	6	0	—	4
Cary D	10	10	5	17	9	—	—	—
Coles D	10	10	5	17	9	5	—	—
Gilmer W	9	10	5	17	5	3	—	—
Goggin W	1	2	0	16	7	3	—	15
Goode D	10	10	5	17	9	2	—	0
Harris D	10	10	5	17	9	5	—	15
Hays D	10	—	5	17	8	5	—	—
Hopkins D	10	10	5	17	9	0	—	—
Hubard D	10	10	5	17	9	5	—	—
Hunter D	10	10	5	17	9	5	—	—
Jones D	10	10	4	17	9	5	—	—
Mallory W	9	10	5	16	7	—	—	—
Powell W	1	0	0	0	5	1	—	14
Steenrod D	10	10	5	17	9	5	—	—
Stuart W	1	3	0	9	4	3	—	4
Summers W	1	3	0	12	6	0	—	15
Taliaferro W	1	5	1	10	6	4	—	15
Wise D	—	10	5	16	9	1	—	—
Senate								
Archer W	9	8	10	4	—	—	6	—
Rives W	3	2	9	4	—	—	6	—

TWENTY-EIGHTH CONGRESS

Name and Party	Expansion	Improvements	Name and Party	Expansion	Improvements
ALABAMA			*Senate*		
House			Bayard W	10	1
Belser D	—	—	Clayton W	9	6
Chapman D	1	—	**GEORGIA**		
Dellett W	5	—	*House*		
Houston D	0	—	Black D	1	—
Lewis D	—	—	Chappell W	1	—
McConnell D	0	—	Clinch W	4	—
Payne D	0	—	Cobb D	4	—
Yancey D	2	—	Haralson D	0	—
Senate			Lumpkin D	2	—
Bagby D	2	9	Stephens W	3	—
King D	—	—	Stiles D	4	—
Lewis D	0	9	*Senate*		
ARKANSAS			Berrien W	10	7
House			Colquitt D	0	—
Cross W	1	—	**ILLINOIS**		
Senate			*House*		
Ashley D	—	1	Douglas D	0	—
Fulton D	0	1	Ficklin D	0	—
Sevier D	0	1	Hardin W	8	—
CONNECTICUT			Hoge D	5	—
House			McClernand D	1	—
Catlin D	7	—	Smith D	1	—
Seymour D	2	—	Wentworth D	1	—
Simons D	2	—	*Senate*		
Stewart D	2	—	Breese D	0	0
Senate			McRoberts D	—	—
Huntington W	11	6	Semple D	0	4
Niles D	3	9	**INDIANA**		
DELAWARE			*House*		
House			Brown D	0	—
Rodney W	9	—	Davis D	0	—

Name and Party	*Exp.*	*Imp.*	Name and Party	*Exp.*	*Imp.*
Henley D	1	—	MAINE		
Kennedy D	0	—	*House*		
Owen D	1	—	Cary D	—	—
Pettit D	1	—	Dunlap D	—	—
Sample W	10	—	Hamlin D	—	—
C. Smith W	10	—	Herrick D	3	—
T. Smith D	0	—	Morse W	10	—
Wright D	0	—	Severance W	10	—
Senate			White D	6	—
Hannegan D	1	0	*Senate*		
White W	8	0	Evans W	11	6
KENTUCKY			Fairfield D	1	9
House			MARYLAND		
Boyd D	0	—	*House*		
Caldwell D	1	—	Brengle W	10	—
Davis W	9	—	Causin W	9	—
French D	0	—	Kennedy W	9	—
Green W	—	—	Preston W	10	—
Grider W	7	—	Spence W	—	—
Stone D	1	—	Wethered D	8	—
Thomasson W	9	—	*Senate*		
Tibbatts D	1	—	Merrick W	6	1
White W	9	—	Pearce W	9	—
Senate			MASSACHUSETTS		
Crittenden W	10	1	*House*		
Morehead W	8	1	Abbott W	10	—
LOUISIANA			Adams W	10	—
House			Baker W	10	—
Bossier D	—	—	Burnell W	—	—
Dawson D	—	—	Grinnell W	—	—
LaBranche D	0	—	Hudson W	10	—
Morse D	—	—	King W	10	—
Slidell D	0	—	Parmenter D	2	—
Senate			Rockwell W	10	—
Barrow W	9	1	Williams D	—	—
Johnson W	9	1	Winthrop W	10	—

Name and Party	*Exp.*	*Imp.*	Name and Party	*Exp.*	*Imp.*
Senate			*Senate*		
Bates W	11	2	Atherton D	2	9
Choate W	11	2	Woodbury D	0	9
MICHIGAN			NEW JERSEY		
House			*House*		
Hunt D	9	—	Elmer D	—	—
Lyon D	2	—	Farlee D	4	—
McClelland D	2	—	Kirkpatrick D	4	—
Senate			Sykes D	6	—
Porter W	10	2	Wright W	10	—
Woodbridge W	10	3	*Senate*		
MISSISSIPPI			Dayton W	11	—
House			Miller W	11	5
Hammett D	3	—	NEW YORK		
Roberts D	2	—	*House*		
Thompson D	0	—	Anderson D	7	—
Tucker D	1	—	Barnard W	10	—
Senate			Beardsley D	—	—
Henderson W	5	—	Benton D	6	—
Walker D	0	—	Carpenter D	—	—
MISSOURI			Carroll W	10	—
House			Cary D	8	—
Bower D	0	—	Clinton D	3	—
Bowlin D	1	—	Dana D	3	—
Hughes D	0	—	Davis D	10	—
Jameson D	0	—	Ellis D	4	—
Relfe D	1	—	Fish W	10	—
Senate			Green D	—	—
Atchison D	0	1	Hubbell D	2	—
Benton D	1	3	Hungerford D	3	—
Linn D	—	—	Hunt W	10	—
NEW HAMPSHIRE			King D	6	—
House			Leonard D	3	—
Burke D	0	—	Maclay D	5	—
Hale D	7	—	Moseley W	10	—
Norris D	3	—	Murphy D	5	—
Reding D	4	—	Patterson W	10	—

Name and Party	Exp.	Imp.	Name and Party	Exp.	Imp.
Phoenix W	9	—	Dean D	1	—
Pratt D	6	—	Duncan W	2	—
Purdy D	—	—	Florence W	10	—
Rathbun D	—	—	Giddings W	10	—
Robinson D	6	—	Hamlin W	—	—
Rogers W	10	—	Harper W	10	—
Russell D	6	—	Johnson W	10	—
Seymour D	—	—	McCauslen D	2	—
Smith R	10	—	McDowell D	1	—
Stetson D	7	—	Mathews D	2	—
Strong D	3	—	Moore D	—	—
Tyler W	10	—	Morris D	2	—
Wheaton D	7	—	Potter D	1	—
Senate			St. John D	0	—
Dickinson D	—	—	Schenck W	10	—
Dix D	—	—	Stone D	2	—
Foster W	10	—	Tilden W	10	—
Tallmadge W	—	—	Vance W	10	—
Wright D	1	2	Van Meter W	8	—
NORTH CAROLINA			Vinton W	10	—
House			Weller D	0	—
Arrington D	0	—	*Senate*		
Barringer W	9	—	Allen D	1	0
Clingman W	9	—	Tappan D	1	0
Daniel D	1	—	PENNSYLVANIA		
DeBerry W	10	—	*House*		
McKay D	3	—	Bidlack D	0	—
Rayner W	—	—	Black D	0	—
Reid D	0	—	Brodhead D	2	—
Saunders D	3	—	Brown W	—	—
Senate			Buffington W	10	—
Haywood D	3	8	Darragh W	10	—
Mangum W	8	8	Dickey W	10	—
OHIO			Foster D	0	—
House			Frick W	—	—
H. Brinkerhoff D	—	—	Fuller D	—	—
J. Brinkerhoff D	5	—	Hays D	0	—

Name and Party	*Exp.*	*Imp.*	Name and Party	*Exp.*	*Imp.*
C. Ingersoll D	0	—	*Senate*		
J. Ingersoll W	10	—	Huger D	3	9
Irvin W	10	—	McDuffie D	4	9
Jenks W	10	—	TENNESSEE		
McIlvaine W	10	—	*House*		
Morris W	9	—	Ashe W	4	—
Nes Ind.	10	—	Blackwell D	1	—
Pollock W	8	—	A. Brown D	0	—
Ramsey W	8	—	M. Brown W	4	—
Read D	—	—	Collom D	0	—
Reed W	—	—	Dickinson W	—	—
Ritter D	2	—	A. Johnson D	3	—
Smith D	3	—	C. Johnson D	0	—
Stewart W	10	—	Jones D	5	—
Wilkins D	—	—	Peyton W	9	—
Yost D	—	—	Senter W	9	—
Senate			*Senate*		
Buchanan D	2	0	Foster W	9	—
Sturgeon D	0	0	Jarnagin W	9	6
RHODE ISLAND			VERMONT		
House			*House*		
Cranston W	—	—	Collamer W	10	—
Potter W	10	—	Dillingham D	7	—
Senate			Foot W	10	—
Francis W	11	2	Marsh W	10	—
Simmons W	11	2	*Senate*		
Sprague W	—	—	Phelps W	11	5
SOUTH CAROLINA			Upham W	11	2
House			VIRGINIA		
Black D	1	—	*House*		
Burt D	1	—	Atkinson D	0	—
Campell D	—	—	Bayly D	0	—
Holmes D	4	—	Chapman D	0	—
Rhett D	1	—	Chilton W	9	—
Simpson D	2	—	Coles D	1	—
Woodward D	1	—	Dromgoole D	1	—

Name and Party	*Exp.*	*Imp.*	Name and Party	*Exp.*	*Imp.*
Gilmer D	—	—	Steenrod D	0	—
Goggin W	9	—	Summers W	9	—
Hopkins D	0	—	Taylor D	4	—
Hubard D	1	—	Wise D	—	—
Jones D Speaker of the House			*Senate*		
Lucas D	1	—	Archer W	10	9
Newton W	5	—	Rives W	9	—

TWENTY-NINTH CONGRESS

Name and Party	Tariff	Land	Expansion	Improvements	War	War (2d Sess.)	Slavery (2d Sess.)	Land (2d Sess.)	Tariff (2d Sess.)
ALABAMA									
House									
Bowdon D	—	—	—	—	—	0	0	—	0
Chapman D	2	0	7	19	0	2	0	—	0
Cottrell D	—	—	—	—	—	2	0	—	0
Dargan D	0	0	13	19	3	5	1	—	0
Hilliard W	4	—	8	19	0	8	0	—	6
Houston D	0	0	0	19	3	0	1	—	0
McConnell D	1	0	1	19	0	—	—	—	—
Payne D	1	0	7	19	0	0	0	—	0
Yancey D	0	0	—	19	—	—	—	—	—
Senate									
Bagby D	1	0	5	9	0	1	—	2	—
Lewis D	0	0	11	9	0	5	—	—	—
ARKANSAS									
House									
Newton W	—	—	—	—	—	—	2	—	—
Yell D	—	—	1	13	—	—	—	—	—
Senate									
Ashley D	0	0	5	5	0	3	—	4	—
Sevier D	—	0	5	7	0	1	—	0	—
CONNECTICUT									
House									
Dixon W	7	7	12	0	—	—	8	—	7
Hubbard W	7	7	12	0	6	11	8	—	7
Rockwell W	7	7	12	0	5	7	8	—	6
Smith W	7	7	12	0	5	11	8	—	7
Senate									
Huntington W	8	9	11	1	6	10	—	7	—
Niles D	8	8	3	8	0	1	—	0	—

Name and Party	*Tar.*	*Land*	*Exp.*	*Imp.*	*War*	*War(2)*	*Slav.(2)*	*Land(2)*	*Tar.(2)*
DELAWARE									
House									
Houston W	7	7	13	1	1	9	8	—	7
Senate									
J. Clayton W	8	9	11	1	5	9	—	6	—
T. Clayton W	8	9	11	1	6	8	—	6	—
FLORIDA									
House									
Brockenbrough D	2	0	4	19	0	0	0	—	—
Senate									
Westcott D	1	0	9	—	1	0	—	7	—
Yulee D	2	0	7	9	0	4	—	0	—
GEORGIA									
House									
Cobb D	0	0	0	19	0	2	1	—	0
Haralson D	0	0	2	19	0	1	1	—	0
Jones D	0	—	2	19	0	0	1	—	0
King W	—	7	2	4	0	8	0	—	7
Lumpkin D	0	0	1	19	0	2	1	—	2
Stephens W	7	7	—	—	0	8	0	—	—
Toombs W	7	7	13	—	0	8	0	—	—
Towns D	0	—	—	—	0	2	0	—	—
Senate									
Berrien W	7	8	11	1	4	9	—	6	—
Colquitt D	2	—	7	—	0	0	—	—	—
ILLINOIS									
House									
Baker W	—	—	8	0	—	—	—	—	—
Douglas D	2	0	0	0	0	0	1	—	0
Ficklin D	0	0	2	18	0	1	2	—	0
Henry W	—	—	—	—	—	—	8	—	0
Hoge D	2	0	0	19	0	0	8	—	4
McClernand D	2	0	0	18	0	0	2	—	0
Smith D	3	0	2	2	3	0	1	—	2

Name and Party	*Tar.*	*Land*	*Exp.*	*Imp.*	*War*	*War(2)*	*Slav.(2)*	*Land(2)*	*Tar.(2)*
Wentworth D	—	0	0	2	3	1	8	—	2
Senate									
Breese D	1	0	1	2	0	0	—	2	—
Semple D	1	0	0	4	0	—	—	—	—
INDIANA									
House									
Cathcart D	0	0	0	3	3	1	6	—	3
Davis D	Speaker of the House								
Henley D	0	0	0	2	4	0	6	—	2
Kennedy D	0	—	0	—	3	0	6	—	2
McGaughey W	7	7	11	0	5	11	8	—	7
Owen D	—	0	1	15	3	3	3	—	2
Pettit D	—	—	0	—	1	—	8	—	
C. Smith W	7	7	—	0	—	11	8	—	7
T. Smith D	0	0	0	13	3	1	8	—	2
Wick D	0	0	0	4	3	0	3	—	3
Senate									
Bright D	1	0	2	3	0	0	—	2	—
Hannegan D	0	0	0	4	—	3	—	2	—
IOWA									
House									
Hastings D						2	8	—	3
Leffler D						1	6	—	3
Senate									
Vacant									
KENTUCKY									
House									
Bell W	7	7	7	18	0	8	1	—	6
Boyd D	0	0	1	18	0	0	1	—	0
Davis W	7	7	—	0	0	8	0	—	7
Grider W	7	7	8	0	5	8	1	—	6
Martin D	0	0	2	19	0	0	2	—	3
McHenry W	7	7	8	1	0	8	1	—	6
Thomasson W	7	—	5	0	3	8	1	—	6
Tibbatts D	3	0	0	2	0	1	1	—	3
Trumbo W	7	7	7	4	1	9	1	—	6

Name and Party	*Tar.*	*Land*	*Exp.*	*Imp.*	*War*	*War(2)*	*Slav.(2)*	*Land(2)*	*Tar.(2)*
Young D	7	7	7	0	0	8	1	—	6
Senate									
Crittenden W	8	9	10	0	5	10	—	6	—
Morehead W	8	9	11	1	5	9	—	6	—
LOUISIANA									
House									
Harmanson D	1	—	0	19	0	0	0	—	0
LaSere D	0	0	1	15	0	0	0	—	0
Morse D	1	0	5	19	1	0	1	—	0
Slidell D	—	—	—	—	—	—	—	—	—
Thibodeaux W	7	7	7	2	3	7	0	—	7
Senate									
Barrow W	8	2	9	0	5	—	—	—	—
Johnson W	7	3	9	0	5	7	—	5	—
Soule D	—	—	—	—	—	2	—	—	—
MAINE									
House									
Dunlap D	2	0	1	8	5	0	6	—	4
Hamlin D	1	0	1	19	5	0	8	—	5
McCrate D	0	1	5	19	3	0	6	—	—
Sawtelle D	1	3	1	19	3	1	6	—	4
Scammon D	0	1	0	19	3	0	6	—	—
Severance W	7	7	10	0	6	11	8	—	7
Williams D	0	1	1	19	3	0	6	—	5
Senate									
Evans W	8	9	11	0	6	10	—	7	—
Fairfield D	0	1	1	9	—	2	—	0	—
MARYLAND									
House									
Chapman W	—	7	13	1	0	8	0	—	0
Constable D	1	—	7	5	0	—	—	—	—
Giles D	4	0	4	3	0	2	1	—	0
Ligon D	—	2	4	19	3	1	1	—	0
Long W	7	7	—	2	0	8	0	—	6
Perry D	7	—	7	16	0	0	0	—	4

Name and Party	*Tar.*	*Land*	*Exp.*	*Imp.*	*War*	*War(2)*	*Slav.(2)*	*Land(2)*	*Tar.(2)*
Senate									
R. Johnson	8	2	10	—	3	—	—	—	—
Pearce	8	9	11	—	—	10	—	7	—
MASSACHUSETTS									
House									
Abbott W	7	7	13	2	6	11	8	—	7
Adams W	7	7	10	0	6	—	—	—	—
Ashmun W	7	7	13	0	6	11	8	—	7
Grinnell W	7	7	—	1	6	11	8	—	7
Hale W	—	—	—	—	—	11	8	—	7
Hudson W	7	7	—	2	6	11	8	—	7
King W	7	7	—	0	6	11	8	—	7
Rockwell W	7	7	12	0	6	11	8	—	7
Thompson W	7	—	13	1	—	11	8	—	7
Winthrop W	7	7	13	0	5	11	8	—	6
Senate									
Davis W	8	9	10	2	6	10	—	7	—
Webster W	7	—	11	—	—	10	—	7	—
MICHIGAN									
House									
Chipman D	1	0	0	5	4	0	2	—	2
Hunt D	1	—	0	7	4	4	6	—	3
McClelland D	2	0	0	3	3	2	6	—	2
Senate									
Cass D	1	1	1	3	0	1	—	2	—
Woodbridge W	8	9	10	1	5	10	—	6	—
MISSISSIPPI									
House									
Adams D	0	0	3	19	0	0	1	—	0
Davis D	0	—	1	18	3	—	0	—	—
Ellett D	—	—	—	—	—	4	2	—	—
Roberts D	1	0	2	18	0	0	1	—	0
Thompson D	0	0	1	18	0	0	1	—	0
Senate									
Chalmers D	8	0	8	—	—	2	—	3	—
Speight D	3	—	11	1	0	3	—	2	—

Name and Party	Tar.	Land	Exp.	Imp.	War	War(2)	Slav.(2)	Land(2)	Tar.(2)
MISSOURI									
House									
Bowlin D	2	0	1	2	0	0	1	—	—
McDaniel D	—	—	—	—	—	0	1	—	—
Phelps D	2	0	2	13	0	0	1	—	—
Price D	—	—	1	12	—	—	—	—	—
Relfe D	2	0	0	2	3	3	1	—	—
Sims D	0	0	7	19	0	0	2	—	—
Senate									
Atchison D	2	0	0	5	0	3	—	2	—
Benton D	1	0	6	7	0	2	—	0	—
NEW HAMPSHIRE									
House									
Johnson D	4	0	0	19	6	0	8	—	2
Moulton D	4	0	0	19	3	0	8	—	2
Norris D	4	0	0	19	4	0	6	—	2
Senate									
Atherton D	0	1	3	9	0	0	—	0	—
Cilley W	8	9	—	9	—	10	—	7	—
Jenness D	—	—	2	—	0	—	—	—	—
NEW JERSEY									
House									
Edsall D	7	7	1	—	4	2	6	—	4
Hampton W	7	7	11	0	5	8	8	—	7
Runk W	7	—	10	2	6	11	8	—	6
Sykes D	7	7	1	3	6	1	6	—	—
Wright W	7	7	13	0	—	—	8	—	6
Senate									
Dayton W	8	9	10	—	5	9	—	7	—
Miller W	8	9	10	2	—	9	—	6	—
NEW YORK									
House									
Anderson D	5	—	0	19	4	0	8	—	2
Benton D	0	2	1	19	3	0	6	—	4
Campbell A	7	7	10	1	5	8	0	—	6
Carroll W	7	—	—	0	5	10	8	—	7

Name and Party	Tar.	Land	Exp.	Imp.	War	War(2)	Slav.(2)	Land(2)	Tar.(2)
Collen D	0	3	1	18	3	0	6	—	0
Culver W	7	7	11	0	6	11	—	—	7
DeMott D	1	7	0	5	3	0	6	—	4
Ellsworth D	1	6	—	3	3	0	6	—	4
Goodyear D	1	5	5	5	4	5	—	—	0
Gordon D	0	6	0	19	3	0	6	—	0
Grover D	1	7	1	19	3	0	8	—	4
Herrick W	—	—	—	0	4	—	—	—	—
Holmes W	7	7	13	0	5	11	7	—	7
Hough D	1	0	1	7	3	0	6	—	3
Hungerford D	7	—	1	10	3	0	6	—	4
Hunt W	7	7	10	0	6	11	8	—	6
Jenkins D	7	7	2	5	3	4	6	—	4
King D	1	6	0	5	4	4	8	—	4
Lawrence D	1	—	1	9	—	1	6	—	0
Lewis W	7	7	10	1	5	11	8	—	7
Maclay D	1	0	0	19	4	1	8	—	2
Miller W	7	7	—	1	5	11	8	—	6
Moseley W	7	7	—	0	5	11	8	—	6
Niven D	—	7	5	6	4	3	6	—	—
Rathbun D	6	7	0	5	4	4	8	—	4
Ripley W	—	—	—	—	—	11	8	—	7
Russell D	7	—	—	—	—	0	6	—	—
Seaman A	7	7	10	7	6	11	0	—	6
Smith R	7	7	10	1	5	10	8	—	7
Strong D	1	0	2	4	3	0	3	—	2
Wheaton D	0	7	0	17	4	0	8	—	—
White R	7	7	10	0	6	11	8	—	7
Wood D	1	—	—	8	3	0	8	—	4
Woodruff D	7	7	10	2	—	11	—	—	—
Woodworth D	—	—	6	3	—	1	6	—	2
Senate									
Dickinson D	1	1	1	6	—	2	—	—	—
Dix D	0	1	5	7	0	1	—	0	—
NORTH CAROLINA									
House									
Barringer W	7	7	7	19	0	7	1	—	6

Name and Party	*Tar.*	*Land*	*Exp.*	*Imp.*	*War*	*War(2)*	*Slav.(2)*	*Land(2)*	*Tar.(2)*
Biggs D	0	2	1	19	1	2	—	—	0
Clark D	0	—	1	19	0	0	1	—	0
Daniel D	0	1	1	19	0	0	1	—	3
Dobbin D	0	1	2	19	0	3	1	—	—
Dockery W	7	7	7	19	0	9	0	—	6
Graham W	7	7	7	19	0	7	0	—	6
McKay D	0	0	1	19	0	0	1	—	0
Reid D	0	1	0	19	0	1	1	—	0
Senate									
Badger W	—	—	—	—	—	9	—	6	—
Haywood D	—	—	11	8	—	—	—	—	—
Mangum W	8	9	9	0	5	8	—	6	—
OHIO									
House									
J. Brinkerhoff D	5	—	1	2	3	4	8	—	5
Cummins D	—	2	0	16	3	4	6	—	5
Cunningham D	0	0	2	0	1	0	3	—	0
Delano W	7	7	11	0	—	11	8	—	7
Faran D	2	0	0	2	3	0	8	—	2
Fries D	1	0	0	3	3	0	6	—	2
Giddings W	7	7	11	4	6	11	8	—	—
Harper W	7	7	10	0	5	10	8	—	6
McDowell D	0	0	1	2	3	0	5	—	4
Morris D	0	0	0	2	3	1	3	—	—
Parrish D	1	0	2	3	3	1	1	—	0
Perrill D	1	0	0	13	3	0	6	—	3
Root W	7	7	10	2	6	11	8	—	7
St. John D	4	—	0	6	3	0	—	—	—
Sawyer D	—	0	0	4	3	0	3	—	2
Schenck W	7	7	10	0	5	11	8	—	7
Starkweather D	4	0	2	2	3	0	6	—	2
Thurman D	2	2	0	2	3	0	6	—	2
Tilden W	7	7	10	1	6	11	—	—	7
Vance W	7	5	11	—	6	11	8	—	7
Vinton W	7	7	12	1	5	11	8	—	6
Senate									
Allen D	0	0	1	3	0	0	—	2	—

Name and Party	Tar.	Land	Exp.	Imp.	War	War(2)	Slav.(2)	Land(2)	Tar.(2)
Corwin W	8	9	10	1	5	10	—	6	—
PENNSYLVANIA									
House									
Black D	7	—	2	19	3	0	3	—	3
Blanchard W	7	7	10	0	5	7	8	—	6
Brodhead D	7	7	1	4	3	3	3	—	3
Buffington W	7	7	11	7	5	9	8	—	7
Campbell W	7	7	6	0	4	8	7	—	6
Darragh W	7	—	11	3	3	—	8	—	—
Erdman D	7	7	1	19	3	0	3	—	3
Ewing W	7	7	10	0	5	11	8	—	7
Foster D	7	7	2	4	3	0	3	—	3
Garvin D	7	7	2	14	3	0	6	—	3
C. Ingersoll D	7	7	1	0	3	0	3	—	3
J. Ingersoll W	7	7	—	2	3	8	8	—	6
Leib D	7	7	6	5	3	1	—	—	4
Levin A	7	—	9	0	4	8	8	—	—
McClean D	7	7	1	19	3	0	3	—	3
McIlvaine W	7	7	11	0	6	11	8	—	—
Pollock W	7	—	9	1	3	7	8	—	6
Ramsey W	7	7	11	1	2	8	8	—	6
Ritter D	7	7	1	19	3	1	6	—	3
Stewart W	7	7	10	0	5	7	8	—	6
Strohm W	7	7	12	7	6	10	8	—	6
Thompson D	7	7	4	3	3	0	5	—	—
Wilmot D	5	2	2	19	6	1	8	—	—
Yost D	7	7	1	19	3	4	6	—	3
Senate									
Buchanan D	—	—	—	—	—	—	—	—	—
Cameron D	8	9	4	—	0	5	—	5	—
Sturgeon D	8	9	0	4	0	1	—	5	—
RHODE ISLAND									
House									
Arnold W	7	7	11	0	4	8	8	—	6
Cranston W	7	7	—	0	—	11	8	—	7
Senate									
Greene W	8	9	11	4	—	10	—	6	—

Name and Party	Tar.	Land	Exp.	Imp.	War	War(2)	Slav.(2)	Land(2)	Tar.(2)
Simmons W	8	9	10	1	5	9	—	4	—
SOUTH CAROLINA									
House									
Black D	1	0	1	19	0	1	1	—	1
Burt D	0	0	13	19	0	6	0	—	0
Holmes D	0	2	—	18	0	3	0	—	0
Rhett D	1	0	—	19	0	7	0	—	—
Simpson D	0	0	—	19	1	6	0	—	0
Sims D	0	—	7	19	0	1	2	—	2
Woodward D	0	0	—	19	0	7	0	—	0
Senate									
Butler D	—	—	—	—	—	5	—	0	—
Calhoun D	2	0	9	9	4	5	—	7	—
McDuffie D	2	1	10	9	5	—	—	—	—
TENNESSEE									
House									
M. Brown W	7	7	7	14	4	9	1	—	6
Chase D	0	0	1	19	0	0	1	—	0
Cocke D	7	7	7	17	4	7	1	—	6
Crozier W	7	7	7	17	0	7	0	—	6
Cullom D	0	0	1	19	1	0	1	—	0
Ewing W	7	7	10	0	5	8	8	—	6
Gentry W	7	7	7	—	3	8	1	—	6
A. Johnson D	3	—	0	19	0	6	1	—	1
Jones D	0	0	1	19	3	0	1	—	0
Martin D	0	0	1	19	0	0	1	—	0
Peyton W	—	—	—	—	—	—	—	—	—
Stanton D	0	0	5	11	1	0	1	—	0
Senate									
Jarnagin W	4	—	10	0	2	9	—	5	—
Turney D	—	1	5	9	0	0	—	2	—
TEXAS									
House									
Kaufman D	1	0	—	—	0	0	2	—	—
Pilsbury D	1	0	—	—	0	0	1	—	3
Senate									
Houston D	1	0	5	0	0	3	—	1	—

Name and Party	Tar.	Land	Exp.	Imp.	War	War(2)	Slav.(2)	Land(2)	Tar.(2)
Rusk D	2	0	6	3	0	3	—	0	—
VERMONT									
House									
Collamer W	7	7	12	1	—	11	8	—	6
Dillingham D	7	4	2	19	3	3	6	—	5
Foot W	7	7	—	0	5	11	8	—	—
Marsh W	7	7	12	1	5	11	8	—	7
Senate									
Phelps W	8	9	11	—	—	8	—	7	—
Upham W	8	9	11	1	5	9	—	6	—
VIRGINIA									
House									
Atkinson D	1	1	3	19	0	1	1	—	2
Bayly D	1	2	—	19	0	2	0	—	0
Bedinger D	1	0	5	19	0	1	0	—	1
Brown D	0	0	0	18	3	0	1	—	0
Chapman D	1	0	13	19	3	1	—	—	4
Dromgoole D	1	0	1	19	1	1	2	—	5
Hopkins D	0	1	6	19	0	1	2	—	2
Hubard D	1	0	13	19	0	1	2	—	0
Hunter D	1	1	—	19	0	2	1	—	0
Johnson D	0	1	1	19	0	0	1	—	1
Leake D	1	0	7	19	1	0	0	—	0
McDowell D	2	1	2	19	0	0	1	—	1
Pendleton W	7	7	13	0	5	7	0	—	6
Seddon D	1	0	—	19	—	2	0	—	2
Taylor D	—	—	—	—	—	—	—	—	—
Tredway D	1	0	5	19	3	0	0	—	0
Senate									
Archer W	7	9	11	—	5	8	—	3	—
Mason D	—	—	—	—	—	2	—	0	—
Pennybacker D	0	1	4	9	0	—	—	—	—

THIRTIETH CONGRESS

Name and Party	*War*	*Improvements*	*Slavery*	Name and Party	*War*	*Improvements*	*Slavery*
ALABAMA				DELAWARE			
House				*House*			
Bowdon D	3	10	—	Houston W	8	0	—
Cobb D	0	10	0	*Senate*			
Gayle W	8	0	0	Clayton W	—	0	6
Harris D	3	10	0	Spruance W	—	0	6
Hilliard W	9	—	0	Wales W	—	—	—
Houston D	0	10	0	FLORIDA			
Inge D	2	10	0	*House*			
Senate				Cabell W	9	0	0
Bagby D	2	6	—	*Senate*			
Fitzpatrick D	—	—	—	Westcott D	2	5	0
King D	—	—	1	Yulee D	3	6	0
Lewis D	3	—	0	GEORGIA			
ARKANSAS				*House*			
House				Cobb D	0	10	0
Johnson D	1	8	0	Haralson D	2	10	0
Senate				Iverson D	—	9	0
Ashley D	2	—	—	Jones W	7	0	0
Borland D	—	3	1	King W	9	0	0
Sebastian D	—	—	2	Lumpkin D	2	10	0
Sevier D	0	—	—	Stephens W	8	0	0
CONNECTICUT				Toombs W	9	1	0
House				*Senate*			
Dixon W	10	0	12	Berrien W	7	—	1
Hubbard W	11	0	11	Colquitt D	—	—	—
Rockwell W	9	0	12	Johnson D	1	6	2
Smith W	11	0	9	ILLINOIS			
Senate				*House*			
Baldwin W	7	—	13	Ficklin D	2	10	2
Huntington W	—	—	—	Lincoln W	9	0	9
Niles D	6	1	10	McClernand D	1	10	2

Name and Party	War	Imp.	Slav.
Richardson D	2	—	2
Smith D	2	5	11
Turner D	1	2	—
Wentworth D	3	0	12
Senate			
Breese D	2	3	6
Douglas D	2	3	5
INDIANA			
House			
Cathcart D	3	4	11
Dunn W	8	0	9
Embree W	7	0	10
Henley D	3	5	11
Pettit D	—	6	7
Robinson D	3	10	4
Rockhill D	3	6	12
C. Smith W	10	0	10
Thompson W	10	4	9
Wick D	1	10	—
Senate			
Bright D	3	3	6
Hannegan D	3	2	4
IOWA			
House			
Leffler D	1	2	—
Thompson D	2	—	—
Senate			
Dodge D	—	—	—
Jones D	—	—	—
KENTUCKY			
House			
Adams W	9	0	2
Boyd D	0	10	0
Buckner W	10	0	1
Clarke D	1	10	1
Duncan W	7	1	0
French D	3	7	0

Name and Party	War	Imp.	Slav.
Gaines W	8	—	1
Morehead W	10	0	1
Peyton D	2	8	1
Thompson W	9	1	2
Senate			
Crittenden W	7	—	—
Metcalfe W	—	—	3
Underwood W	7	0	3
LOUISIANA			
House			
Harmanson D	3	10	1
LaSere D	3	10	0
Morse D	2	—	1
Thibodeaux W	9	2	0
Senate			
Downs D	3	1	3
Johnson W	6	0	3
MAINE			
House			
Belcher W	11	2	12
Clapp D	—	—	12
Clark D	2	9	3
Hammons D	0	10	9
Smart D	4	9	10
Wiley D	1	9	3
Williams D	1	9	3
Senate			
Bradbury W	2	—	9
Fairfield D	—	—	—
Hamlin D	—	—	12
Moore W	3	—	—
MARYLAND			
House			
Chapman W	10	0	0
Crisfield W	8	0	0
Evans W	7	0	0
Ligon D	4	10	0

Name and Party	*War*	*Imp.*	*Slav.*
McLane D	1	10	0
Roman W	—	1	0
Senate			
Johnson W	0	0	6
Pearce W	7	6	2
MASSACHUSETTS			
House			
Abbott W	11	0	12
Adams W	10	—	—
Ashmun W	11	1	—
Grinnell W	10	—	12
Hale W	11	1	11
Hudson W	11	0	12
King W	11	0	11
Mann W	—	1	12
Palfrey W	11	0	12
Rockwell W	11	0	11
Winthrop W	Speaker of the House		
Senate			
Davis W	7	0	13
Webster W	7	—	13
MICHIGAN			
House			
Bingham D	2	2	12
McClelland D	2	2	11
Stuart D	2	2	10
Senate			
Cass D	2	—	—
Felch D	2	3	12
Fitzgerald D	—	—	8
MISSISSIPPI			
House			
Brown D	2	10	0
Featherston D	3	10	0
Thompson D	2	10	0
Tompkins W	9	0	0

Name and Party	*War*	*Imp.*	*Slav.*
Senate			
Davis D	2	2	0
Foote D	2	2	1
Speight D	—	—	—
MISSOURI			
House			
Bowlin D	2	2	1
Green D	2	9	0
Hall D	3	9	1
Jameson D	0	9	1
Phelps D	2	10	0
Senate			
Atchison D	2	3	2
Benton D	—	2	7
NEW HAMPSHIRE			
House			
Johnson D	3	10	12
Peaslee D	2	10	11
Tuck Ind.	11	1	12
Wilson W	11	2	12
Senate			
Atherton D	1	6	6
Hale D	7	6	13
NEW JERSEY			
House			
Edsall D	—	4	—
Gregory W	10	0	11
Hampton W	9	0	11
Newell W	8	0	12
Van Dyke W	9	2	11
Senate			
Dayton W	7	—	12
Miller W	7	—	12
NEW YORK			
House			
Birdsall D	2	3	4
Blackmar W	—	—	12

Name and Party	War	Imp.	Slav.
Collins D	2	2	12
Conger W	10	0	12
Duer W	8	4	12
Gott W	10	0	12
Greeley W	—	—	12
Hall W	10	0	12
Holmes W	10	0	12
Hunt W	10	0	12
Jenkins D	2	2	12
Kellogg W	10	0	12
Lawrence, S. D	2	2	12
Lawrence, W. W	10	0	12
Lord W	10	10	8
Maclay D	2	3	—
Marvin W	10	0	12
Mullin R	8	0	12
Murphy D	1	—	—
Nelson W	10	0	11
Nicoll D	3	3	11
Petrie R	1	2	11
Putnam W	8	0	12
Reynolds W	8	1	12
Rose W	—	0	—
Rumsey W	10	0	12
St. John D	9	1	11
Sherrill W	8	0	12
Silvester W	9	0	12
Slingerland R	10	0	12
Starkweather D	2	2	12
Tallmadge W	10	0	11
Warren W	10	0	11
White R	10	0	12
Senate			
Dickinson D	2	6	5
Dix D	2	1	12

Name and Party	War	Imp.	Slav.
NORTH CAROLINA			
House			
Barringer W	8	1	0
Boyden W	11	0	2
Clingman W	9	0	0
Daniel D	0	10	0
Donnell W	9	0	2
McKay D	1	10	0
Outlaw W	8	0	0
Shepperd W	9	4	0
Venable D	2	10	0
Senate			
Badger W	7	0	2
Mangum W	7	—	3
OHIO			
House			
Camby W	11	0	10
Crowell W	11	0	12
Cummins D	2	10	—
Dickinson D	11	2	7
Duncan W	10	1	12
Edwards W	10	1	11
Evans W	10	0	—
Faran D	4	4	12
Fisher W	11	0	12
Fries D	2	10	11
Giddings W	11	0	12
Kennon D	0	10	2
Lahm D	3	6	11
Miller D	0	10	2
Morris D	3	2	—
Ritchey D	0	6	7
Root W	11	0	12
Sawyer D	0	—	6
Schenck W	10	1	—

Name and Party	*War*	*Imp.*	*Slav.*	Name and Party	*War*	*Imp.*	*Slav.*
Taylor W	9	0	9	Thurston D	2	2	12
Vinton W	10	0	9	*Senate*			
Senate				Clarke W	7	0	13
Allen D	2	3	9	Greene W	7	0	13
Corwin W	7	0	12	SOUTH CAROLINA			
PENNSYLVANIA				*House*			
House				Black D	4	—	—
Blanchard W	10	0	12	Burt D	2	10	0
Brady W	10	0	9	Holmes D	—	—	0
Brodhead D	0	10	4	Rhett D	4	10	0
Brown D	0	10	2	Simpson D	5	10	0
Butler W	9	1	10	Sims D	2	10	—
Dickey W	10	0	12	Wallace D	—	10	0
Eckert W	10	1	12	Woodward D	2	10	0
Farrelly W	9	0	12	*Senate*			
Freedley W	10	0	11	Butler D	0	6	2
Hampton W	9	0	12	Calhoun D	7	4	0
C. Ingersoll D	2	3	1	TENNESSEE			
J. Ingersoll D	9	0	—	*House*			
Irvin W	7	0	10	Barrow W	9	1	1
Levin A	—	0	0	Chase D	1	9	—
McIlvaine W	10	1	12	Cocke D	9	0	1
Mann D	1	10	7	Crozier W	8	0	0
Nes Ind.	9	0	11	Gentry W	9	0	0
Pollock W	8	0	10	Haskell W	9	—	—
Stewart W	9	5	—	Hill D	0	10	0
Strohm W	10	0	12	Johnson D	2	9	1
Strong D	2	—	9	Jones D	1	9	1
Thompson D	1	2	11	Stanton D	3	—	0
Wilmot D	—	—	12	Thomas D	2	10	0
Senate				*Senate*			
Cameron D	3	—	—	Bell W	7	0	5
Sturgeon D	0	1	4	Turney D	2	6	0
RHODE ISLAND				TEXAS			
House				*House*			
Cranston W	10	0	12	Kaufman D	0	10	0

Name and Party	*War*	*Imp.*	*Slav.*	Name and Party	*War*	*Imp.*	*Slav.*
Pilsbury D	1	9	0	Botts W	10	2	0
Senate				Brown D	2	10	1
Houston D	—	2	4	Flournoy W	—	0	0
Rusk D	4	—	1	Fulton W	6	2	0
VERMONT				Goggin W	7	0	0
House				McDowell D	2	10	0
Collamer W	10	0	12	Meade D	1	10	0
Henry W	10	0	12	Pendleton W	10	—	0
Marsh W	10	0	12	Preston W	9	0	0
Peck D	2	2	12	Thompson W	—	1	0
Senate				*Senate*			
Phelps W	—	0	11	Hunter D	0	6	0
Upham W	7	0	13	Mason D	4	6	3
VIRGINIA				WISCONSIN			
House				*House*			
Atkinson D	—	10	1	Darling D	—	2	—
Bayly D	3	10	0	Lynde D	—	2	—
Beale D	2	10	0	*Senate*			
Bedinger D	2	10	1	Dodge D	—	—	12
Bocock D	2	10	0	Walker D	—	—	12

THIRTY-FIRST CONGRESS

Name and Party	Sectionalism	Compromise	Land	Improvements	Improvements (2d. Sess.)	Postage	Govt. Operations
ALABAMA							
House							
Alston W	13	1	—	1	—	—	—
Bowden D	13	13	—	0	9	—	7
Cobb D	13	0	0	0	8	—	—
Harris D	13	12	—	0	—	—	7
Hilliard W	13	0	2	0	—	—	0
Hubbard D	13	12	2	0	—	—	—
Inge D	13	13	2	1	8	—	7
Senate							
Clemens D	—	1	—	—	10	6	—
Fitzpatrick D	—	—	—	—	—	—	—
King D	18	1	—	—	7	6	—
ARKANSAS							
House							
Johnson D	13	12	2	0	1	—	7
Senate							
Borland D	—	—	—	—	—	6	—
Sebastian D	18	1	—	—	0	6	—
CALIFORNIA							
House							
Gilbert D	—	—	—	0	5	—	0
Wright Ind.	—	—	—	—	—	—	0
Senate							
Fremont D	—	—	—	—	—	—	—
Gwin D	—	—	—	—	10	3	—
CONNECTICUT							
House							
Booth FS	0	13	0	7	7	—	1
Butler W	0	8	0	1	—	—	—
Cleveland D	—	—	—	4	8	—	4
Waldo D	0	8	0	—	7	—	1

Name and Party	*Sec.*	*Comp.*	*Land*	*Imp.*	*Imp.(2)*	*Post.*	*G.Op.*
Senate							
Baldwin W	1	10	—	—	1	4	—
Smith W	4	10	—	—	1	6	—
DELAWARE							
House							
Houston W	9	0	5	2	0	—	2
Senate							
Spruance W	6	7	—	—	2	5	—
Wales W	6	7	—	—	0	5	—
FLORIDA							
House							
Cabell W	13	2	—	0	—	—	7
Senate							
Morton D	18	2	—	—	7	6	—
Yulee D	17	4	—	—	9	6	—
GEORGIA							
House							
Cobb D	Speaker of the House						
Hackett	—	—	—	—	—	—	—
Haralson D	13	7	0	9	8	—	7
Jackson D	13	7	2	0	8	—	7
King W	—	—	—	—	—	—	—
Owen W	13	1	—	—	—	—	—
Stephens W	—	—	5	3	9	—	—
Toombs W	13	1	5	—	8	—	7
Wellborn D	13	1	3	—	—	—	7
Senate							
Berrien W	16	2	—	—	—	6	—
Dawson D	16	1	—	—	10	6	—
ILLINOIS							
House							
Baker W	3	9	—	1	—	—	—
Bissell D	7	1	3	0	—	—	—
Harris D	7	0	3	0	4	—	7
McClernand D	8	0	0	0	—	—	—
Richardson D	7	1	3	0	4	—	—

Name and Party	*Sec.*	*Comp.*	*Land*	*Imp.*	*Imp.(2)*	*Post.*	*G.Op.*
Wentworth D	0	8	0	1	1	—	0
Young D	7	0	1	0	8	—	0
Senate							
Douglas D	11	5	—	—	0	1	—
Shields D	9	6	—	—	0	—	—
INDIANA							
House							
Albertson D	7	0	2	0	9	—	6
Brown D	7	0	0	1	9	—	—
Dunham D	7	0	0	2	8	—	7
Fitch D	2	2	0	0	1	—	4
Gurman D	7	0	3	0	8	—	7
Harlan D	2	9	0	0	—	—	7
Julian FS	0	13	0	0	2	—	4
McDonald D	7	1	0	—	8	—	4
McGaughey W	7	10	0	0	1	—	3
Robinson D	2	0	0	0	8	—	7
Senate							
Bright D	10	1	—	—	5	—	—
Whitcomb D	10	1	—	—	6	2	—
IOWA							
House							
Leffler D	7	0	0	0	0	—	4
Miller W	—	—	—	—	1	—	0
Thompson D	—	—	0	—	—	—	—
Senate							
Dodge D	12	6	—	—	0	0	—
Jones D	12	7	—	—	0	4	—
KENTUCKY							
House							
Boyd D	13	1	1	9	6	—	7
Breck W	10	0	—	1	0	—	4
Caldwell D	13	1	2	8	8	—	7
Johnson W	12	0	2	—	0	—	4
Marshall W	12	1	0	9	2	—	1
Mason D	12	3	0	2	—	—	7

Name and Party	Sec.	Comp.	Land	Imp.	Imp.(2)	Post.	G.Op.
McLean W	12	1	—	—	2	—	5
Morehead W	12	0	3	4	3	—	3
Stanton D	13	3	0	0	9	—	7
Thompson W	12	0	—	1	1	—	6
Senate							
Clay W	12	0	—	—	1	5	—
Underwood W	13	3	—	—	0	4	—
LOUISIANA							
House							
Bullard W	—	—	—	—	—	—	7
Conrad W	—	—	—	—	—	—	—
Harmanson D	—	—	—	—	—	—	—
LaSere D	13	7	0	0	9	—	5
Morse D	13	11	3	1	9	—	1
Penn D	—	—	—	—	9	—	6
Senate							
Downs D	18	1	—	—	10	2	0
Soule D	17	2	—	—	10	4	—
MAINE							
House							
Fuller D	7	0	2	7	8	—	7
Gerry D	7	0	—	7	9	—	4
Goodenow W	—	—	0	7	3	—	2
Littlefield D	7	0	0	7	8	—	4
Otis W	0	9	5	5	0	—	2
Sawtelle D	0	8	3	9	7	—	2
Stetson D	0	8	0	7	7	—	2
Senate							
Bradbury W	5		—	—	7	5	—
Hamlin D	2	10	—	—	8	—	—
MARYLAND							
House							
Bowle W	11	0	2	0	0	—	7
Evans W	—	—	—	7	0	—	2
Hamilton D	12	—	2	9	9	—	6
Hammond D	—	2	—	9	9	—	2

Name and Party	*Sec.*	*Comp.*	*Land*	*Imp.*	*Imp.(2)*	*Post.*	*G.Op.*
Kerr W	11	0	—	7	0	—	5
McLane D	12	0	2	0	0	—	5
Senate							
Johnson W	—	—	—	—	—	—	—
Pearce W	15	3	—	—	4	5	—
Pratt W	17	1	—	—	0	4	—
Stewart W	—	—	—	—	—	—	—
MASSACHUSETTS							
House							
Allen FS	0	13	5	4	1	—	3
Ashmun W	—	—	5	0	0	—	0
Duncan W	2	4	1	3	0	—	2
Eliot W	7	0	—	0	0	—	1
Fowler FS	0	—	0	7	1	—	2
Grinnell W	6	0	0	2	0	—	1
King W	0	—	0	—	—	—	—
Mann W	0	11	0	0	1	—	2
Rockwell W	0	9	0	7	0	—	0
Winthrop W	—	—	0	—	—	—	—
Senate							
Davis W	2	10	—	—	1	4	—
Rantoul D	—	—	—	—	0	—	—
Webster W	—	9	—	—	—	—	—
Winthrop W	1	—	—	—	—	—	—
MICHIGAN							
House							
Bingham D	0	11	0	0	1	—	4
Buel D	7	0	0	0	0	—	4
Sprague W	0	8	0	0	0	—	0
Senate							
Cass D	14	0	—	—	6	1	—
Felch D	11	7	—	—	0	2	—
MISSISSIPPI							
House							
Brown D	13	13	1	0	8	—	7
Featherston D	13	11	2	0	8	—	7

Name and Party	Sec.	Comp.	Land	Imp.	Imp.(2)	Post.	G.Op.
McWillie D	13	7	—	3	8	—	7
Thompson D							
Senate							
Davis D	17	3	—	—	8	6	—
Foote D	16	1	—	—	10	—	—
MISSOURI							
House							
Bay D	11	0	—	0	—	—	7
Bowlin D	11	1	4	0	4	—	—
Green D	13	2	0	0	—	—	—
Hall D	8	0	0	0	8	—	—
Phelps D	9	8	0	0	7	—	6
Senate							
Atchison D	18	1	—	—	9	4	—
Benton D	12	8	—	—	—	—	—
NEW HAMPSHIRE							
House							
Hibbard D	7	0	0	8	8	—	—
Morrison D	—	—	—	—	9	—	—
Peaslee D	4	0	0	7	8	—	2
Tuck Ind.	0	10	0	7	0	—	2
Wilson W	9	0	—	—	—	—	—
Senate							
Hale D	0	—	—	—	2	1	—
Norris D	11	6	—	—	10	4	—
NEW JERSEY							
House							
Hay W	—	—	0	6	0	—	0
King W	0	8	3	4	0	—	1
Newell W	1	8	0	—	—	—	—
Van Dyke W	1	8	0	5	0	—	1
Wildrick D	7	0	2	9	8	—	—
Senate							
Dayton W	4	10	—	—	—	1	—
Miller W	—	10	—	—	1	1	—

Name and Party	*Sec.*	*Comp.*	*Land*	*Imp.*	*Imp.(2)*	*Post.*	*G.Op.*
NEW YORK							
House							
Alexander W	1	11	0	7	0	—	0
Andrews W	6	0	0	3	1	—	1
Bennett W	0	13	—	—	1	—	1
Bokee W	7	0	5	3	1	—	1
Briggs W	7	0	0	2	0	—	1
Brooks W	7	0	5	2	—	—	1
Burrows W	0	8	0	4	0	—	1
Clarke W	1	13	—	7	1	—	3
Conger W	—	8	5	—	1	—	1
Duer W	7	2	—	—	1	—	1
Gott W	0	—	0	0	1	—	0
Gould W	2	8	0	6	3	—	1
Halloway W	0	8	0	3	0	—	1
Jackson W	2	9	—	9	0	—	1
J. King W	0	8	4	2	0	—	1
P. King D	0	13	0	7	—	—	2
McKissock W	0	13	3	2	0	—	1
Matteson W	2	13	3	2	0	—	0
Nelson W	0	2	4	7	0	—	1
Phoenyx W	7	0	1	0	—	—	1
Putnam W	1	8	—	3	0	—	1
Reynolds W	1	9	0	7	1	—	0
Risley W	—	—	0	0	0	—	0
Rose W	7	0	2	1	0	—	2
Rumsey W	0	10	0	7	0	—	1
Sackett W	0	13	0	5	1	—	0
Schermerhorn W	0	8	1	3	—	—	1
Schoolcraft W	0	13	0	3	2	—	1
Silvester W	0	8	0	—	0	—	1
Spaulding W	—	—	0	4	1	—	0
Thurman W	2	0	3	6	0	—	0
Underhill W	0	3	0	0	0	—	1
Walden D	7	0	0	1	1	—	1

Name and Party	*Sec.*	*Comp.*	*Land*	*Imp.*	*Imp.(2)*	*Post.*	*G.Op.*
White Repub.	6	0	5	3	0	—	1
Senate							
Dickinson D	14	0	—	—	5	0	—
Seward W	0	10	—	—	0	0	—
NORTH CAROLINA							
House							
Ashe D	13	11	5	9	—	—	7
Caldwell W	12	0	—	1	6	—	—
Clingman D	13	6	5	3	—	—	7
Daniel D	13	13	5	9	9	—	7
Deberry W	13	0	5	9	8	—	2
Outlaw W	13	0	2	7	1	—	7
Shepperd W	13	0	3	—	0	—	2
Stanly W	9	0	—	3	1	—	1
Venable D	13	11	5	9	—	—	7
Senate							
Badger W	17	1	—	—	1	4	—
Mangum W	16	1	—	—	1	—	—
OHIO							
House							
Bell W	—	—	—	—	—	—	—
Cable D	1	13	0	9	8	—	—
Campbell W	0	13	—	9	1	—	2
Cartter D	1	8	0	9	2	—	7
Corwin W	2	8	0	0	1	—	2
Crowell W	0	10	5	6	1	—	1
Dickinson D	—	—	—	—	—	—	—
Disney D	1	0	—	9	—	—	6
Evans W	0	12	5	7	1	—	2
Giddings W	0	—	4	—	2	—	4
Hoagland D	7	0	—	0	8	—	4
Hunter W	0	—	0	8	2	—	2
Miller D	—	—	2	9	8	—	—
Morris D	0	8	0	9	2	—	0
Olds D	4	9	3	—	—	—	0
Potter D	2	1	2	0	—	—	0

Name and Party	*Sec.*	*Comp.*	*Land*	*Imp.*	*Imp.(2)*	*Post.*	*G.Op.*
Root W	0	13	5	7	1	—	2
Schenck W	1	13	—	—	—	—	2
Sweetser D	4	8	3	—	1	—	7
Taylor W	5	2	0	3	1	—	1
Vinton W	0	8	5	7	0	—	1
Whittlesey D	0	5	0	0	7	—	4
Wood D	—	—	0	3	—	—	—
Senate							
Chase FS	0	10	—	—	0	0	—
Corwin W	—	10	—	—	—	—	—
Ewing W	8	—	—	—	1	2	—
PENNSYLVANIA							
House							
Brisbin W	—	—	—	—	9	—	4
Butler W	7	0	3	7	—	—	—
Calvin W	0	8	0	3	1	—	4
Casey W	—	0	0	4	3	—	2
Chandler W	2	4	1	3	0	—	4
Danner W	2	4	1	3	8	—	4
Dickey W	2	10	1	7	0	—	4
Dimmick D	7	0	0	9	9	—	5
Freedley W	0	8	0	4	9	—	5
Gilmore D	7	1	—	9	8	—	0
Hampton W	—	—	4	7	0	—	2
Howe FS	0	13	0	7	1	—	4
Levin Amer.	7	0	—	0	0	—	6
McLanahan D	7	1	2	8	8	—	5
Mann D	7	0	4	9	7	—	5
Moore W	2	8	3	7	0	—	4
Ness Ind.	—	—	—	—	—	—	—
Ogle W	4	8	1	7	1	—	4
Pitman W	8	0	0	3	1	—	2
Reed W	0	8	0	7	1	—	4
Robbins D	7	0	2	7	8	—	5
Ross D	8	1	—	9	8	—	7
Stevens W	1	13	0	7	—	—	—

Name and Party	*Sec.*	*Comp.*	*Land*	*Imp.*	*Imp.(2)*	*Post.*	*G.Op.*
Strong D	—	0	2	7	7	—	—
Thompson D	6	1	2	9	7	—	6
Wilmot D	—	—	0	—	—	—	—
Senate							
Cooper W	5	0	—	—	1	1	—
Sturgeon D	13	0	—	—	8	2	—
RHODE ISLAND							
House							
Dixon W	0	8	5	7	—	—	—
King W	0	5	5	4	0	—	—
Senate							
Clarke W	7	10	—	—	2	2	—
Greene W	3	10	—	—	1	3	—
SOUTH CAROLINA							
House							
Burt D	13	13	1	9	—	—	7
Colcock D	13	13	—	9	8	—	7
Holmes D	13	12	—	—	—	—	1
McQueen D	13	13	2	0	8	—	7
Orr D	13	13	2	1	8	—	7
Wallace D	13	13	2	9	8	—	7
Woodward D	13	13	2	8	—	—	—
Senate							
Barnwell D	17	—	—	—	—		—
Butler D	18	2	—	—	10		—
Calhoun D	—	—	—	—	—		—
Elmore D	—	—	—	—	—		—
Rhett D	—	—	—	—	10		—
TENNESSEE							
House							
Anderson W	12	0	0	1	1	—	—
Ewing D	12	0	3	1	8	—	7
Gentry W	8	0	—	3	—	—	—
Harris D	13	1	1	9	8	—	7
Johnson D	12	0	2	9	8	—	7
Jones D	13	0	3	9	8	—	7

Name and Party	*Sec.*	*Comp.*	*Land*	*Imp.*	*Imp.(2)*	*Post.*	*G.Op.*
Savage D	13	1	2	9	7	—	7
Stanton D	—	5	2	0	0	—	0
Thomas D	13	3	3	9	8	—	7
Watkins W	11	0	2	7	1	—	—
Williams W	11	0	0	0	0	—	7
Senate							
Bell W	15	3	—	—	1	6	—
Turney D	18	3	—	—	10	6	—
TEXAS							
House							
Howard D	13	3	3	1	0	—	7
Kaufman D	13	0	—	3	—	—	7
Senate							
Houston D	18	1	—	—	10	4	—
Rusk D	18	1	—	—	—	4	—
VERMONT							
House							
Hebard W	0	13	3	7	—	—	—
Henry W	0	8	5	7	1	—	2
Marsh W	—	—	—	—	—	—	—
Meacham W	0	6	0	7	1	—	2
Peck D	1	13	3	—	—	—	4
Senate							
Phelps W	3	10	—	—	—	—	—
Upham W	0	10	—	—	2	1	—
VIRGINIA							
House							
Averett D	13	12	4	9	8	—	7
Bayly D	13	1	4	7	7	—	7
Beale D	13	1	5	9	9	—	7
Bocock D	—	—	4	—	9	—	7
Edmundson D	13	1	—	9	9	—	7
Haymond W	8	0	2	4	2	—	1
Holladay D	13	—	5	9	9	—	7
McDowell D	13	0	3	9	9	—	5
McMullen D	13	0	—	9	8	—	7

Name and Party	*Sec.*	*Comp.*	*Land*	*Imp.*	*Imp.(2)*	*Post.*	*G.Op.*
Meade D	13	12	—	9	9	—	7
Millson D	13	11	4	7	9	—	7
Morton W	13	0	4	5	9	—	1
Newman D	—	—	—	—	—	—	—
Parker D	13	0	2	9	8	—	7
Powell D	13	11	—	9	9	—	7
Seddon D	13	12	2	7	9	—	—
Senate							
Hunter D	18	2	—	—	8	6	—
Mason D	18	2	—	—	10	6	—
WISCONSIN							
House							
Cole W	0	13	4	0	0	—	0
Doty D	0	13	0	0	1	—	0
Durkee FS	0	13	—	0	1	—	0
Senate							
Dodge D	0	10	—	—	1	0	—
Walker D	3	10	—	—	—	0	—

THIRTY-SECOND CONGRESS

Name and Party	Sectionalism	Improvements	Land	For. Relations
ALABAMA				
House				
Abercrombie W	—	1	2	5
Bragg D	7	—	7	0
Cobb D	6	—	0	2
Harris D	—	1	4	0
Houston D	7	—	2	2
Smith UW	7	0	2	1
White UW	6	1	2	2
Senate				
Clemens D	5	5	—	8
Fitzpatrick D	—	—	—	—
King D	5	6	4	7
ARKANSAS				
House				
Johnson D	7	0	0	—
Senate				
Borland D	5	6	4	—
Sebastian D	5	—	4	—
CALIFORNIA				
House				
McCorkle D	7	0	0	—
Marshall D	7	—	1	2
Senate				
Gwin D	5	4	0	4
Weller D	5	—	—	—
CONNECTICUT				
House				
Chapman W	0	12	4	—
Cleveland D	—	17	1	—
Ingersoll D	7	16	2	0
Seymour D	7	16	7	0

Name and Party	Sec.	Imp.	Land	F.R.
Senate				
Smith W	5	3	4	6
Toucey D	5	—	4	—
DELAWARE				
House				
Riddle D	7	11	—	3
Senate				
Bayard W	5	4	4	—
Spruance W	5	0	4	7
FLORIDA				
House				
Cabell W	7	0	0	3
Senate				
Mallory D	5	12	4	1
Morton D	—	7	—	8
GEORGIA				
House				
Bailey D	0	—	7	—
Chastain D	—	19	7	3
Hillyer D	7	19	—	4
Jackson D	7	19	7	2
Johnson U	7	1	—	5
Murphey D	—	19	7	2
Stephens W	—	—	—	5
Toombs W	—	—	—	—
Senate				
Berrien W	—	—	4	—
Charlton D	—	12	—	—
Dawson D	5	—	4	8
ILLINOIS				
House				
Allen D	7	0	0	2
Bissell D	—	1	0	—
Campbell D	0	6	0	1
Ficklin D	7	0	0	0
Molony D	0	0	0	1
Richardson D	6	0	0	1

Name and Party	*Sec.*	*Imp.*	*Land*	*F.R.*
Yates W	0	0	0	3
Senate				
Douglas D	5	4	1	0
Shields D	3	4	4	0
INDIANA				
House				
Brenton W	0	2	—	2
Davis D	7	8	0	2
Dunham D	7	19	—	2
Fitch D	7	1	0	0
Gorman D	7	5	0	2
Hendricks D	7	2	0	2
Lockhart D	7	0	0	1
Mace D	—	0	0	2
Parker W	4	1	0	4
Robinson D	7	—	0	2
Senate				
Bright D	—	10	2	1
Cathcart D	—	—	—	—
Pettit D	—	—	—	—
Whitcomb D	—	—	—	0
IOWA				
House				
Clark D	7	0	7	0
Henn D	7	0	2	0
Senate				
Dodge D	5	5	2	0
Jones D	5	5	3	0
KENTUCKY				
House				
Boyd D	Speaker of the House			
Breckinridge D	7	11	7	0
Ewing W	6	19	2	—
Grey W	7	8	3	0
Marshall W	7	0	7	2
Mason D	7	16	6	1
Preston W	—	—	—	—

Name and Party	*Sec.*	*Imp.*	*Land*	*F.R.*
Stanton D	7	1	0	2
Stone D	7	3	1	0
Ward W	6	2	0	3
White W	6	2	1	—
Senate				
Clay W	—	—	—	—
Dixon W	—	—	—	—
Meriwether D	—	10	4	—
Underwood W	5	0	4	—
LOUISIANA				
House				
Landry W	7	0	7	—
Moore W	7	0	0	3
Penn D	7	1	0	—
St. Martin D	7	1	3	0
Senate				
Downs D	5	—	3	2
Soule D	5	7	4	—
MAINE				
House				
Andrews D	—	—	—	—
Appleton D	—	3	7	2
Fuller D	7	19	7	2
Goodenow W	0	12	—	4
McDonald D	7	—	—	0
Reed W				
Smart D	0	17	—	1
Washburn W	0	16	7	—
Senate				
Bradbury W	5	—	4	0
Hamlin D	2	—	4	3
MARYLAND				
House				
Bowie W	7	2	—	3
Coffman W	—	—	2	—
Evans W	—	4	7	3

Name and Party	*Sec.*	*Imp.*	*Land*	*F.R.*
Hamilton D	6	19	7	2
Hammond D	7	19	—	—
Walsh W	7	1	3	3
Senate				
Pearce W	5	—	4	—
Pratt W	5	0	4	—
MASSACHUSETTS				
House				
Allen FS	—	4	2	4
Appleton W	7	—	—	3
Davis W	1	12	3	4
Duncan W	—	12	7	—
Fay W	—	—	—	—
Fowler FSW	0	12	2	4
Goodrich W	0	3	4	—
Little D				
Mann W	0	13	5	4
Rantoul D	0	0	—	—
Sabine W				
Scudder W	0	12	—	4
Thompson W	0	12	—	3
Senate				
Davis W	2	0	4	4
Sumner FS	0	4	1	2
MICHIGAN				
House				
Conger W	0	1	7	4
Penniman W	0	0	0	4
Stuart D	7	2	—	0
Senate				
Cass D	5	4	2	1
Felch D	5	5	4	0
MISSISSIPPI				
House				
Brown D	6	0	1	1
Freeman U	7	0	—	0

Name and Party	*Sec.*	*Imp.*	*Land*	*F.R.*
Nabers W	7	0	—	0
Wilcox UW	7	0	—	0
Senate				
Adams D	5	—	4	—
Brooke D	5	—	4	—
Davis D	—	—	—	—
Foote D	—	0	—	1
McRae	—	—	—	—
MISSOURI				
House				
Darby W				
Hall D	7	10	0	4
Miller W	7	0	0	3
Phelps D	7	0	4	4
Porter W	7	1	0	3
Senate				
Atchison D	5	12	4	—
Geyer W	5	5	4	6
NEW HAMPSHIRE				
House				
Hibbard D	7	19	7	2
Peaslee D	7	19	7	2
Perkins W	0	12	6	
Tuck Ind.	0	—	4	4
Senate				
Hale FS	0	2	3	—
Norris D	5	11	4	0
NEW JERSEY				
House				
Brown W	6	1	7	—
Price D	7	4	—	2
Skelton D	—	19	1	2
Stratton D	0	—	1	0
Wildrick D	—	19	7	0
Senate				
Miller W	5	—	4	5

Name and Party	*Sec.*	*Imp.*	*Land*	*F.R.*
Stockton D	—	—	2	1
NEW YORK				
House				
Babcock D	1	16	2	2
Bennett W	1	17	—	4
Bowne W	—	8	—	3
Boyd W	—	16	—	—
Briggs W	7	0	2	3
Brooks W	5	0	3	3
Buell D	0	19	3	1
Burrows W	—	12	7	3
Dean D	0	16	—	0
Floyd D	0	19	3	—
Hart D	7	18	—	0
Hascell W	—	14	4	3
Haven W	7	5	—	3
Haws W	7	1	—	3
Horsford W	0	12	7	3
Howe D	—	18	7	3
Ives D	0	18	4	2
Jenkins D	0	18	7	3
Jones D	0	19	0	1
P. King D	0	19	7	—
Martin W	6	18	7	5
Murray D	1	17	—	0
Robie D	—	17	—	—
Russell D	1	—	—	—
Sackett W	0	1	0	3
Schemerhorn W	7	4	—	—
Schoolcraft W	0	4	2	3
Schoonmaker W	—	16	—	4
Seymour D	1	10	7	1
Snow D	1	16	4	—
Stephens D	—	1	4	4
Sutherland D	6	19	—	—
Walbridge W	0	12	2	3

Name and Party	*Sec.*	*Imp.*	*Land*	*F.R.*
Wells W	0	12	—	3
Senate				
Fish W	4	0	4	4
Seward W	1	0	1	4
NORTH CAROLINA				
House				
Ashe D	0	19	—	—
Caldwell W	—	19	—	5
Clingman D	0	5	7	3
Daniel D	7	19	—	1
Dockery W	6	—	7	3
Morehead W	7	16	7	—
Outlaw W	6	4	7	3
Stanly W	7	1	5	3
Venable D	3	19	—	1
Senate				
Badger W	5	—	4	8
Mangum W	5	1	4	—
OHIO				
House				
Barrerre W	0	11	7	3
Bell W	—	6	7	4
Busby D	7	18	0	1
Cable D	0	7	2	—
Campbell W	0	0	—	4
Cartter D	—	4	2	1
Disney D	—	2	2	—
Edgerton D	0	4	—	1
Gaylord D	0	11	0	0
Giddings W	—	13	1	4
Green D	—	2	0	—
Harper W	0	6	7	3
Hunter W	1	14	—	3
Johnson Ind.	0	0	0	1
Newton W	0	—	1	4
Olds D	3	1	2	3

Name and Party	*Sec.*	*Imp.*	*Land*	*F.R.*
Stanton W	0	4	2	—
Sweetser D	0	11	—	0
Taylor W	—	4	6	3
Townshend D	—	4	0	1
Welch W	—	1	7	3
Senate				
Chase FS	0	5	2	2
Wade D	0	2	0	2
PENNSYLVANIA				
House				
Allison W	0	16	1	4
Bibighaus W	—	12	—	3
Chandler W	1	1	2	3
Curtis D	—	13	2	0
Dawson D	7	14	2	2
Dimmick D	—	17	—	2
Florence D	7	1	2	0
Fuller W	7	2	—	3
Gamble D	7	15	4	1
Gilmore D	—	10	3	—
Grow D	0	—	2	1
J. Howe FSW	3	4	6	4
T. Howe W	0	13	—	4
Jones D	—	18	6	0
Kuhns W	5	3	—	3
Kurtz D	7	18	1	1
McLanahan D	7	18	—	2
McNair D	—	10	0	0
Moore W	—	3	2	3
Morrison D	—	19	—	1
Parker D	—	17	—	1
Robbins D	7	18	2	2
Ross D	7	19	7	—
Stevens W	—	—	—	—
Senate				
Brodhead D	5	10	—	1

Name and Party	Sec.	Imp.	Land	F.R.
Cooper W	5	—	—	—
RHODE ISLAND				
House				
King W	1	12	7	3
Thurston D	—	13	1	2
Senate				
Clarke W	5	0	3	6
James D	—	1	3	4
SOUTH CAROLINA				
House				
Aiken D	0	19	7	1
Burt D	—	—	—	—
Colcock D	—	19	7	0
McQueen D	0	19	7	—
Orr D	0	—	7	0
Wallace D	0	19	7	1
Woodward D	0	19	7	5
Senate				
Butler D	—	12	4	—
DeSaussure D	5	12	4	—
Rhett D	—	—	—	5
TENNESSEE				
House				
Churchwell D	—	16	0	1
Cullom W	—	7	1	4
Gentry W	6	2	3	3
Harris D	—	19	7	0
Johnson D	7	19	0	2
Jones D	6	19	2	2
Polk D	7	8	1	1
Savage D	7	19	2	0
Stanton D	6	3	3	2
Watkins W	7	4	0	3
Williams W	6	1	3	5
Senate				
Bell W	—	1	4	—
Jones W	—	6	4	—

Name and Party	*Sec.*	*Imp.*	*Land*	*F.R.*
TEXAS				
House				
Howard D	7	0	—	0
Scurry D	7	0	2	0
Senate				
Houston D	—	10	—	—
Rusk D	5	6	4	—
VERMONT				
House				
Bartlett D	0	—	1	0
Hebard W	—	12	7	4
Meacham W	0	—	—	4
Miner W	0	5	6	4
Senate				
Foot W	3	—	2	4
Phelps W	—	—	—	—
Upham W	3	0	4	8
VIRGINIA				
House				
Averett D	3	19	7	5
Bayly D	7	19	7	0
Beale D	4	19	7	3
Bocock D	—	19	7	1
Caskie D	7	19	7	0
Clemens D	—	—	—	—
Edmundson D	7	19	7	0
Faulkner D	7	19	7	0
Holladay D	0	19	7	0
Letcher D	7	19	7	0
McMullan D	4	19	4	0
Meade D	6	19	—	1
Millson D	0	19	7	2
Powell D	3	19	—	—
Strother W	7	1	—	1
Thompson D	7	—	2	2
Senate				
Hunter D	5	10	4	8

Name and Party	*Sec.*	*Imp.*	*Land*	*F.R.*
Mason D	5	11	—	—
WISCONSIN				
House				
Doty D	0	0	0	2
Durkee FS	0	0	2	1
Eastman D	0	0	0	0
House				
Dodge D	1	7	1	0
Walker D	5	6	0	0

Notes

Bibliographic Note

NOTES

PREFACE

1. Thomas J. Pressly, *Americans Interpret Their Civil War* (Princeton, 1954), Chap. 8.

2. Richard P. McCormick, "Conference on Early American Political History," Soc. Sci. Res. Council *Items*, XI (December 1957), 49.

3. Lee Benson, "Research Problems in American Political Historiography," in Mirra Komarovsky, ed., *Common Frontiers of the Social Sciences* (Glencoe, Ill., 1957), 113–83; Samuel P. Hays, "History as Human Behavior," *Iowa Jour. of Hist. and Politics*, LVIII (July 1960), 193–206, and "Archival Sources for American Political History," *American Archivist*, XXVIII (January 1965), 17–30; George Daniels, "Immigrant Vote in the Election of 1860: The Case of Iowa," *Mid-America*, XLIV (July 1962), 146–62; Robert Swierenga, "The Ethnic Voter and the First Lincoln Election," *Civil War Hist.*, XI (March 1965), 27–43; J. Rogers Hollingsworth, "The Historian, Presidential Elections, and 1896," *Mid-America*, XLVI (July 1964), 185–92. The reference to "documentary determinism" is in a review by Geoffrey Blodgett of Stanley P. Jones, *The Presidential Election of 1896*, in *Jour. of Amer. Hist.*, LI (December 1964), 523.

4. "Verifying claims concerning popular support for, or in opposition to, certain government actions is a crucial, preliminary step in the verification of historical explanations that emphasize the impact of public opinion upon events. . . . Unfortunately, at present, historians are poorly equipped to demonstrate the state of public opinion on any issue." Lee Benson, "Causation and the American Civil War," *History and Theory*, I (1961), 173.

5. Samuel P. Hays has called the use of statistical methods "the most promising current methodological innovation in the social analysis of political history." "New Possibilities for American Political History: The So-

cial Analysis of Political Life," paper presented at the meeting of the American Historical Association, Washington, D.C., December 29, 1964, and mimeographed by the Inter-University Consortium for Political Research (Ann Arbor, 1964), 36. See also Hayward Alker, Jr., *Mathematics and Politics* (New York, 1965).

6. Lee Benson, *The Concept of Jacksonian Democracy: New York As a Test Case* (Princeton, 1961); Charles Grier Sellers, Jr., "The Equilibrium Cycle in Two-Party Politics," *Public Opinion Qtly.*, xxix (Spring 1965), 16–38; Richard P. McCormick, "New Perspectives on Jacksonian Politics," *Amer. Hist. Rev.*, lxv (January 1960), 288–301, and "Suffrage Classes and Party Alignments: A Study in Voter Behavior," *Miss. Valley Hist. Rev.*, xlvi (December 1959), 397–410; David Donald, *The Politics of Reconstruction* (Baton Rouge, 1965); Samuel P. Hays, "The Social Analysis of American Political History, 1880–1920," *Pol. Sci. Qtly.*, lxxi (Fall 1965), 373–92; Samuel T. McSeveney, "The Politics of Depression: Voting Behavior in Connecticut, New York and New Jersey, 1893–1896," (Ph.D. diss., Univ. of Iowa, 1965); V. O. Key, "A Theory of Critical Elections," *Jour. of Politics*, xvii (February 1955), 1–18; Carl N. Degler, "American Political Parties and the Rise of the City: An Interpretation," *Jour. of Amer. Hist.*, li (June 1964), 41–59; Duncan MacRae and James Meldrum, "Critical Elections in Illinois, 1880–1958," *Amer. Pol. Sci. Rev.*, liv (September 1960), 669–83; Paul Lazarsfeld et al., *The People's Choice* (New York, 1948); Angus Campbell et al., *The American Voter* (New York, 1960); Heinz Eulau, *Class and Party in the Eisenhower Years* (New York, 1962); V. O. Key and Milton Cummings, Jr., *The Responsible Electorate* (Cambridge, 1966); Samuel Lubell, *The Future of American Politics* (New York, 1952).

CHAPTER ONE

1. Frederick Jackson Turner, *The Significance of Sections in American History* (New York, 1932), especially 22–51, 183–206, 287–339. The quotes are from 36–37 and 50.

2. Ibid., 40–41, 198–205.

3. See the essays by Fullmer Mood, "The Origin, Evolution and Application of the Sectional Concept, 1750–1900," and Vernon Carstensen, "The Development and Application of Regional-Sectional Concepts, 1900–1950," in Merrill Jensen, ed., *Regionalism in America* (Madison, 1951), 5–98 and 99–118 respectively.

4. See the measurement and appreciation of Turner's influence by Merle Curti, "The Section and the Frontier in American History: The Methodological Concepts of Frederick Jackson Turner," in Stuart A. Rice, ed., *Methods in Social Science: A Casebook* (Chicago, 1931), 353–67; Avery O. Craven, "Frederick Jackson Turner," in William T. Hutchinson, ed., *Marcus W. Jernegan Essays in American Historiography* (Chicago, 1937), 252–70.

More apparent manifestations of the influence of the sectional concept can be noted from the number of courses offered on sectional themes in graduate schools and colleges and the various sectional journals and histories published.

5. See Frederick Jackson Turner, *The United States, 1830–1850: The Nation and Its Sections* (New York, 1935), and *The Rise of the New West, 1819–1829* (New York, 1906).

Gerald Capers has pointed out that at the time of his death Turner was contemplating a biography of John C. Calhoun, a prime practitioner of the interplay of sectional forces. Gerald Capers, *John C. Calhoun—Opportunist: A Reappraisal* (Gainesville, Fla., 1960), v.

6. Turner, *Significance of Sections*, Chap. 2, especially 47–51.

7. The point of view of these historians can be seen in the following statement of Professor Frank Lawrence Owsley of Vanderbilt University. "The North and the South had joined together under the Constitution fully conscious that there were thus united two divergent economic and social systems, two civilizations in fact." Quoted in Edwin Rozwenc, ed., *The Causes of the American Civil War* (Boston, 1961), 125. To Avery Craven the emergence of the two civilizations was a later occurrence and was developmental and evolutionary in nature. Between 1830 and 1860, he writes, "two distinct and differing social-economic systems were evolving side by side in the United States. One was primarily agricultural; in the other commerce, industry and finance were increasingly important." Avery O. Craven, "Democracy in Crisis," *Alabama Review*, VII (October 1955), 265.

8. Most of this discussion of Craven is drawn from his major synthesis, *The Coming of the Civil War* (2d ed., Chicago, 1957). In addition, his *The Growth of Southern Nationalism, 1848–1861* (Baton Rouge, 1953) should be noted.

Craven also led many students to investigate various phases of the problem. Typical of his students' work in this field is Thomas Stirton, "Party Disruption and the Rise of the Slavery Extension Controversy, 1840–1846" (Ph.D. diss. Univ. of Chicago, 1956). See note 12 for others.

9. An interest which may also be deduced from the titles, and contents, of two books by Craven, *The Growth of Southern Nationalism, 1848–1861*, and *Civil War in the Making, 1815–1860* (Baton Rouge, 1959).

10. Craven, *Coming of Civil War*, Chaps. 8–10.

11. No attempt is made here to suggest the extent of their influence which is certainly familiar to American historians. It might suffice to note the first two volumes of a new series designed "to make the best of historical scholarship available to the general reader." They are Charles Wiltse, *The New Nation, 1800–1845* (New York, 1961), and Roy F. Nichols, *The Stakes of Power, 1845–1877* (New York, 1961). Wiltse's last two chapters are "Half-Slave and Half-Free" and "Sectionalism and Democracy." Nichols' first chapter is "E Pluribus Duo."

12. In addition to Craven's work, note some of the Ph.D. dissertations undertaken at the University of Chicago at his direction: Stirton, "Party Disruption"; Aaron M. Boom, "The Development of Sectional Attitudes in Wisconsin, 1848–1861" (1949); David Bradford, "The Background and Formation of the Republican Party in Ohio, 1844–1861" (1948); Roger H. Van Bolt, "The Rise of the Republican Party in Indiana, 1840–1856" (1951); John S. Wright, "The Background and Formation of the Republican Party in Illinois, 1846–1860" (1947); Helen M. Cavanagh, "Anti-Slavery Sentiment and Politics in the Northwest, 1844–1860" (1938).

13. Some of these points are discussed in Thomas C. Cochran, "The Presidential Synthesis in American History," *Amer. Hist. Rev.*, LIII (July 1948), 748–59; Lee Benson, "Research Problems in American Political Historiography," in Mirra Komarovsky, ed., *Common Frontiers in the Social Sciences* (Glencoe, 1957), 113–83; Joel H. Silbey, "The Civil War Synthesis in American Political History," *Civil War Hist.*, X (June 1964), 130–40.

14. In *U.S., 1830–1850*, Turner discusses the six subregions or sections.

15. Craven, *Coming of Civil War*; Henry Clyde Hubbart, *The Older Middle West, 1840–1880* (New York, 1936), passim.

16. David Truman has suggested the high cohesion of state representatives with each other despite other attachments in certain circumstances. "State Delegations and Voting Alignments," in John Wahlke and Heinz Eulau, eds., *Legislative Behavior* (Glencoe, 1959), 204–18.

17. Turner, *U.S., 1830–1850*. See also Turner's letter to Charles O. Paullin, circa 1931, which is quoted by Carstensen, "Regional-Sectional Concepts," in Jensen, ed., *Regionalism*, 114–15. He says, in part, "Sectionalism in the larger sense has not been adequately treated. Formerly it was

conceived of as North against South, or less often East against West, but these big sections mislead the reader."

18. *Significance of Sections*, 48–49. For a development of this idea see Ulrich Bonnell Phillips, *Life and Labor in the Old South* (Boston, 1929). Phillips was one of Turner's graduate students. See also Frank Owsley's list of factors which make up a section in "Sectionalism," *The Dictionary of American History* (New York, 1940), v, 53–55.

19. See Craven, *Coming of Civil War*, passim.

20. Ibid., 244; Charles Wiltse, *John C. Calhoun, Sectionalist, 1840–1850* (Indianapolis, 1951), 382–88.

21. Charles Grier Sellers, Jr., "Who Were the Southern Whigs?" *Amer. Hist. Rev.*, LIX (January 1954), 335–46.

22. Thomas P. Govan, "Americans Below the Potomac," in Charles Grier Sellers, Jr., ed., *The Southerner As American* (Chapel Hill, 1960), 19–39.

23. The literature of political behavior is extensive. Useful introductions to the field can be found in Heinz Eulau, Samuel Eldersveld, and Morris Janowitz, eds. *Political Behavior: A Reader in Theory and Research* (Glencoe, 1956); Seymour Martin Lipset, "Political Sociology," in Robert K. Merton, Leonard Broom, and Leonard S. Cottrell, Jr., eds., *Sociology Today* (New York, 1959); and Wahlke and Eulau, eds., *Legislative Behavior*.

24. The great variety of problems to be solved in the understanding of the political process are suggested in the two books of readings edited by Eulau, Eldersveld, and Janowitz, and by Wahlke and Eulau. See also Nelson Polsby, Robert Deutler, and Paul Smith, *Politics and Social Life* (New York, 1963).

25. Angus Campbell et al., *The American Voter* (New York, 1960), 120–61.

26. *Cong. Globe*, 29 Cong., 1 Sess., 530, has the original vote to pass the bill. The vote to override the veto is on 1189.

27. David Truman has suggested the importance of these worthies in *The Congressional Party* (New York, 1959), passim.

28. Campbell, et al., *American Voter*, passim. See also their "Stability and Change in 1960: A Reinstating Election," *Amer. Poli. Sci. Rev.*, LV (June 1961), 269–80.

29. The factual background for the 1840's can be gleaned from Glyndon G. Van Deusen, *The Jacksonian Era, 1828–1848* (New York, 1959); Lee Benson, *The Concept of Jacksonian Democracy: New York As a Test Case*

(Princeton, 1961); George Rogers Taylor, *The Transportation Revolution* (New York, 1951).

30. Albert K. Weinberg, *Manifest Destiny* (Baltimore, 1935), 100–89; Richard Van Alstyne, *The Rising American Empire* (New York, 1960).

31. These points are succinctly summed up in Craven, *Coming of Civil War*, 175–325; and Charles Sydnor, *The Growth of Southern Sectionalism, 1819–1848* (Baton Rouge, 1948), passim.

32. "Historians differ as to the exact date when the South became an entity, recognized by itself and other areas as a distinct section. Although some scholars claim that the states below the Potomac realized they had separate interests as early as the Constitutional Convention, most put the time much later. There is pretty general agreement that the phenomenon we know as the South was at least taking shape by the 1830's." T. Harry Williams, *Romance and Realism in Southern Politics* (Athens, 1964), 7–8; "How far the South had come towards sectionalism or nationalism by the late 1840's depends on the meaning ascribed to these words." Sydnor, *Southern Sectionalism*, 331; perusal of any of the other works so far cited will reveal a multitude of answers ranging from vagueness to precise dates, usually different.

33. *Significance of Sections*, 40, 198. In *U.S., 1830–1850*, Turner used and mapped several Congressional votes to prove his assertions. See, for instance, 400–1, 408, 421, 495, 505–6, 532, 553, 557, and end maps.

34. Truman, *Congressional Party*, 12.

35. There are frequent indications of the congressmen's perusal of their local and state party newspapers in the manuscripts of these congressmen and in the newspapers themselves. The Washington newspapers also reprinted much material on party meetings and editorial opinion from the local and state newspapers which the congressmen were sure to see. Finally, the printed documents of the Congresses of the period were filled with petitions from constituents to their congressman.

36. See William E. Dodd, "The Principle of Instructing United States Senators," *South Atlantic Qtly.*, I (October 1902), 326–32; and William H. Riker, "The Senate and American Federalism," *Amer. Poli. Sci. Rev.* XLIX (June 1955), 452–69. At the critical point in the vote on the Tariff of 1846, the vote of the Whig Senator, Spencer Jarnagin of Tennessee, helped to pass the tariff. Jarnagin was against the bill but he felt bound by the instructions of the Tennessee legislature that he vote aye. Ibid., 461.

37. See Orrin G. Libby, "A Plea for the Study of Votes in Congress," *Annual Report of the American Historical Association for 1896* (Washington, 1897), I, 323–34. Libby was a student of Turner's.

38. See Turner's use of such votes in *U.S., 1830–1850.*

39. I have tried to develop this point in an unpublished paper, "John C. Calhoun As the Leader of the Southern Congressmen, 1841–1850."

40. See the discussion of this point by Stuart A. Rice, *Quantitative Methods in Politics* (New York, 1927), 71–91.

41. Rice used the following example to demonstrate this idea. On a tariff issue there may be five possible positions which a legislator can take: free trade, tariff for revenue, low protection, high protection, isolation (prohibitive duties). Given these five positions, each of which will be supported by a group of legislators, those voting for the bill would depend on the character of the bill as presented to them. If a low protective tariff bill was introduced and an amendment was offered to raise its rates 5%, this would draw some of the high protective people to it because they would view the bill as now better than it was. And some of the low protective people might now vote against it because its duties are now too high. In the voting on the final passage of the bill, however, if the 5% raise had remained in, most of the low protection tariff people would vote for it in order to get some legislation. Similarly, if an amendment to lower rates was offered it would be supported by some of the low protection people as well as the revenue groups and free traders. Although there were only two positions on final passage, by considering the amendments and the voting on them we can see the five groups present. Ibid., 77–80

42. See the discussion of attitude measurement in such works as Paul Lazarsfeld et al., *The People's Choice* (2d ed., New York, 1948); Angus Campbell et al., *The Voter Decides* (Evanston, 1954).

43. The concept of the scalogram was originally set forth in Samuel Stouffer et al., *The American Soldier* (Princeton, 1949), IV, "Measurement and Prediction." Its use in roll-call analysis is set forth in George Belknap, "A Method for Analyzing Legislative Behavior," *Midwest Jour. of Pol. Sci.,* II (November 1958), 377–402; Duncan Macrae, Jr., *Dimensions of Congressional Voting* (Berkeley, 1958).

44. Ibid., Chap. 1.

45. How this is done can be seen in the following simplified example. When the Tyler administration sent the Webster-Ashburton treaty to the Senate for ratification in August, 1842, there was a concerted attempt to defeat it and substitute more aggressive proposals. On August 19, Senator Williams of Maine moved a resolution that the treaty be recommited to the Foreign Relations Committee and a resolution be substituted directing the President to take immediate possession of the disputed territory in Maine without a treaty or reference to England's claims. This was defeated the

same day 8–31, the 8 being the smallest bloc present on any of the foreign policy roll-calls in this Congress (*Senate Journal*, 27 Cong., 2 Sess., 696). These 8 men are therefore placed on a chart as follows:

		Roll-Call
Senators		1
Allen	D-Ohio	+
Bagby	D-Ala.	+
Walker	D-Miss.	+
Fulton	D-Ark.	+
Linn	D-Mo.	+
Williams	D-Me.	+
Smith	D-Conn.	+
Sturgeon	D-Pa.	+

On the following day, after a series of other votes the treaty was ratified 39–9, the 9 being the next largest group of senators voting in one bloc (ibid., 699). Preliminary inspection indicates that among these 9 are almost all of the senators from the first group. The men in the second group are therefore added to the chart, which now looks as follows:

		Roll-Call	
Senators		1	2
Allen	D-Ohio	+	+
Bagby	D-Ala.	+	+
Linn	D-Mo.	+	+
Fulton	D-Ark.	+	
Smith	D-Conn.	+	+
Sturgeon	D-Pa.	+	+
Walker	D-Miss.	+	
Williams	D-Me.	+	+
Benton	D-Mo.		+
Buchanan	D-Pa.		+
Conrad	W-La.		+

We have thus separated two blocs on the foreign relations issue, one group willing to risk war with England by seizing Maine, and also opposed to ratifying the Webster-Ashburton treaty, and a second group, willing to vote against the treaty but unwilling to go as far as seizing the disputed area. This process is then continued through all of the available roll-calls on foreign affairs until all of them have been placed on the scale. After refinements are made to deal with absences, ambiguous voting patterns or roll-calls, and votes which add no information to the scale are removed, we have as the final product, a scalogram of the foreign relations issue in the 27th Congress. This is included as Appendix One.

46. William O. Aydelotte, "Parties and Issues in Early Victorian England," unpublished ms., forthcoming in *Jour. of British Studies*, 14. In the scale there will not be absolute regularity, as this rarely happens in legislative voting. However, there is a test to determine if there are so many irregularities as to make the scale meaningless. This is done by dividing the number of vote responses by the same number minus all irregular votes. The result, called the coefficient of reproducibility, is deemed to show a relevant scale if it is .90 or better. See Belknap, "Method for Analyzing Legislative Behavior."

47. "These scales provided, of course, a ranking of members on the dimension embodied in the scale far superior to that yielded by the crude indices employed in . . . earlier studies." V. O. Key, *Public Opinion and American Democracy* (New York, 1961), 488.

48. A concise, clear statement as to the value of such methodological tools in answering the question of what precisely happened is in William O. Aydelotte, "A Statistical Analysis of the Parliament of 1841: Some Problems of Method," Ins. for Hist. Res. *Bulletin*, xxvii (1954), 141–55. Professor Aydelotte has made fuller use of the scalogram technique in his research than any other historian. In addition to this article and the one cited in note 46, also see "Voting Patterns in the British House of Commons in the 1840's," *Comparative Studies in Society and History*, v (January 1963), 134–63; "Notes on the Problem of Historical Generalization," in Louis Gottschalk, ed., *Generalization in the Writing of History* (Chicago, 1963), 145–77, especially 172–77; "Quantification in History," *Amer. Hist. Rev.,* lxxi (April 1966), 803–25. In addition, Professor Aydelotte is working on a short monograph on the use of the scalogram in legislative analysis.

49. See note 21 above and the citations in Chapter 2.

50. See Charles Grier Sellers, Jr., "The Equilibrium Cycle in Two-Party Politics." *Public Opinion Qtly.*, xxix (Spring 1965), 16. In this study, Sellers relied heavily on Campbell et al., *American Voter.*

CHAPTER TWO

1. "Most members of the electorate feel some degree of psychological attachment to one of the major parties. This partisan identification is remarkably resistant to passing political events and typically remains

constant through the life of the individual. It exercises an important influence on perceptions, attitudes, and behavior." Angus Campbell, "Voters
and Elections—Past and Present," *Jour. of Politics,* xxvi (November
1964), 747. This is developed in more detail in Angus Campbell et al., *The
American Voter* (New York, 1960), 120–21 and passim.

2. David Truman, *The Congressional Party* (New York, 1959), vi–vii
and passim.

3. V. O. Key, *Public Opinion and American Democracy* (New York,
1961), 432–33.

4. Professor Charles Sydnor has written, for example, that party politics
in the 1840's had "the hollow sound of a stage duel with tin swords."
The Development of Southern Sectionalism, 1819–1848 (Baton Rouge,
1948), 316.

5. Lee Benson, *The Concept of Jacksonian Democracy: New York
As a Test Case* (Princeton, 1961), passim; William Carleton, "Political
Aspects of the Van Buren Era," *South Atlantic Qtly.,* L (April 1951),
167–85; Charles Grier Sellers, Jr., "Who Were the Southern Whigs?"
Amer. Hist. Rev., LIX (January 1954), 335–46; Glyndon G. Van Deusen,
The Jacksonian Era, 1828–1848 (New York, 1959), 112.

6. The early attempts to unify the Democratic party and give it leadership and coherence can be traced in Richard M. Brown, "Southern Planters
and Plain Republicans of the North: Martin Van Buren's Formula for
National Politics" (Ph.D. diss., Yale Univ., 1955); and Robert V. Remini,
Martin Van Buren and the Founding of the Democratic Party (New York,
1959).

7. The history of the Whig party can be traced in Eber M. Carroll,
Origins of the Whig Party (Philadelphia, 1925); Arthur Charles Cole,
The Whig Party in the South (Washington, 1913); Charles Wiltse, *John
C. Calhoun, Nullifier, 1829–1839* (Indianapolis, 1949); George R. Poage,
Henry Clay and the Whig Party (Chapel Hill, 1936).

8. Richard P. McCormick, "New Perspectives on Jacksonian Politics,"
Amer. Hist. Rev., LXV (January 1960), 288–301. McCormick indicates
that by 1840 evenly balanced parties had emerged in almost every state.

9. Although the Democrats won three elections and the Whigs two
during this period, the margins of victory of both parties on the national
level averaged only 4.2%. This discussion is drawn from charts and com-
putations in W. Dean Burnham, *Presidential Ballots, 1836–1892* (Baltimore, 1955); *The Whig Almanac and United States Register* (New York,
1841–1852); and from returns published in various newspapers.

10. McCormick, "New Perspectives," 300–1.

11. As Burnham did in his compilation. Burnham, *Presidential Ballots*, xv.

12. "After 1828 there was a steady and rapid movement towards equilibrium between the parties in all sections." Charles G. Sellers, Jr., "The Equilibrium Cycle in Two-Party Politics," *Public Opinion Qtly.*, XXIX (Spring 1965), 31.

13. Some historians and political scientists have also been very impressed with the very high levels of voter turnout in pre-Civil War elections, particularly after 1840. They see in this extensive participation real interest and concern with the results of elections, and a recognition of basic differences, of policy and otherwise, between the parties. McCormick, "New Perspectives"; W. Dean Burnham, "The Changing Shape of the Political Universe," *Amer. Pol. Sci. Rev.*, LIX (January 1965), 7–28; Thomas Flinn, "Continuity and Change in Ohio Politics," *Jour. of Politics*, XXIV (August 1962), 521–44.

14. No attempt is made here to identify and analyze those individuals and groups which made up the leadership and following of each party. This would involve several additional separate studies and is beyond the scope of this work. Such analyses would be most important for an understanding of American politics on all levels in this period.

15. For a discussion of these points in both the general context and in specific reference to the 1840's, see Benson, *Jacksonian Democracy*, 270–87; Campbell et al., *American Voter*, 120–61.

16. Sydnor, *Southern Sectionalism*, 316.

17. Thomas Stirton, "Party Disruption and the Rise of the Slavery Extension Controversy, 1840–1846" (Ph.D. diss., Univ. of Chicago, 1956), 84, 309.

18. Glyndon G. Van Deusen, "Some Aspects of Whig Thought and Theory in the Jacksonian Period," *Amer. Hist. Rev.*, LXIII (January 1958), 322.

19. See especially, Sellers, "Southern Whigs," passim.; Gerald Capers, *Stephen A. Douglas, Defender of the Union* (Boston, 1959), 25.

20. Alexander Bowie to John C. Calhoun, April 13, 1847, in J. Franklin Jameson, ed., "Correspondence of John C. Calhoun," *Annual Report of the American Historical Association for 1899* (Washington, 1900); William Gilmore Simms to Calhoun, February 19, 1849, in Chauncey S. Boucher and Robert P. Brooks, eds., "Correspondence Addressed to John C. Calhoun, 1837–1849," *Annual Report of the American Historical Association for 1929* (Washington, 1930), 498–99.

21. See Geoffrey Blodgett's review of Stanley Jones, *The Presidential*

Election of 1896 (Madison, 1964), for a brief and insightful consideration of the problems of "documentary determinism." *Jour. of Amer. Hist.*, LI (December 1964), 523.

22. For a general criticism of the viewpoint of American political historians see Thomas C. Cochran, "The Presidential Synthesis in American History," *Amer. Hist. Rev.*, LIII (July 1948), 748–59; Lee Benson, "Research Problems in American Political Historiography," in Mirra Komarovsky, ed., *Common Frontiers of the Social Sciences* (Glencoe, Ill., 1957), 113–83; Samuel P. Hays, "History as Human Behavior," *Iowa Jour. of Hist.*, LVIII (July 1960), 193–206.

23. Benson, *Jacksonian Democracy*, 281 and Chap. 13.

24. Some examples of this in action can be found in Seymour Martin Lipset, *Political Man: The Social Bases of Politics* (New York, 1958), 345–46.

25. See Avery Leiserson, *Party Politics* (New York, 1958), 345–46; Roland Young, *The American Congress* (New York, 1958), 32–39; V. O. Key, *Politics, Parties and Pressure Groups* (4th ed., New York, 1958), 736–37.

26. Lee Benson discusses the methodology here employed, although his book appeared after it was so employed, in *Jacksonian Democracy,* Chap. 11. The note on "saturation" appears on page 217.

27. Ibid., 216–17.

28. This discussion is taken from George Rogers Taylor, *The Transportation Revolution* (New York, 1951); Paul Wallace Gates, *The Farmer's Age, Agriculture, 1815–1860* (New York, 1960); Douglass C. North, *The Economic Growth of the United States, 1790–1860* (Englewood Cliffs, 1961).

29. North, 189–90.

30. Ibid., 204–06; Walt Whitman Rostow, "The Take-Off into Self-Sustained Growth," *Economic Journal,* LXVI (March 1956), 25–48.

31. All of these figures are drawn from U.S., Bureau of the Census, *Historical Statistics of the United States from Colonial Times to 1957* (Washington, 1960), 7, 13.

32. For the optimism apparent within the country in this era see Ralph Henry Gabriel, *The Course of American Democratic Thought* (New York, 1940), Part I, 3–100. The government's role in achieving the best development of the United States is discussed in a series of works reviewed by Robert Lively, "The American System: A Review Article," *Business Hist. Rev.* XXIX (March 1955), 81–96.

33. For a discussion of the formation, role, and conflict of interest groups in American life, see David Truman, *The Governmental Process* (New York, 1951).

34. McCormick, "New Perspectives," 299–301. The first major national party platforms were presented by the Democrats in 1840, the Whigs in 1844. Local and state declarations preceded these.

35. See, for example, J. C. N. Paul, *Rift in the Democracy* (Philadelphia, 1951); Oscar Doane Lambert, *Presidential Politics in the United States, 1841–1844* (Durham, 1936); Charles Wiltse, *John C. Calhoun, Sectionalist, 1840–1850* (Indianapolis, 1951).

36. Impressionistic evidence of the unity of the Whig party, despite its states-rights and nationalist wings, can be deduced from, George Gilmer to Thomas W. Gilmer, June 29, 1842, John Tyler Papers, Lib. Cong.; Willis P. Mangum to James Watson Webb, July 30, 1842, in Henry T. Shanks, ed., *The Papers of Willie Person Mangum* (Raleigh, 1950), v, 470; Speech of William Preston of South Carolina, July 27, 1841, in *Cong. Globe*, 27 Cong., 1 Sess., 255.

Historians have noted this tendency also. Van Deusen, *Jacksonian Era*, 167, 180–81; C. Jay Smith, Jr., "John McPherson Berrien," in Horace Montgomery, ed., *Georgians in Profile: Historical Essays in Honor of Ellis Merton Coulter* (Athens, 1958), 181; Howard Braverman, "The Economic and Political Background of the Conservative Revolt in Virginia," *Va. Mag. of Hist. and Biog.*, LX (April 1952), 287; Herbert Pegg, "The Whig Party of North Carolina, 1834–1861" (Ph.D. diss., Univ. of N.C., 1932), 209.

Some idea of the dissensions which did exist and the efforts to present a united front in Congress can be seen in John J. Crittenden to James Harlan, August 16, 1842, John Crittenden Papers, Lib. Cong.

37. These are conveniently reproduced in Kirk H. Porter and Donald Bruce Johnson, eds., *National Party Platforms, 1840–1956* (Urbana, 1956).

38. These platforms can be found reprinted in such party newspapers as the Washington *Globe, Richmond Enquirer, Richmond Whig, National Intelligencer* (Washington), and others, as well as in relevant contemporary periodicals such as the *Whig Review*, whose writers stated the essence of the Whig party program well before the party issued an official national platform.

39. Benson, *Jacksonian Democracy*, 86–109.

40. See the review of this literature in Lively, "American System"; and

Carter Goodrich, *Government Promotion of American Canals and Railroads* (New York, 1960).

41. Oscar Handlin, "Laissez-Faire Thought in Massachusetts, 1790–1860," *Tasks of Econ. Hist.*, III (December 1943), 65. The whole idea is, of course, developed in the Handlins' full length study of Massachusetts economic life and thought, as well as in similar works mentioned in Lively, "American System."

42. William Appleman Williams, *The Contours of American History* (Cleveland, 1961), 234.

43. *Cong. Globe*, 27 Cong., 3 Sess., *Appendix*, 143. The speech was made February 13, 1843.

44. Ibid. A similar statement was made by Lewis Cass of Michigan in a letter to Aaron Hobart on May 11, 1844. Lewis Cass Papers, William E. Clements Lib., Ann Arbor.

45. "The Grounds of Difference Between the Contending Parties," *The Whig Almanac* (1843), 16; Benson, *Jacksonian Democracy*, 237.

46. Such divisions, reflecting as they did, quite real internal divisions in the United States were not confined to this era either. "Since the seventeenth century, financial questions have often been the distinctive form social conflict has taken in America. Periodically . . . differences over currency and the related subject of banking have expressed basic American social and political antagonisms." Irwin Unger, *The Greenback Era: A Social and Political History of American Finance, 1865–1879*, (Princeton, 1964), 3.

47. The whole history is well recounted in Bray Hammond, *Banks and Politics in America from the Revolution to the Civil War* (Princeton, 1957).

48. *Mobile Register*, August 20, 1841.

49. See the discussion by Richard A. Timberlake, Jr., "The Independent Treasury and Monetary Policy before the Civil War," *Southern Econ. Jour.*, XXVII (October 1960), 92–103; Hammond, *Banks and Politics*, Chap. 12–14; and the national and state platforms of the Democratic party in this period.

50. Some examples of this bank hatred can be seen in Jessee Speight to James K. Polk, December 20, 1841, and Archibald Yell to Polk, March 6, 1842, both in James K. Polk Papers, Lib. Cong. The Independent Treasury was passed by the Democratic Congress on June 30, 1840. *Cong. Globe*, 26 Cong., 1 Sess., 495.

51. *Charleston Courier*, June 28, 1841; Leslie Norton, "A History of the Whig Party in Louisiana" (Ph.D. diss., La. State Univ., 1940), 184.

In the gubernatorial election of 1843 in Tennessee, the Whig candidate, James Jones, advocated the establishment of a national bank as an antidote for the depression and attacked the Democrats' willingness to rely on metallic currency only. He told his audiences that he was "for a United States Bank, between this and hard money currency—*choose ye.*" Quoted in Paul Bergeron, "The Election of 1843: A Whig Triumph in Tennessee," *Tenn. Hist. Qtly.*, XXII (June 1963), 129.

52. John C. Calhoun to James Hammond, November 27, 1842, in Jameson, ed., "Calhoun Correspondence," 520–21.

53. The extent and nature of the Democratic party position on the tariff has been drawn from many sources. Typical party positions can be gleaned from Athens (Ga.) *Southern Banner*, October 1, 1841; *Raleigh Standard*, August 3, 1842; *Mobile Register*, September 2, 1842; Columbus *Ohio Statesman*, September 5, November 9, 1842; Springfield *Illinois State Register*, May 5, 1843; *Cong. Globe*, 27 Cong., 2 Sess., 74, 518, 635–36, in speeches by Payne of Alabama, Kennedy of Indiana, and Gwin of Mississippi. In addition, various Democratic state legislatures passed resolutions on tariff policy which are reprinted in the *House* and *Senate Documents* of the 27th Congress.

54. Such divisions over the tariff, as in the case of financial matters mentioned above (see note 46), apparently reflect long standing and continual basic social conflicts in American society.

55. See Chapter 4. Earlier Democratic differences on tariff policy which suggest relevance for the 1840's are recounted in Robert Remini, "Martin Van Buren and the Tariff of Abominations," *Amer. Hist. Rev.*, LXIII (July 1958), 903–917.

56. *Whig Almanac,* "Grounds of Difference."

57. Ibid.; *Alton* (Ill.) *Telegraph and Review*, April 9, August 13, 1842; Columbus *Ohio State Journal*, February 23, March 11, 1842; *Savannah Georgian* quoted in ibid., March 12, 1842; Pegg, "Whigs of North Carolina," 211; Williams, *Contours*, 267; Van Deusen, "Aspects of Whig Thought," 316–17. The resolutions of a convention of "Southern Planters" at Mobile, Alabama, in favor of a protective tariff and a home market for cotton is noted in *Niles National Register* (Baltimore), April 2, 1842.

58. Evidence of this attitude can be found in the *Charleston Courier*, August 8, 13, 1842; William A. Graham to Charles Plummer Green, July 18, 1841, in Henry T. Shanks, ed., *Papers of William Alexander Graham* (Raleigh, 1952), II, 214; U.S., Congress, Senate, 28 Cong., 1 Sess., *Senate Documents*, no. 294.

59. *Historical Statistics*, 239.

60. Henry A. Wise to the Editor of the *Richmond Whig*, February 2, 1841, quoted in the *Richmond Enquirer*, February 6, 1841; *Nashville Union*, September 9, 1841, April 12, 1845; Speech of John C. Calhoun, August 10, 1841, *Cong. Globe*, 27 Cong., 1 Sess., 313–14; speech of Andrew Kennedy, June 30, 1841, ibid., 132.

61. Some manifestations of the sentiment for more liberal land laws and Democratic advocacy of it can be seen in *Cong. Globe*, 27 Cong., 1 Sess., *Appendix*, 310; Little Rock *Arkansas State Gazette*, April 13, 1842. See also George Stephenson, *Political History of the Public Lands* (Boston, 1917).

62. *Whig Almanac*, "Grounds of Difference"; Van Deusen, "Aspects of Whig Thought"; *Charleston Courier*, September 7, 1841; Robert Rayback, *Millard Fillmore, Biography of a President* (Buffalo, 1959), 124–25.

63. *Cong. Globe*, 28 Cong., 2 Sess., *Appendix*, 309. See also the *National Intelligencer*, December 30, 1844.

64. These words, first expressed in the platform of 1840, were repeated exactly in the platforms of 1844, 1848 and 1852. Porter and Johnson, eds., *National Party Platforms*, 2, 3, 10, 16.

65. Benson, *Jacksonian Democracy*, 40–41. Some of the dissent is discussed in Chapter 3. The results of this position and the dissent from it are discussed in Chapter 5.

66. *Whig Almanac*, "Grounds of Difference."

67. Evidence of differences over other matters can be found in the *Cong. Globe* and in many of the local newspapers.

68. See for example, *Charleston Courier*, July 27, 1841; *Ohio State Journal*, December 31, 1842; Rayback, *Fillmore*, 124; Reginald McGrane, *Foreign Bondholders and American State Debts* (New York, 1935), 34–38.

69. *Cong. Globe*, 27 Cong., 3 Sess., 295; N. J. Fulton to Martin Van Buren, February 27, 1844, Martin Van Buren Papers, Lib. of Cong.; Washington *Globe*, March 8, 1842; Charles Sellers, *James K. Polk, Jacksonian, 1795–1843* (Princeton, 1957), 448.

70. Reginald C. McGrane, *The Panic of 1837* (Chicago, 1924); Samuel Rezneck, "The Social History of an American Depression, 1837–1843," *Amer. Hist. Rev.*, XL (July 1935), 662–87.

71. Ibid.; John Bach McMaster, *A History of the People of the United States, from the Revolution to the Civil War* (New York, 1920), VI, 389–420. Cotton which was 17½¢ per pound in 1835 fell to 9¢ in 1840 and 5½¢ in 1845. Wheat fell from $1.92 per bushel in 1838 to $1.05 in 1840 and 97½¢ in 1844. All statistics are from U.S. Census, *Historical Statistics*, 115 ff.

72. Campbell et al., *American Voter*, and Campbell et al., "Election of 1960." The works of Lazarsfeld and others cited in Chapter 1, note 42, bear on this point also.

73. Robert Gunderson, *The Log Cabin Campaign* (Lexington, 1957), 28–29. This can be seen in action, for example, in *Alton Telegraph and Review*, July 31, 1841.

74. See for example, Sellers, *Polk*; Perry H. Howard, *Political Tendencies in Louisiana, 1812–1952* (Baton Rouge, 1957); Clarence C. Norton, *The Democratic Party of Ante-Bellum North Carolina, 1835–1861* (Chapel Hill, 1930).

75. Benson, *Jacksonian Democracy*, 219. See also McCormick, "New Perspectives." In the House in 1841 there were 133 Whigs, 102 Democrats, and 6 "others." In the Senate the Whigs had a 29–22 majority.

76. See for example, *Ohio State Journal*, April 25, 1842.

CHAPTER THREE

1. And in other times as well. As Professor V. O. Key has written, throughout our history "sectional interests have constituted important building blocks for the American parties. Each party has had its roots deep in sectional interest and each has sought to build intersectional combinations powerful enough to govern." *Politics, Parties and Pressure Groups*, (4th ed., New York, 1958), 251.

2. See Chapter 1.

3. "Sectionalism," *Dictionary of American History* (New York, 1940), v, 53–55.

4. Ulrich Bonnell Phillips, *Life and Labor in the Old South* (Boston, 1929), 3.

5. The standard work on Southern economic life remains Lewis C. Gray, *History of Agriculture in the Southern United States to 1860*, 2 vols. (reprinted, New York, 1941). Shorter general treatments from differing points of view may be found in Paul Wallace Gates, *The Farmer's Age: Agriculture, 1815–1860* (New York, 1960); and Douglass C. North, *The Economic Growth of the United States, 1790–1860* (Englewood Cliffs, 1961). I have relied on all three of these works in my discussion.

6. The story of the expansion and development of the cotton industry can be traced in Gray, *History of Agriculture*, ii, 888–907. Figures are based on the chart on page 1026.

7. Gates, *Farmer's Age*, 142.

8. Frank L. Owsley, *Plain Folk of the Old South* (Baton Rouge, 1949).

9. The psychology produced by the Southern agricultural system is analyzed well by Wilbur J. Cash, *The Mind of the South* (2d ed., New York, 1960) especially Book I.

10. Gates, *Farmer's Age*, 160; Louis B. Schmidt, "The Westward Movement of the Corn Growing Industry in the United States," *Iowa Jour. of Hist. and Politics*, XXI (January 1923), 112–41 and "The Westward Movement of the Wheat Growing Industry in the United States," ibid., XVIII (July 1920), 396–412; Paul Henlein, *The Cattle Kingdom in the Ohio Valley* (Lexington, 1959).

11. Gates, *Farmer's Age*, 413; North, *Economic Growth*, 143.

12. The problem of capital formation was particularly relevant to the period before the 1840's. By then the economy itself was helping to produce capital in addition to that gained from foreign investment. See North, *Economic Growth*, passim. The problem of transportation will be more fully discussed below.

13. By 1849 manufacturing employed a million workers and the value added by manufacturing had reached $464,000,000. Of this 75% was in the Northeastern states. North, *Economic Growth*, 159; U.S., Bureau of the Census, *Historical Statistics of the United States from Colonial Times to 1957* (Washington, 1960), 409.

14. Gates, *Farmer's Age*, 152; North, *Economic Growth*, 123–25.

15. Ibid., 140; R. B. Way, "The Commerce of the Lower Mississippi in the Period 1830–1860," Miss. Valley Hist. Assoc. *Proceedings*, X (1918–1919), 57–68.

16. *Cong. Globe*, 29 Cong., 1 Sess., 1124. See also, U.S., Congress, House, "Report of the Secretary of the Treasury," 29 Cong., 1 Sess., *House Executive Documents*, no. 6, 13.

17. U.S. Census, *Historical Statistics*, 124.

18. Thomas B. Odle, "The American Grain Trade of the Great Lakes, 1825–1873" (Ph.D. diss., Univ. of Mich., 1952), 9–10; Herbert J. Wunderlich, "Foreign Grain Trade of the United States, 1835–1860," *Iowa Jour. of Hist. and Politics*, XXIII (January 1925), 75.

19. Much of this discussion is drawn from George Rogers Taylor, *The Transportation Revolution, 1815–1860* (New York, 1951), the best one-volume study of transportation problems in this period.

20. Ulrich Bonnell Phillips, *A History of Transportation in the Eastern Cotton Belt to 1860* (New York, 1913), 1–3.

21. See pages 43–45.

22. The general pattern of proslavery thought is summarized in William S. Jenkins, *Pro-Slavery Thought in the Old South* (Chapel Hill, 1935).

The profitability of a slave-labor plantation system is discussed in Kenneth Stampp, *The Peculiar Institution* (New York, 1956), Chap. 9, especially 412–13.

23. Gray, *History of Agriculture*, I, 446–47, II, 910–11. For a detailed analysis of the impact of soil exhaustion see Avery O. Craven, *Soil Exhaustion as a Factor in the Agricultural History of Virginia and Maryland, 1606–1860* (Urbana, 1926).

24. Cash, *Mind of the South*, 39–40, 68–70 and Book I.

25. The abolitionist mail controversy is summed up in Samuel Flagg Bemis, *John Quincy Adams and the Union* (New York, 1956), 334–35; Charles Wiltse, *John C. Calhoun, Nullifier, 1829–1839* (Indianapolis, 1949), 268–77.

26. The trading position of the South is discussed in North, *Economic Growth*, 67–68, 122.

27. Athens (Ga.) *Southern Banner*, April 14, November 9, 1843; *Raleigh Standard*, July 5, 1843; James Seddon to Robert M. T. Hunter, August 19, 1844, in Charles H. Ambler, ed., "Correspondence of Robert M. T. Hunter, 1826–1876," *Annual Report of the American Historical Association for the Year 1916* (Washington, 1918), 68–69; *Cong. Globe*, 27 Cong., 3 Sess., *Appendix*, 145.

28. Cotton prices fell to 9¢ per pound in 1840 from previous highs of 16¢ and 17¢. By 1845 cotton prices hit their lowest point in the 19th century, 5.6¢ per pound. U.S. Census, *Historical Statistics*, 124.

29. Various aspects of the trade and credit relationships between East and South are discussed in Robert G. Albion, *The Rise of New York Port, 1815–1860* (New York, 1939), Chap. 4; Gray, *History of Agriculture*, II, 711–16; Robert R. Russel, *Economic Aspects of Southern Sectionalism, 1840–1861* (Urbana, 1924), 21–22, 101–10; Ralph W. Haskins, "Planter and Cotton Factor in the Old South: Some Areas of Friction," *Agricultural History*, XXIX (January 1955), 1–14.

30. Gray, *History of Agriculture*, II, 691–696. The importance of the cotton export market is the theme of North, *Economic Growth*. Figures reflecting the greater importance to the South of the English cotton trade over the cotton trade with New England can be gleaned from Taylor, *Transportation Revolution*, 185–86, 243.

31. See the "Report of the Secretary of the Treasury," *House Documents*, 6. The fierceness provoked in the South against a high tariff can be seen in the *Charleston Mercury*, July 24, 1844; and in resolutions of the legislature of Louisiana in, U.S., Congress, House, 27 Cong., 1 Sess., *House Documents*, no. 12.

32. The Southern position on internal improvements can be seen in *Cong. Globe*, 28 Cong., 1 Sess., 529, *Appendix*, 413, 466; *Charleston Mercury*, February 10, 1845. On the matter of land revenue see the debate on the graduation bill, *Cong. Globe*, 28 Cong., 2 Sess., 241–42.

33. Taylor, *Transportation Revolution*, 169–70; Wunderlich, "Foreign Grain Trade."

34. "Report of the Secretary of the Treasury," *House Documents*, 11–13; U.S., Congress, House, "Report of the Secretary of the Treasury," 29 Cong., 2 Sess., *House Documents*, no. 7, 10.

The similarity of interests in regard to the tariff was constantly played up by Southern spokesmen. See Seaborn Jones of Georgia's speech, June 18, 1846, *Cong. Globe*, 29 Cong., 1 Sess., 990; *Southern Qtly. Rev.*, VIII (July 1845), 242.

35. Albert Kohlmeier, *The Old Northwest As the Keystone of the Arch of American Federal Union: A Study in Commerce and Politics* (Bloomington, 1938), 9–10; John B. Appleton, "The Declining Significance of the Mississippi as a Commercial Highway in the Middle of the Nineteenth Century," Geog. Soc. of Philadelphia *Bulletin*, XXVIII (October 1930), 267–70. One Western state's approach to the problems of transportation is recounted in John H. Krenkel, *Illinois Internal Improvements, 1818–1848* (Cedar Rapids, 1958).

36. Gray, *History of Agriculture*, I, 446–51; Gates, *Farmer's Age*, 3–6; Percy W. Bidwell and John I. Falconer, *A History of Agriculture in the Northern United States, 1620–1860* (Washington, 1925), 272–73.

37. See Albert K. Weinberg, *Manifest Destiny: A Study of Nationalist Expansionism in American History* (Baltimore, 1935), Chap. 3 and 149–50.

38. A brief summary of the transition of the New England economy is available in Taylor, *Transportation Revolution*, and North, *Economic Growth*.

39. This is, of course, the point of view developed in the "Second American Revolution" chapter in Charles and Mary Beard, *The Rise of American Civilization* (New York, 1927). See also Frederick Jackson Turner, *The United States, 1830–1850: The Nation and Its Sections* (New York, 1935), 59 ff.

40. Louis Filler, *The Crusade Against Slavery, 1830–1860* (New York, 1960); Julian Bretz, "The Economic Background of the Liberty Party," *Amer. Hist. Rev.*, XXXIV (January 1929), 250–64.

41. Both Avery O. Craven, *The Coming of the Civil War* (2d ed., Chicago, 1957), and Samuel Flagg Bemis, *Adams and the Union*, call

attention to New England's fears of Southern power growing through annexation of new territory and through the three-fifths compromise in the Constitution.

42. Some of the attraction of abolition to New Englanders is discussed in Filler, *Crusade Against Slavery*, Chap. 3.

43. As suggested in Henry Clyde Hubbart, *The Older Middle West, 1840–1880* (New York, 1936), 14.

44. Louis B. Schmidt, "The Internal Grain Trade of the United States, 1850–1860," *Iowa Jour. of Hist. and Politics*, xviii (January 1920), 94–124.

45. And historians have accepted the idea that such an alliance existed. See Chapter 10.

46. Quoted in Jesse T. Carpenter, *The South As a Conscious Minority, 1789–1861: A Study in Political Thought* (New York, 1930), 178–79.

47. S. H. Anderson, "To the Voters of the Second Congressional District," June 11, 1841, in Springfield *Illinois State Register*, June 21, 1841.

48. Charles Wiltse, *John C. Calhoun, Sectionalist, 1840–1850* (Indianapolis, 1951), 72; Turner, *U.S., 1830–1850*, 225–27; Craven, *Coming of Civil War*, 212–13.

49. See Calhoun's letter to an Alabama legislator in 1847 or 1848, quoted in Melvin J. White, *The Secession Movement in the United States, 1847–1852* (New Orleans, n.d.), 72.

50. Taylor, *Transportation Revolution*, 74–80.

51. Ralph Cotterill, "Southern Railroads and Western Trade, 1840–1850," *Miss. Valley Hist. Rev.*, iii (March 1917), 427–41; Phillips, *Transportation in Cotton Belt*, 175–218; G. W. Stephens, "Some Aspects of Early Intersectional Rivalry for the Commerce of the Upper Mississippi Valley," *Washington Univ. Studies, Humanistic Series*, x (April 1923), 297–98.

52. Wiltse, *Calhoun, Nullifier*, 324–27; Cotterill, "Southern Railroads," 429.

53. Paul Wallace Gates, *The Illinois Central Railroad and Its Colonization Work* (Cambridge, 1934).

54. Way, "Commerce of Lower Mississippi," 64; Stephens, "Early Intersectional Rivalry," 278.

55. Calhoun's plans in this direction have been traced in Wiltse, *Calhoun, Nullifier*, 399; *Calhoun, Sectionalist*, 60–61; Turner, *U.S., 1830–1850*, 486; Rayner G. Wellington, *The Political and Sectional Influences of the Public Lands, 1828–1842* (Cambridge, 1914), 92, 117.

56. Krenkel, *Illinois Internal Improvements*, 140–49; Reginald Mc-

Grane, *The Panic of 1837* (Chicago, 1924), 13, 128–30; Carter Goodrich, *Government Promotion of American Canals and Railroads, 1800–1890* (New York, 1960), 164.

57. Appleton, "Declining Significance of Mississippi," 267–70; *Cong. Globe*, 27 Cong., 2 Sess., *Appendix* 155–56.

58. Herbert Wender, *Southern Commercial Conventions, 1837–1859* (Baltimore, 1930), Chap. 3; *Journal of the Proceedings of the Southwestern Convention, Began and Held at the City of Memphis on the 12th of November, 1845* (Memphis, 1845); *The Commercial Review of the South and West*, I (January 1846), 20; *Southern Qtly. Rev.*, X (December 1846), 417.

59. The proceedings of the Convention and the results can be traced in the sources listed in note 58, plus *Cong. Globe*, 29 Cong., 1 Sess., 297–304; U.S., Congress, Senate, "Report of Special Committee on the Memphis Memorial," 29 Cong., 1 Sess., *Senate Documents*, no. 410. The memorial called for federal aid to improve inland rivers. The memorialists claimed that the Mississippi River was an inland sea and therefore entitled to the same type of aid and improvement as the nation's coastal harbors had received from the federal government.

60. Laura A. White, *Robert Barnwell Rhett, Father of Secession* (New York, 1931), 88–90; Mentor L. Williams, "The Background of the Chicago River and Harbor Convention, 1847," *Mid-America*, XXX (October 1948), 219–32; *Charleston Mercury*, October 25, November 29, 1845.

61. The literature on the common "mood" and desire for expansion is extensive. See for example, Weinberg, *Manifest Destiny*, Charles Vevier, "American Continentalism: An Idea of Expansion, 1845–1910," *Amer. Hist. Rev.*, LXV (January 1960), 323–35; Richard Van Alstyne, *The Rising American Empire* (New York, 1960); John Hope Franklin, "The Southern Expansionists of 1846," *Jour. of Southern Hist.*, XXV (August 1959), 323–38.

62. Frederick Jackson Turner, *The Significance of Sections in American History* (New York, 1932), 22–26 and Chap. 2.

63. See the speech of Samuel Vinton of Ohio in the House of Representatives, June 8, 1846, on the Iowa boundaries. *Cong. Globe*, 29 Cong., 1 Sess., 940.

64. "Report of Special Committee on Memphis," *Senate Documents*, 21.

65. *Cong. Globe*, 28 Cong., 1 Sess., 49, *Appendix*, 53; 28 Cong., 2 Sess., *Appendix*, 267; *Warsaw* (Ill.) *Signal*, March 20, 1844.

66. This concept is discussed and applied in Lee Benson, *The Concept of Jacksonian Democracy: New York As a Test Case* (Princeton, 1961), 27, 285.

67. From 1840 to 1850 the Old Northwest had an increase of population of almost two million, or 59%. No other section equalled either figure. The country as a whole increased by 6.1 million, or 36%.

68. Craven, *Coming of Civil War*, 317.

69. By 1846 Buffalo also had passed New Orleans in receipts of wheat and flour received in transit. And New York led New Orleans in the export of such commodities. See Wunderlich, "Foreign Grain Trade," 37; *De Bow's Review*, III (February 1847), 100–7, and VIII (May 1850), 444–50; Appleton, "Declining Significance of Mississippi," 284; Schmidt, "Internal Trade," 108–12; Way, "Commerce of Lower Mississippi," 63–68.

70. The importance of the Mississippi route in 1861 is discussed in Ellis Merton Coulter, "Effects of Secession upon the Commerce of the Mississippi Valley," *Miss. Valley Hist. Rev.*, III (December 1916), 275–301.

71. Kohlmeier, *Old Northwest*, 3, 21, 55–58, 209–10; Craven, *Coming of Civil War*, 313–18; Hubbart, *Older Middle West*, Chap. 5. See also, William Binkley, "The South and the West," *Jour. of Southern Hist.*, XVII (February 1951), 13–14.

72. Wyatt W. Belcher, *The Economic Rivalry Between Chicago and St. Louis, 1850–1880* (New York, 1947), 34; Krenkel, *Illinois Internal Improvements*, passim.

73. U.S., Congress, Senate, 27 Cong., 2 Sess., *Senate Documents*, nos. 112, 223; 27 Cong., 3 Sess., *Senate Documents*, nos. 155, 216; 28 Cong., 1 Sess., *Senate Documents*, no. 153.

74. The unhappiness and bitterness of Southern low-tariff advocates over this was well expressed in the *Charleston Mercury*, October 6, 1845. The writer of this editorial chided Westerners because they "can never resist the temptation of gorging at the expense of the Treasury."

75. Mentor L. Williams, "The Chicago River and Harbor Convention, 1847," *Miss. Valley Hist. Rev.*, XXXV (March 1949), 607–26; Russel, *Economic Aspects*, 125; Craven, *Coming of Civil War*, 125, 321–22; *De Bow's Review*, IV (July 1847), 123.

76. James Shields to Sidney Breese, April 12, 1844, Sidney Breese Papers, Ill. State Hist. Soc.; *Cong. Globe*, 28 Cong., 1 Sess., 322, *Appendix*, 187; U.S., Congress, House, 28 Cong., 1 Sess., *House Documents*, no. 157; ibid., 2 Sess., *House Documents*, no. 56; *Chicago Democrat*, April 3, 1844; *Charleston Courier*, February 28, 1844.

77. *Cong. Globe*, 27 Cong., 3 Sess., 199–200; *Appendix*, 139–41; Sidney Breese to Martin Van Buren, March 21, 1843, Martin Van Buren Papers, Lib. Cong.

78. Roy M. Robbins, *Our Landed Heritage: The Public Domain, 1776–1936* (Princeton, 1943), Chap. 6.

79. Ibid., 116; George M. Stephenson, *A Political History of the Public Lands from 1840 to 1862* (Boston, 1917), 121.

80. Bemis, *Adams and the Union*, 446–47, indicates some of the opposition to the three-fifths clause.

CHAPTER FOUR

1. James D. Richardson, ed., *A Compilation of the Messages and Papers of the Presidents, 1789–1905* (Washington, 1907), IV, 1876, 1893 ff. The session had been originally called by President Harrison who had died in the interim.

2. Ibid., 1893–1904. Interestingly enough, Tyler, according to his most recent biographer, later moved closer to the Whig view on the tariff in a vain effort to compromise some of the differences that had developed between him and the party. Robert Seager II, *And Tyler Too* (New York, 1963), 169–70.

3. There were 133 Whigs, 102 Democrats and 6 "Independents" in the House. In the Senate there were 29 Whigs and 22 Democrats.

4. Some indications of Whig factionalism can be seen in speeches by Thomas Gilmer of Virginia, June 14, 1842, *Cong. Globe*, 27 Cong., 2 Sess., 629; by William Merrick of Maryland, August 27, 1842, ibid., *Appendix*, 762. See also John J. Crittenden to James Harlan, August 16, 1842, quoted in Mrs. Chapman Coleman, *The Life of John J. Crittenden* (Philadelphia, 1873), I, 193–94.

5. Clay's leadership position in Congress was noted by the New York *Herald*, quoted by the *Richmond Enquirer*, June 4, 1841; A. O. P. Nicholson to James K. Polk, June 14, 1841, James K. Polk Papers, Lib. Cong.; Glyndon G. Van Deusen, *The Jacksonian Era, 1828–1848* (New York, 1958), 155; George Rawlings Poage, *Henry Clay and the Whig Party* (Chapel Hill, 1936), 42–43. Clay himself did express some qualms about his legislative hopes in a letter to Francis Brooke, July 4, 1841, in Calvin Colton, ed., *Works of Henry Clay, Comprising His Life, Correspondence and Speeches* (New York, 1897), IV, 454.

6. Both the distribution bill and the bankruptcy bill were introduced on June 10, 1841. *Cong. Globe*, 27 Cong., 1 Sess., 38.

7. On June 10, 1842. Ibid., 2 Sess., 615.

8. See for example, Poage, *Henry Clay*, 33–106; Oliver Perry Chitwood, *John Tyler, Champion of the Old South* (New York, 1938), 208–68; Seager, *Tyler Too*, 147–71.

9. The Congressional Whig-Tyler split was completed at a Whig caucus

in September, 1841, when the Whigs assailed the President and read him out of the party.

10. Robert J. Rayback is one of the few historians who have sought to go behind the drama of the party split and trace the larger operations of the congressmen in the midst of depression. See his book, *Millard Fillmore, Biography of a President* (Buffalo, 1959).

11. Political scientists have been very interested in the relation between the legislative leader and his followers and that between the legislator and his constituency. See for example, David Truman, *The Congressional Party* (New York, 1958); Duncan Macrae, Jr., *Dimensions of Congressional Voting* (Berkeley, 1958); Julius Turner, *Party and Constituency: Pressures on Congress* (Baltimore, 1951).

12. Throughout this book I am using the term partisan in the sense that most students of politics use it—to indicate loyalty to a political party —rather than in the more general dictionary sense indicating devoted loyalty to some cause. See the term's use, for example, in Angus Campbell et al., *The American Voter* (New York, 1960).

13. See for example, the *Charleston Courier,* June 28, 1841; the *Alton* (Ill.) *Telegraph and Review,* July 31, 1841. The same sort of appeals are to be found in Congressional speeches.

14. See the speech of Andrew Kennedy of Indiana, June 30, 1841, *Cong. Globe,* 27 Cong., 1 Sess., 132; *Mobile Register,* March 4, 1842; *Detroit Free Press,* June 26, 1841.

15. April 21, 1842.

16. See for example, *Cong. Globe,* 27 Cong., 1 Sess., 210, 236, 403; 2 Sess., *Appendix,* 518; Columbus *Ohio State Journal,* March 11, 1842.

17. Compare the statements of Andrew Kennedy of Indiana and Jacob Weller of Ohio in *Cong. Globe,* 27 Cong., 2 Sess., 663, and Appendix, 633, with the *Ohio State Journal,* March 11, 1842. Also compare *Niles National Register* (Baltimore), December 3, 1842, and *Cong. Globe,* 27 Cong., 2 Sess., *Appendix,* 915, with the *Mobile Register,* March 4, 1842.

18. Some of the material included in this section was presented in a paper, "The Politics of Recovery; Congressional Behavior, 1841–1845," at the April, 1961, meeting of the Mississippi Valley Historical Association at Detroit, Michigan.

19. There were, of course, other votes during these two Congresses. However, either there were not enough votes on an issue to form a scale, or the related bills (e.g. appropriations) involved so many different determinants as to make a scale impossible. Nonetheless, the issues used in this chapter encompass so much of the whole area of Congressional action that they give an accurate picture of that action.

20. The "group of issues" or "policy areas" referred to here were not, of course, intuitively or capriciously chosen. Rather they were separated into such groups through the utilization of the Guttman scalogram. At first, as explained in Appendix I, *all* of the roll-calls that appear to fit into the same policy area are brought together. As the scale is constructed, some of these are eliminated because they add nothing to the scale; that is, the inclusion of a particular roll-call vote will not delineate further than already done the different voting blocs present. Others are eliminated because, despite appearances, an occasional vote does not belong with the other issues on the scale; that is, the voting influence that affected the congressmen during that particular roll-call was different from the influences operating during the rest of the roll-calls. See the discussion of the scaleogram in Chapter 1, and in Appendix I.

21. The scale included votes to repeal the Independent Treasury, to re-establish it, to pass each of two different bank bills, to recharter the District of Columbia banks, to override Tyler's veto of the second bank bill, and similar financial matters.

22. The scale position of every congressman on all of the issues considered between 1841 and 1852 may be found in Appendix II.

23. For the sake of analytic brevity and clarity, throughout this book I have divided the scales into "pro," "moderate," and "anti" groups, or some comparable tri-partite division. Obviously there were as many groups as there were different issues on each scale. However, separating the congressmen into all of the component groups on the chart, while admittedly further refining our knowledge of the voting blocs, would also, it seems to me, add a certain amount of difficulty in handling the material without adding very much to the results shown.

24. The 9 Whig moderates included 1 Northerner—Slade of Vermont; 7 Southerners—Meriwether and Nisbet of Georgia, Johnson and Pearce of Maryland, Rayner of North Carolina, Gentry of Tennessee, and Butler of South Carolina; and George Profitt of Indiana. The 8 Whigs in the anti-bank position were Irwin of Pennsylvania, Dawson and Foster of Georgia, Mason of Maryland, Cushing of Massachusetts, Dean of Ohio, and Gilmer and Mallory of Virginia. At the same time, the bulk of Southern, Western, and Northern Whigs did not deviate from the party position. The reasons which prompted these men to act contrary to their party's position—loyalty to the President, local conditions, lightness of party reins on them—lie outside the scope of this study. They could serve as subjects for future study now that they are identified, but our concern is still with

the larger party, sectional, and regional blocs, not with the voting deviant.

25. The sections are defined simply: the Northwest included the states northwest of the Ohio River; the South, all of the slave states; the North, New England and the Middle Atlantic states.

26. The East was New England, the Middle Atlantic states, Virginia, Maryland, Delaware, the Carolinas, and Georgia. The West was all else. The regional breakdowns used throughout this study were derived from Turner: New England, Middle Atlantic, South Atlantic, South Central, and North Central. Frederick Jackson Turner, *The United States, 1830–1850: The Nation and Its Sections* (New York, 1935).

27. There were nine roll-calls on this scale. They included votes on some of the same questions as in the House. In addition there were votes on various other motions such as that the bank submit an annual statement of debt and discount operations to Congress, that the government directors have access to all transactions of the bank, and that only residents of the country and citizens be allowed to buy bank stock.

28. Financial issue, party division, 27th Congress, Senate:

	Scale Type	Whigs		Democrats	
		No.	%	No.	%
Pro-bank	(7–9)	21	87.5	—	
Moderate	(3–6)	3	12.5	—	
Anti-bank	(0–2)	—		20	100

29. Financial issue, sectional division:

	North	South	West	East	West
Pro-bank	53.9	46.0	43.0	64.0	26.3
Moderate	7.7	8.0	—	8.0	5.3
Anti-bank	38.5	46.0	57.0	28.0	68.4

30. The tariff scales in both houses included motions to lower or raise rates, exempt specific products from duties, and votes on engrossment and passage. The land issue included various votes on distribution, graduation, pre-emption rights for settlers, and attempts to tie land policy in with the level of the public debt. The relief issue included votes on a bankruptcy bill, federal assumption of state debts, a treasury note bill, and a loan bill.

31. Special note should be taken of the Southern Whigs in the House of Representatives. Some historians have suggested that the Southern Whigs were low-tariff men. Turner, *U.S., 1830–1850*, 506–7. In the voting to pass the highest tariff up to that time in American history, the Southern Whigs were somewhat splintered: 21 high, 11 moderate, and 12 low. Each of these groups came from all parts of the South. Any suggestion that

Southern Whigs were less "Whiggish" on the tariff than their cohorts from other sections is obviously open to modification.

32. See Chapter 2.

33. *Cong. Globe,* 27 Cong., 3 Sess., 48; 28 Cong., 1 Sess., 50, 529, *Appendix,* 413, 466, 776–77; *Charleston Mercury,* February 12, 1845.

34. Wentworth's speech was on April 6, 1844. *Cong. Globe,* 28 Cong., 1 Sess., 487. Other sectional and local evocations can be found ibid., 49, 310, 538–39; *Appendix,* 53. See also *Wheeling Gazette,* December 14, 1842, quoted in Washington *Globe,* December 21, 1842; U.S., Congress, Senate, 27 Cong., 3 Sess., *Senate Documents,* nos. 155, 216.

35. See the exchange between Stephen A. Douglas and Robert Barnwell Rhett on April 17, 1844. *Cong. Globe,* 28 Cong., 1 Sess., 528–29.

36. The scale included votes to continue the Cumberland Road, to appropriate money for river improvements on various Western rivers, to appropriate money for coastal defenses, etc.

37. The 5 Democratic congressmen from the slave states who voted in the moderate position on this scale included the 3 Democrats from Kentucky, the 1 from Louisiana and the 1 from Missouri.

38. The votes were taken on similar motions to those in the House. The scale contained votes on both an Eastern Harbors improvement bill and a Western Harbors improvement bill.

39. Improvements issue, sectional divisions:

	North		*South*		*West*		*East*		*West*	
	No.	%	No.	%	No.	%	No.	%	No.	%
Pro	8	50.0	7	35	6	75	10	40	11	57.9
Moderate	2	12.5	1	5	2	25	2	8	3	15.8
Anti	6	37.5	12	60			13	52	5	26.3

40. The 2 Missouri Democrats, Thomas Hart Benton and David Rice Atchison, were the Southern dissenters.

41. The apportionment scale contained votes to limit or extend the workings of the bill. The foreign relations scale contained various votes on the Webster-Ashburton treaty, on a motion to take immediate possession of Maine, to appropriate money for a China mission, and to take up the Oregon question. The use of the term "aggressive" in this chart is a descriptive reference to the mood of the congressmen, especially in relation to the tactics they advocated against England.

42. The divisions within the Democratic party were not sectional. The Northern Democrats divided: 2 pro, 2 moderate, none anti; the Southerners divided: 3, 4, 7, respectively; and the Westerners split: 2, 1, 1.

43. In addition there were votes to censure Joshua Giddings for inter-

fering with domestic slavery, to censure John Quincy Adams, and to grant full civil rights to free Negroes.

44. George Harris to James K. Polk, June 18, 1841, Cave Johnson to Polk, December 30, 1843, February 25, 1844, Polk to Silas Wright, February 9, 1844, Polk Papers; *Nashville Union*, June 28, 1841; Athens *Southern Banner*, January 11, March 14, 1844; *Ohio State Journal*, March 5, 1844. This condition was noted in Chauncey S. Boucher, "*In Re*: That Aggressive Slavocracy," *Miss. Valley Hist. Rev.*, VIII (June 1921), 17.

45. *Cong. Globe*, 27 Cong., 1 Sess., 54, 60; *National Intelligencer* (Washington), June 10, 1841; *Charleston Courier*, June 21, 1841; *Richmond Enquirer*, July 2, 1841.

46. *Chicago Democrat*, August 14, December 18, 1844; *Charleston Mercury*, January 21, 1845; *Cong. Globe*, 28 Cong., 1 Sess., 235, Appendix, 70.

47. The two Western Democrats on this scale split between the moderate and anti-Negro positions.

48. The Whigs broke down as follows:

	Northern	*Southern*	*Western*
Pro-Negro	63	3	14
Moderate	1	6	3
Anti-Negro	—	22	1

George Profitt, Whig of Indiana, commented that "he was willing to go with the South and to show his love for that section of the country." *Cong. Globe*, 27 Cong., 1 Sess., 54.

49. This point is further developed in Chapter 7.

50. Charles Wiltse, *John C. Calhoun, Sectionalist, 1840–1850* (Indianapolis, 1951), 156, 171.

51. Nationwide expansionist sentiment can be gleaned from *Cong. Globe*, 28 Cong., 2 Sess., 201, 216, *Appendix*, 171; H. Yoakum to James K. Polk, March 4, 1845, Polk Papers; circular from "Oregon General Committee of Ohio," March 22, 1843, and a circular from a meeting in Ghent, Carrol County, Ky., November 25, 1843, both in Martin Van Buren Papers, Lib. Cong.; W. O. Butler to Robert J. Walker, February 24, 1844, Robert J. Walker Papers, N.Y. Hist. Soc.; Andrew Jackson to Lewis Cass, July 8, 1843, Lewis Cass Papers, William E. Clements Lib., Ann Arbor.

52. *Cong. Globe*, 28 Cong., 2 Sess., *Appendix*, 342; Henry Clay to Stephen Miller, July 1, 1844, in Colton, ed., *Works of Henry Clay*, IV, 491; W. H. Herndon to John Hardin, April 3, 1844, John Hardin Papers, Chicago Hist. Soc.; *Ohio State Journal*, March 15, 1842; *National Intelligencer*,

March 23, December 14, 1844; *Louisville Journal,* quoted in *National Intelligencer,* April 20, 1844; Frankfort *Kentucky Yeoman,* April 11, 1844.

53. M. W. Cluskey, ed., *Speeches, Messages and Other Writings of the Honorable Albert G. Brown* (Philadelphia, 1859), 66.

54. *Cleveland Plain Dealer,* July 18, 1845.

55. The two states were Iowa and Florida. The different votes on Oregon and Texas varied in anti-British belligerency and activity.

56. These 15 Democrats, 11.4% of their total party membership, broke down as follows: 8 of 20 from New York, 4 of 12 from New England, and 1 each from Maryland, Illinois and Ohio. The 4 Whigs were 2 Georgians, and 1 each from Tennessee and Ohio.

57. The votes were on similar matters to those voted on in the House and included ratification of the Texas annexation treaty.

58. These party unity percentages are also impressive when compared with those computed by George Belknap for the 81st Congress. There was a higher degree of party cohesion in the 1841–1845 period. See George Belknap, "A Study of Senatorial Voting by Scale Analysis" (Ph.D. diss., Univ. Chicago, 1951), 76, 79–80, 84.

59. The same is true when the regions used by Turner are broken down and analyzed.

60. Using the Southern Whigs as an example here, since they are sometimes characterized as less Whiggish than other regional blocs in the party, we find that the pattern of dissent suggests otherwise.

61. On the Democratic side in the Senate, for example, the two Pennsylvanians, Buchanan and Sturgeon, bolted on the tariff and relief issues— but to different degrees—yet they rejoined their party colleagues on the other issues. Niles of New Hampshire, McDuffie of South Carolina, Haywood of North Carolina, and Dickinson of New York,, voted differently from the bulk of their party colleagues on the expansion issue.

62. Although written at a later time, the comment of a Southern newspaper editor succinctly sums up the political situation in Congress during the first half of the 1840's: "The antipathies of Whig and Democrat are too strong in Washington and their exercise forms too much the habit of men's lives there." *Charleston Mercury,* January 22, 1849.

63. In addition to the issues discussed in the text, the members of the 28th Congress also voted once more on financial and tariff matters. The results of their voting were similar to the patterns of the 27th Congress. They have not been included here since they add nothing further to the argument that, in the years between 1841 and 1845, Congressional voting reflected an intense partisan division in American politics.

CHAPTER FIVE

1. There were 143 Democrats and 77 Whigs in the House of Representatives. In the Senate were 31 Democrats and 25 Whigs.

2. Avery O. Craven, *The Coming of the Civil War* (2d ed., Chicago, 1957), 206–19; Charles Wiltse, *John C. Calhoun, Sectionalist, 1840–1850* (Indianapolis, 1951), 246; Gerald Capers, *Stephen A. Douglas, Defender of the Union* (Boston, 1959), 40; Thomas Stirton, "Party Disruption and the Rise of the Slavery Extension Controversy, 1840–1846," (Ph.D. diss., Univ. of Chicago, 1956), 300.

3. Polk's first annual message can be found conveniently in James D. Richardson, ed., *A Compilation of the Messages and Papers of the Presidents, 1789–1905* (Washington, 1907), v, 2235–66.

4. Ibid., 2253–8.

5. The Democratic platform of 1844, containing these suggestions, is available in Kirk H. Porter and Donald Bruce Johnson, eds., *National Party Platforms, 1840–1956* (Urbana, 1956), 3–4.

6. Richardson, ed., *Messages and Papers*, 2236–52. The Democratic pressure on Polk in these matters and the favorable response to the message can be followed in various clippings and letters in the James K. Polk Papers, Lib. Cong.; and in the Columbus *Ohio Statesman*, December 10, 1845; *Raleigh Standard*, March 19, 1846; Springfield *Illinois State Register*, January 15, 1846; *Cong. Globe*, 29 Cong., 1 Sess., 87; U.S., Congress, Senate, 29 Cong., 1 Sess., *Senate Documents*, no. 150.

7. The rest of Polk's message advoted a more liberal land policy in the direction of graduation and pre-emption, and some government interest in the development of steamships for commerce and war.

8. See for example, the *Chicago Daily Journal*, January 7, February 4, 1846; "Resolutions of the General Assembly of Ohio," January 22, March 2, 1846, in the William Allen Papers, Lib. Cong.

9. Representative Tibbatts introduced a rivers and harbors bill into the House of Representatives on December 31, 1845. In addition Representative Smith introduced the Cumberland Road bill in the House on January 8, 1846. *Cong. Globe*, 29 Cong., 1 Sess., 120, 164.

10. For a different approach, emphasizing a sectional viewpoint on these policies, see Wiltse, *Calhoun, Sectionalist*, 221.

11. The different attitudes on this question can be traced throughout the debates of 1846. See for example, *Cong. Globe*, 29 Cong., 1 Sess., 275–76, 584, 647, 667, 669, 895, *Appendix*, 82, 494, 1018. Other mani-

festations of this view can be found in the personal correspondence, memoirs, and newspapers of the period.

12. *Cong. Globe*, 29 Cong., 1 Sess., 206, 379; *Washington Union*, November 18, 1845; *Ohio Statesman*, January 5, 1846; Athens (Ga.) *Southern Banner*, February 10, 1846.

13. The major demands were coming from the ports of the Great Lakes concerned with their commercial ties with the East. However, questions dealing with the rivers and roads of the West were also brought up at this session. *Illinois State Register*, September 5, 1846; *Chicago Democrat*, March 17, April 7, 1846; *Chicago Daily Journal*, January 7, February 4, 1846; "Resolutions of Ohio," Wm. Allen Papers; *Cong. Globe*, 29 Cong., 1 Sess., 354, *Appendix*, 560. For a general statement of the problem see John H. Krenkel, *Illinois Internal Improvements, 1818–1848* (Cedar Rapids, 1958), passim; Bessie L. Pierce, *A History of Chicago* (New York, 1937), I, 394.

14. *Charleston Mercury*, March 8, October 23, 1845, March 25, July 18, 1846; *Richmond Enquirer*, March 24, August 4, 1846; *Illinois State Register*, March 21, 1846; *Cong. Globe*, 29 Cong., 1 Sess., 420, 428–29, 438, 472, 486, *Appendix*, 399, 402–10, 996; John Wentworth, *Congressional Reminiscences . . .* (Chicago, 1882), 37.

15. Wiltse, *Calhoun, Sectionalist*, 235–40; Herbert Wender, *Southern Commercial Conventions, 1837–1859* (Baltimore, 1930), 49–69.

16. See the speech of Robert McClelland of Michigan, February 26, 1846, *Cong. Globe*, 29 Cong., 1 Sess., *Appendix*, 330; Duff Green to John C. Calhoun, September 24, 1845, in J. Franklin Jameson, ed., "Correspondence Addressed to John C. Calhoun," *Annual Report of the American Historical Association for 1899* (Washington, 1900), 1055.

17. *Cong. Globe*, 29 Cong., 1 Sess., 420, 428–29, 438; *Richmond Enquirer*, November 22, 1845; *Southern Banner*, December 2, 1845. John Van Deusen in *Economic Bases of Disunion in South Carolina* (New York, 1928), 131, suggests that Calhoun was nearly instructed against such improvements by the South Carolina legislature.

Even in the West there was some Democratic distress at the Memphis position. *Illinois State Register*, March 27, 1846.

18. Wiltse, *Calhoun, Sectionalist*, 178–81, 217–32; Eugene I. McCormac, *James K. Polk* (Berkeley, 1922), 212–351; John A. Garraty, *Silas Wright* (New York, 1949), 232–308. Polk was unhappily aware of the resentment over his appointment policy and its effect on the party. Polk to Silas Wright, July 8, 1845, Polk Papers.

19. The Independent Treasury was also in this area, but it passed in

both houses with too few votes to make a valid scale possible. *Cong. Globe,* 29 Cong., 1 Sess., 595, 1172, 1176.

20. These included several motions to table the bill, to end the floor debate, to add salt to the free entry list, etc.

21. The Democratic chairman of the committee was David McKay of North Carolina. He was assisted by George Dromgoole (D–Va.), Orville Hungerford (D–N.Y.), George S. Houston (D–Ala.), Seaborn Jones (D–Ga.), Moses Norris (D–N.H.), Robert Winthrop (W–Mass.), Samuel Vinton (W–Ohio), and Joseph Ingersoll (W–Pa.).

22. The roll-calls included votes on various parts of a land graduation bill, to grant pre-emption rights on certain land, and to reduce land prices. The term "liberal" here is a subjective descriptive identification of the positions taken, i.e., the Democrats were liberal because they wanted to reduce and graduate the price of land and to grant pre-emption rights to settlers.

23. Compare the party cohesion of over 98% on this issue with that in the 27th and 28th Congresses. See Chapter 4.

24. On the land issue there were 24 Democrats on the conservative end of the scale. These included 10 of 16 New York Democrats, 10 of 11 from Pennsylvania, and the 2 Democrats from New Jersey. They were joined by 1 each from Kentucky and Tennessee. On the tariff issue the New Jersey and Pennsylvania Democratic delegations were unanimous at the high-tariff end of the scale. They were joined by 6 of 20 New Yorkers and 1 each from Ohio, Vermont, Kentucky, and Tennessee.

25. The issue orientation which sometimes broke party ties is underlined by recalling the one previous issue, internal improvements in the 28th Congress, where there had been deviants from party unity. In that case the dissenters were the Western Democrats. See Chapter 4.

26. The tariff scale in the Senate included votes on motions to delay the bill or send it back to committee, to pass a special duty on railroad iron, to pass the Warehouse bill, and on final passage of the tariff. The land scale contained similar votes to those in the House as well as on motions to delay the bill.

27. The 2 Pennsylvania Democrats, Buchanan and Sturgeon, as well as Senator Niles of Connecticut, left their party on both issues. Senators Chalmers and Speight of Mississippi joined them on the tariff issue.

28. By the beginning of the 29th Congress Texas had been annexed and was awaiting admission as a state, which was soon forthcoming. U.S., Congress, House, 29 Cong., 1 Sess., *House Journal*, 113–14. The position of Oregon at this time is summed up in Norman A. Graebner, *Empire on the Pacific* (New York, 1955), 103–7.

29. This was during the 30th Congress in 1848. See Chapter 6. Allan Nevins, *Ordeal of the Union* (New York, 1947), I, 25.

30. *Cong. Globe*, 29 Cong., 1 Sess., 164–65, 287, 983; Milo M. Quaife, ed., *Diary of James K. Polk During His Presidency, 1845–1849* (Chicago, 1910), I, 140–41; *Charleston Mercury*, November 4, 1845, February 17, 18, 1846; *Raleigh Standard*, January 12, 21, 1846; *Chicago Weekly Democrat*, January 27, April 24, 1846; "Oregon and the Oregon Question," *Southern Qtly., Rev.*, VIII (July 1845), 239–41; Norman A. Graebner, "Maritime Factors and the Oregon Compromise," *Pacific Hist. Rev.*, XX (November 1951), 336.

31. See Chapter 4. On this point also see John Hope Franklin, "The Southern Expansionists of 1846," *Jour. of Southern Hist.*, XXV (August 1959), 323–38.

32. While the administration and Democratic spokesmen asserted our claims to various parts of the territory, several of the Whigs were cautiously opposing acquiring Oregon and deprecating the value of that "barren strip of land." They suggested that we greatly limit our claims since the area was worth so little. *Cong. Globe*, 29 Cong., 1 Sess., 50, 56, 58, 139, 160, 195; *National Intelligencer* (Washington), December, 1845, various issues.

33. These included votes on several belligerent notices to England in regard to Oregon, to admit Texas, to pass the Oregon notice, as well as various delaying votes.

34. The Democratic anti-expansionists included 2 of 10 Virginians, 1 of 3 South Carolinians, 1 of 5 Alabamians, and a New Yorker. In the moderate position were Democrats from New York, Pennsylvania, Maryland, Maine, South Carolina, Alabama, Louisiana, Kentucky, and Tennessee.

35. The Senate votes on expansion included several similar roll-calls to those in the House (see note 33), as well as to ratify the Oregon treaty, to end England's navigation rights on the Columbia River, and to warn Europe not to interfere in the Western hemisphere.

36. These were the 2 senators from South Carolina, the 2 from Mississippi, and single senators from Florida, Alabama, and North Carolina.

37. *Cong. Globe*, 29 Cong., 1 Sess., *Appendix* 85–87; George McDuffie to James K. Polk, February 25, 1856, Polk Papers; *Charleston Mercury* quoted in *Niles National Register* (Baltimore), May 16, 1846.

38. See Chapter 4.

39. The scales in both houses included votes on various appropriations for different improvements, on the Cumberland Road, and on a motion not

to use any money appropriated for these purposes until the government was out of debt.

40. The Whig breakdown by section was:

	North	*South*	*West*
House			
Pro	39	12	10
Moderate	2	—	—
Anti	—	7	—
Senate			
Pro	6	9	2
Moderate	1	—	—
Anti	1	—	—

41. In the Senate these included both Texas senators and single senators from Mississippi, Arkansas, Illinois, Indiana, Ohio, and Michigan. In the House, the Democratic dissenters were several of the representatives from New York, Pennsylvania, Illinois, Indiana, Ohio, Michigan, Kentucky, and Missouri.

42. In the Senate, for example, one Illinois Democrat was pro-improvements while the other was moderate. A similar pattern existed in the House. See Table 5.9.

43. The *Allegan Recorder*, a Michigan Democratic paper, characterized Polk's veto as "worthy only of a sectional despot of the nullification stamp." Quoted in the *National Intelligencer*, September 19, 1846. See also, the speech of Stephen A. Douglas, *Cong. Globe*, 29 Cong., 1 Sess., 1184.

44. Ibid., 1186; *Cleveland Plain Dealer*, August 5, 1846.

45. See for example, Craven, *Coming of Civil War*, 217–19, 222, 224; Wiltse, *Calhoun, Sectionalist*, 246.

46. The war scales included votes on motions to limit the President's power to appoint volunteers, to prosecute the war to a successful conclusion, that the war is by act of Mexico, to appoint additional troops and appropriate additional money.

47. In the House, the sectional breakdown was:

	North	*South*	*West*	*North*	*South*	*East*	*West*
Pro	—	70	6	6	70	41	35
Moderate	46	14	23	69	14	50	33
Anti	35	3	8	43	2	36	10

48. In the six highly partisan issues of the 27th and 28th Congresses the Whig party unity percentage averaged 86.8%.

49. In the six highly partisan issues of the 27th and 28th Congresses the House Whigs had a party unity average of 79.4%.

50. Wiltse, *Calhoun, Sectionalist*, 281–86.

51. See, for example, James Hunt of Michigan to James G. Birney, June 2, 1846, in Dwight L. Dumond, ed., *Letters of James Gillespie Birney, 1831–1857* (New York, 1938), ii, 1024.

CHAPTER SIX

1. Milo M. Quaife, ed., *The Diary of James K. Polk During His Presidency, 1845–1849* (Chicago, 1910), ii, 340, iv, 265; *Charleston Courier*, March 5, 1847; S. H. Laughlin to Polk, February 5, 1847, James K. Polk Papers, Lib. Cong.; *Cong. Globe*, 29 Cong., 2 Sess., 312, 342. Polk did have support among some of the Democrats in Congress. See ibid., 264; *Appendix*, 159, 403; Gerald A. Capers, *Stephen A. Douglas, Defender of the Union* (Boston, 1959), 33.

2. See Chapter 5. Stephen A. Douglas wrote to his senatorial colleague, Sidney Breese, that in Northern Illinois the Oregon issue and the Rivers and Harbors Bill were "the great measures of the day." Douglas to Breese, October 20, 1846, Sidney Breese Papers, Ill. State Hist. Soc.

3. Polk did try to patch up the fissures within the party. He had several meetings with a few of the Western Democratic leaders to confirm them in their support of the administration. Quaife, ed., *Polk Diary*, ii, 339; Capers, *Stephen Douglas*, 33. A leading Western Democrat, William Wick of Indiana, upbraided the dissidents and upheld Polk. *Cong. Globe*, 29 Cong., 2 Sess., 264; *Appendix*, 159.

4. See Chapter 5.

5. Wilmot introduced the Proviso on August 8, 1846. *Cong. Globe*, 29 Cong., 1 Sess., 1214–17. A recent study of the split in the Democratic party and its relationship to the Wilmot Proviso is Champlain Morrison, "The Wilmot Proviso and the Democratic Party, 1846–1848" (Ph.D. diss., Univ. of N.C., 1963).

6. Avery O. Craven, *The Coming of the Civil War* (2d ed., Chicago, 1957), 222–26.

7. Ibid.; Charles B. Going, *David Wilmot, Free-Soiler* (New York, 1924), 35–36.

8. See the comments by various Southern congressmen in the *Cong. Globe*, 29 Cong., 2 Sess., 120, 136, 386, 424.

9. Ibid., *Appendix*, 159, 311; Springfield *Illinois State Register*, February 5, 1847; Eugene I. McCormac, *James K. Polk: A Political Biography* (Berkeley, 1922), 620.

10. Mentor L. Williams, "The Chicago River and Harbor Convention, 1847," *Miss. Valley Hist. Rev.*, xxxv (March 1949), 607–26.

11. The proceedings can be followed in Robert Fergus, comp., *Chicago River and Harbor Convention, July 5th, 6th, and 7th, 1847* (Chicago, 1882); and John Wentworth, *Congressional Reminiscences . . .* (Chicago, 1882).

12. Charles Wiltse, *John C. Calhoun, Sectionalist, 1840–1850* (Indianapolis 1951), 312; Thomas D. Odle, "The American Grain Trade of the Great Lakes, 1825–1873" (Ph.D. diss., Univ. of Mich., 1952), 123–27.

13. S. Adams to George Wallace Jones, December 22, 1846, George Wallace Jones Papers, Iowa Hist. Dept.; *National Intelligencer* (Washington), December 12, 1846, January 15, 1848; *Chicago Journal*, September 6, 1847, June 29, 1848; *St. Louis Union*, December 1, 1847.

14. President Polk's annual message at the beginning of this session emphasized the fact and called for help in fighting the war. James D. Richardson, ed., *A Compilation of the Messages and Papers of the Presidents, 1789–1905* (Washington, 1907), v, 2322–45.

15. The course of these differences can be followed in part in S. Adams to George Wallace Jones, December 22, 1846, Jones Papers; *Nashville Union*, May 6, October 15, 1847; Iowa City *Iowa Capital Reporter*, March 3, 1847; *National Intelligencer*, January 15, 1848; Lynchburg *Virginia Patriot*, quoted in *Richmond Enquirer*, February 29, 1848; *Cong. Globe*, 30 Cong., 1 Sess., *Appendix*, 856. The *Louisville Journal*, a Whig paper, called the war "one of the most iniquitous . . . recorded in the dark and bloody annals of mankind." Quoted in the *Nashville Union*, May 28, 1847.

16. U.S., Congress, House, 30 Cong., 1 Sess., *House Miscellaneous Documents*, no. 88. During the debates on the causes of the war, Abraham Lincoln, serving his single term as congressman from Illinois, gained a measure of notoriety through his attacks on the Democrats and their war policy. See for example, Donald Riddle, *Congressman Abraham Lincoln* (Urbana, 1957).

17. The scales on this issue included votes on motions to enlist more volunteers, to thank General Taylor, to condemn General Taylor, to appoint a Lieutenant-General, to pass a loan bill, to limit war aims so as not to acquire territory, to inquire into the removal of General Scott, and to withdraw American troops to the Rio Grande River.

18. In the House of Representatives the highest sectional percentage on these issues was 71.1 and was usually much lower. In addition, each of the sections had substantial blocs of voters at each end of the scale of attitudes, unlike the party breakdowns. In the Senate the highest sectional

percentage was 62.5. Here again, most of the time the rest of the section's senators were at the opposite end of the scale.

19. Some of these differences were obviously still present and did emerge on the question of a war tax on tea and coffee. However, they were smoothed over in the general voting. See Don E. Fehrenbacher, *Chicago Giant: A Biography of "Long John" Wentworth* (Madison, 1957), 65.

20. These included votes on various provisions to limit or extend a military bounty bill for service in the Mexican War. The discussions and the votes centered over how much land should be given or whether or not negotiable land scrip should be given instead of actual land.

21. The issues on this scale included rivers improvements in both East and West as well as railroad land grants, particularly to the Illinois Central Railroad.

22. The issues on the tariff scale included, in addition to particular duties on goods, a treasury loan bill. The improvements issue was concerned with rivers and harbors projects, Congress' right to legislate in this area, and the inadequacy of the President's reasoning in his vetoes.

23. See Chapters 4 and 5.

24. January 27, 1848. The Northern Democratic paper, the Columbus *Ohio Statesman*, echoed similar resolves on September 6, 1848.

25. *Cong. Globe*, 30 Cong., 2 Sess., 557. See also the speech of John Berrien of Georgia at Dahlonega, Ga., in *Niles National Register*, (Baltimore), October 23, 1847.

26. Craven, *Coming of Civil War*, 231.

27. *Cong. Globe*, 30 Cong., 1 Sess., 545, *Appendix*, 747; *Charleston Mercury*, January 12, 1847; Milledgeville (Ga.) *Federal Union*, November 23, 1849.

28. C. S. Tarpley to James K. Polk, November 8, 1847, Polk Papers; George London, "George Edmund Badger and the Compromise of 1850," *N.C. Hist. Rev.*, xv (April 1938), 101.

29. See for example, the legislative resolutions of various Southern states reprinted in the Congressional documents of the 30th Congress.

30. Milwaukee *Weekly Wisconsin*, June 27, 1849; *Alabama Argus*, quoted in *Cleveland Plain Dealer*, April 30, 1849.

31. The Wilmot Proviso was added to the Oregon territorial bill and to several appropriations bills, provoking fights on these bills within a slavery versus antislavery framework. In addition, there was a motion declaring that slavery was excluded from Oregon because it was north of 36° 30'.

32. See the speech of John McClernand of Illinois, January 15, 1847, *Cong. Globe*, 29 Cong., 2 Sess., *Appendix*, 103.

33. Ibid., 134, 311, 427; *Illinois State Register*, March 26, April 2, 1847.

For their position, these Northern Democrats were warmly commended by Southern congressmen. *Cong. Globe*, 29 Cong., 2 Sess., 386, *Appendix*, 119, 153; *Raleigh Standard*, March 10, 1847.

34. In the speakership contest there was a tendency on the part of the Whigs from both North and South not to support Robert Winthrop of Massachusetts for the post. He had taken a position on the Proviso which pleased neither side. See George W. Julian, *The Life of Joshua Giddings* (Chicago, 1892), 218–23; *Charleston Mercury*, January 11, 1848.

35. *Cong. Globe*, 29 Cong., 2 Sess., 148; Columbus *Ohio State Journal*, June 15, 1847; Thomas Stevenson to John J. Crittenden, September 7, 1848, John J. Crittenden Papers, Lib. Cong.; *National Intelligencer*, February 29, 1848. The Democratic senator, James Westcott of Florida, took this stand publicly also. *Cong. Globe*, 29 Cong., 2 Sess., 410.

36. *Richmond Enquirer*, October 1, 1847; *Chicago Democrat*, January 4, February 5, 1848; *Cong. Globe*, 29 Cong., 2 Sess., *Appendix*, 159.

37. Ibid., 30 Cong., 2 Sess., 950.

38. These scales included votes on the Oregon bill, on a motion declaring that Congress cannot interfere with slavery where it exists, nor keep it out of new territories, on the Clayton Compromise, to extend the Missouri Compromise line, to abolish slavery in the territories, and to end the slave trade in the District of Columbia.

39. This was not as true in the Senate as in the House. It is possible that since representatives faced more frequent elections in smaller constituencies than did senators, the former were more quickly responsive to shifts in public opinion. For a general discussion of this possibility see Lewis N. Froman, Jr., *Congressman and Constituency* (New York, 1963).

40. These were:

War issue, 29th Cong.	86.8%
War issue, 30th Cong.	93.2
Tariff issue, 29th Cong.	97.0
Improvements issue, 30th Cong.	94.7

41. These were:

War issue, 29th Cong.	91.7%
War issue, 30th Cong.	100.0
Land issue, 29th Cong.	82.7
Improvements issue, 30th Cong.	92.9

42. In the 27th and 28th House of Representatives, Whig unity was 74.0%. In the first session of the 29th Congress, it was 82.3%. For the Senate, the figures were, in the 27th and 28th, 82.5%, and in the 29th, 1st session, 91.3%. See Chapters 4 and 5.

43. Southern Whigs, war issue:

	29th Congress		30th Congress	
	House	*Senate*	*House*	*Senate*
Prowar	—	—	—	1
Moderate	5	2	5	—
Antiwar	17	9	30	8

44. Democratic party unity in the House:

War issue, 29th Cong.	87.2%
War issue, 30th Cong.	91.0
Tariff issue, 29th Cong.	63.3
Improvements issue, 30th Cong.	62.6

45. Democratic party unity in the Senate:

War issue, 29th Cong.	62.1%
War issue, 30th Cong.	64.7
Land issue, 29th Cong.	74.1
Improvements issue, 30th Cong.	46.4

46. In the 27th and 28th Houses, Democratic unity averaged 88.4%. In the first session of the 29th Congress, it was 68.0%. In the Senate the figures were 87.0% and 70.2% respectively. See Chapters 4 and 5.

47. It was from among the unhappy Western Democrats that much of the breaking of party ties took place. See Morrison, "Wilmot Proviso," passim.

48. These broke down as follows:

	House, 29, 2d Sess.	*Senate, 30*	*House, 30*
South	97.7%	80.0%	100.0%
North	55.0	68.0	83.3

49. In the House of Representatives of the 29th Congress, the North was only 55.0% united. In the 30th, it was 83.3% united.

50. These deviants in the Senate were, in the South, from Delaware, Maryland, Missouri, Tennessee, and Texas. In the North they were from New Hampshire, New York, Pennsylvania, Michigan, Illinois, and Indiana. In the House the 2 Southern deviants were from Tennessee and Delaware. The Northerners were primarily from New York, Illinois, Indiana, Ohio, and Michigan.

51. Senator Douglas added a California territorial bill to the appropriations bill and would not voluntarily delete it. He said he would prefer that the appropriations bill failed than that the 30th Congress end without California having a government. *Cong. Globe*, 30 Cong., 2 Sess., 685. See also, for the pressures present, the reports of a Washington correspondent in the *Charleston Courier*, December 11, 16, 1848.

CHAPTER SEVEN

1. February 22, 1848.

2. See for example, ibid., December 4, 1847.

3. During the abolitionist gag-rule controversy of 1837–1838, Calhoun sought united sectional action against this danger. Charles M. Wiltse, *John C. Calhoun, Nulifier, 1829–1839* (Indianapolis, 1949), 367–70. Calhoun continued to advocate such a course. See John C. Calhoun to Robert M. T. Hunter, December 29, 1844, Calhoun to James E. Calhoun, July 9, 1848, in J. Franklin Jameson, ed., "The Correspondence of John C. Calhoun," *Annual Report of the American Historical Association for 1899* (Washington, 1900), 636, 759.

4. Two of these were noted in the *Charleston Mercury*, December 8, 1847, March 8, 1848.

5. The prospectus for this newspaper is in the Samuel Gouverneur Papers, N.Y. Public Lib. See also James Gadsden to Gouverneur, August 31, 1848, ibid.

6. This point of view can be traced in James G. Birney to the Editor of the *Albany Evening Journal*, May 19, 1845; Theodore Foster to Birney, October 16, 1845, in Dwight L. Dumond, ed., *The Letters of James Gillespie Birney, 1831–1857* (New York, 1938), II, 938–42, 980–81. The abolitionist argument against the South is developed also in Julian Bretz, "The Economic Background of the Liberty Party," *Amer. Hist. Rev.*, XXXIV (January 1929), 250–64.

7. In 1840 the Liberty party received 6,225 votes, .003% of the total vote. In 1844 the figures were 61,999 and 2.4%.

8. As we have seen, some Northern congressmen and newspapers violently criticized the South in 1846 and thereafter for its alleged failure to support Northern interests. See Chapter 5.

9. Some Southern examples of this point of view can be found in Jefferson Davis to C. J. Searles, October 12, 1847, in Dunbar Rowland, ed., *Jefferson Davis, Constitutionalist: His Letters, Papers and Speeches* (Jackson, 1923), I, 95; and in William King's speech to the Alabama Democratic state convention, May 3, 1847, in *Charleston Mercury*, May 8, 1847; Isaac Holmes to Howell Cobb, August 21, 1847, in Ulrich B. Phillips, ed., "The Correspondence of Robert Toombs, Alexander H. Stephens, and Howell Cobb," *Annual Report of the American Historical Association for 1911* (Washington, 1913), 88.

Northern unity expressions may be found in the speech of Joshua R.

Giddings of Ohio, February 13, 1847, *Cong. Globe*, 29 Cong., 2 Sess., *Appendix*, 404. See also, David Donald, *Charles Sumner and the Coming of the Civil War* (New York, 1960), 137–40.

10. See the resolutions of the Democrats of the Sixth Congressional District of Georgia in the *Washington Union*, June 17, 1847; the resolutions of the Alabama state Democratic convention, February, 1848, in ibid., February 25, 1848; Athens (Ga.) *Southern Banner*, April 6, 1847; Montgomery *Tri-Weekly Flag and Advertiser*, June 22, 1848.

11. *Southern Banner*, September 30, 1847; *Flag and Advertiser*, March 30, 1847. I have developed some of these ideas and extended the chronological limits of the discussion in an article, "The Southern National Democrats, 1746–1861," *Mid-America*, XLVII (July 1965), 176–90.

12. Wiltse, *Calhoun, Nullifier*, 115 ff., and *John C. Calhoun, Sectionalist, 1840–1850* (Indianapolis, 1951), 21, 217 ff.

13. *Washington Union*, April 5, 1847; *Southern Banner*, May 18, 1848; Milledgeville (Ga.) *Federal Union*, May 30, 1848; *Nashville Union*, February 23, June 5, 1847.

14. Robert Toombs commented on Calhoun's attempts at Southern unity that "hereafter, treachery itself will not trust him." Toombs to John J. Crittenden, September 27, 1848, in Phillips, ed., "Correspondence," 129.

15. Wilson Lumpkin to John C. Calhoun, August 25, 1848, in Chauncey Boucher and R. P. Brooks, eds., "Correspondence addressed to John C. Calhoun, 1837–1849," *Annual Report of the American Historical Association for 1929* (Washington, 1930), 471; John C. Calhoun to Wilson Lumpkin, September 1, 1848, John C. Calhoun Papers, Lib. Cong.

16. *Cleveland Plain Dealer*, September 10, 1846; speech of Thomas Corwin, September 18, 1847, in Daryl Pendergraft, "The Public Career of Thomas Corwin" (Ph.D. diss., Univ. of Iowa, 1943), II, 452.

17. *Cleveland Plain Dealer*, March 30, 1847; Richard Solberg, "Joshua Giddings, Politician and Idealist" (Ph.D. diss., Univ. of Chicago, 1952), 270, 321; Donald, *Charles Sumner*, 137, 148.

18. The failure to organize the territories can be followed conveniently in Allan Nevins, *Ordeal of the Union*, (New York, 1947), I, Chap. 1.

19. *Cong. Globe*, 30 Cong., 1 Sess., 545, *Appendix*, 747; U.S., Congress, House, 30 Cong., 2 Sess., *House Miscellaneous Documents*, no. 58.

20. These legislative resolutions were reprinted in the Congressional documents of the 30th Congress.

21. Manifestations of this view and actions taken in support of it can be found in *Charleston Mercury*, various issues in 1848; *Abbeville* (S.C.)

Banner, September 9, 1848, (quoted by *Charleston Mercury,* September 12, 1848); *Raleigh Standard,* October 20, 1847; *Federal Union,* June 27, 1848; *Washington Union,* May 5, 1848; *Niles National Register* (Baltimore), January 8, 1848; Herbert Doherty, *The Whigs of Florida* (Gainesville, 1959), 27.

22. *Charleston Mercury,* February 21, June 28, 1848; *Southern Banner,* November 30, 1848.

23. See Chapter 6.

24. The Alabama platform is printed in *The Journal of the Democratic Convention Held in the City of Montgomery on the 14th and 15th of February, 1848* (Montgomery, 1848), 11–13. For background of the movement, see Clarence Phillips Denman, *The Secession Movement in Alabama* (Montgomery, 1933), 1–13.

25. *Charleston Mercury,* February 11, June 1, 1848; *Southern Banner,* April 27, 1848.

26. See Frank B. Woodford, *Lewis Cass, The Last Jeffersonian* (New Brunswick, 1950), 252–54. The Democratic platform of 1848 warned against Congressional interference with slavery as leading to "the most alarming and dangerous consequences." Kirk H. Porter and Donald B. Johnson, eds., *National Party Platforms, 1840–1956* (Urbana, 1956), 11.

27. W. W. Harlee to John C. Calhoun, June 8, 1848, in Boucher and Brooks, eds., "Correspondence," 439–40; Avery O. Craven, *The Growth of Southern Nationalism, 1848–1861* (Baton Rouge, 1953); Nevins, *Ordeal.*

28. The Taylor movement was anti-Clay in character and stimulated by Whig forces throughout the country. See Holman Hamilton, *Zachary Taylor, Soldier in the White House* (Indianapolis, 1951), 63.

29. Ibid., 104–5; Craven, *Southern Nationalism,* 50.

30. The process of Whig organization on a national, nonsectional basis in 1848 can be followed in Hamilton, *Zachary Taylor,* 52–133. Some Southern Whigs violently opposed the overthrow of basic Whig principles and the resort to a sectional appeal by the people behind the Taylor candidacy. See John Minor Botts, *To the Whigs of Virginia, March 8, 1848,* (Richmond, 1848), 14–15.

31. There is no published history of the Free-Soil party. The movement of various components of the party can be followed, however, in such monographs as, Herbert D. A. Donovan, *The Barnburners* (New York, 1925); Donald, *Charles Sumner;* Martin Duberman, *Charles Francis Adams, 1807–1886* (Boston, 1961); Betty Fladeland, *James Gillespie*

Birney (Ithaca, 1955); Frank Otto Gatell, *John Gorham Palfrey* (Boston, 1963); Richard Sewell, *John P. Hale and the Politics of Abolition* (Boston, 1964).

32. See the Free-Soil platform reprinted in Porter and Johnson, eds., *National Party Platforms*, 13–14.

33. The organization of the Free-Soilers can be followed in Nevins, *Ordeal*, I, 202–8.

34. The Free-Soilers drew 291,263 votes in 1848, 9.7% of the total vote cast, a growth over the Liberty party's totals in 1844. Students of this movement consider that these votes were drawn from both parties.

35. This point of view is developed in Norman A. Graebner, "1848: Southern Politics at the Crossroads," *The Historian*, xxv (November 1962), 14–35.

36. *Washington Union*, July 14, 1848; *Southern Banner*, June 22, 1847; *Savannah Georgian* quoted in *Southern Banner*, April 19, 1848; *Raleigh Standard*, June 7, October 25, 1848; *Journal of Alabama Democratic Convention*, 10–11; Chaplain Morrison, "The Wilmot Proviso and the Democratic Party, 1846–1848" (Ph.D. diss., Univ. of N.C., 1963), 125–26, 157, 183–84.

37. See the reports of different meetings and individuals, as well as editorial comment, reported in the *Nashville Union*, December 7, 1847; *Washington Union*, April 11, July 6, 1848; *Charleston Mercury*, July 15, August 3, 21, 1848; *Cong. Globe*, 30 Cong., 1 Sess., 907, 964; John Y. Mason to Lewis Cass, September 25, 1848, Lewis Cass Papers, William E. Clements Lib., Ann Arbor; Howell Cobb et al. to their constituents, February 26, 1849, in R. P. Brooks, ed., "Howell Cobb Papers," *Ga. Hist. Qtly.*, v (June 1921), 42.

38. As the *Richmond Enquirer* put it in regard to the Wilmot Proviso, "General Cass has declared for and taken his stand with the South." Issue of September 22, 1848. See also James Seddon to Robert M. T. Hunter, June 16, 1848, in Charles Ambler, ed., "Correspondence of R. M. T. Hunter, 1826–1876," *Annual Report of the American Historical Association for 1916* (Washington, 1918), 91.

39. *Southern Banner*, June 8, 1848, also April 27, 1848; *Charleston Mercury*, June 1, 1848. In response to these appeals more and more Democrats, including some earlier spokesmen for Southern unity such as the *Charleston Mercury*, announced their support for the national Democratic ticket.

40. *Cleveland Plain Dealer*, June 6, 12, 1848; *Chicago Democrat*, December 22, 1848; Columbus *Ohio State Journal*, August 10, 1848.

41. Many Provisoists such as John Wentworth, Thomas Corwin, Isaac Walker, and Benjamin Wade, did not desert their party in 1848. See John Wentworth to E. S. Kimberly, June 26, 27, 1848, E. S. Kimberly Papers, Chicago Hist. Soc.; Hans Trefousse, *Benjamin Franklin Wade, Radical Republican from Ohio* (New York, 1963), 54–57.

42. Columbus *Ohio Statesman*, July 1, September 14, 1848; *Ohio State Journal*, June 20, October 21, 1848; *Chicago Journal*, September 15, November 13, 1848; Milwaukee *Weekly Wisconsin*, June 28, August 30, 1848.

43. The two national parties received 90.3% of the popular vote in 1848 as compared with 97.7% in 1844. Both parties lost votes but maintained their national character, receiving votes in all sections of the Union.

44. Stephen Adams to James K. Polk, November 15, 1858, James K. Polk Papers, Lib. Cong.; Hamilton, *Zachary Taylor*, 99–104.

45. Even before the election campaign ended John C. Calhoun was thinking in such terms. He expected the agitation to continue and the South to be defeated on slavery extension. Then he expected that Southern political leaders would come together with a sectional convention as their only hope. John C. Calhoun to Wilson Lumpkin, September 1, 1848, Calhoun Papers.

46. See Hamilton, *Zachary Taylor*, 142–43, 177–78; Wiltse, *Calhoun, Sectionalist*, 374.

47. *Cong. Globe*, 30 Cong., 2 Sess., passim; *Flag and Advertiser*, January 18, 1859; *Chicago Democrat*, April 17, 1849.

48. *Cong. Globe*, 30 Cong., 2 Sess., 83.

49. Ibid., 84.

50. Wilson Lumpkin to John C. Calhoun, January 3, 1849, in Boucher and Brooks, eds., "Correspondence," 492–93.

51. Wiltse, *Calhoun, Sectionalist*, 378 ff.

52. Ibid. See also John C. Calhoun et al., *The Address of the Southern Delegates in Congress to their Constituents* (Washington, 1849).

53. *Charleston Mercury*, November 21, December 19, 20, 27, 1848; *Raleigh Standard*, December 27, 1848; *Federal Union*, January 9, 1849; *Washington Union*, January 16, 1849; *Flag and Advertiser*, February 17, 1849.

54. The proceedings of the meeting may be followed in *Richmond Enquirer*, January 30, February 9, 1849; *Flag and Advertiser*, January 27, 1849; Nevins, *Ordeal*, I, 223–24; Wiltse, *Calhoun, Sectionalist*, 378 ff.

55. Thomas Metcalfe to John J. Crittenden, January 14, 1849, John J. Crittenden Papers, Lib. Cong.

56. Robert Toombs to John J. Crittenden, January 22, 1849, in Mrs.

Chapman Coleman, ed., *The Life of John J. Crittenden* . . . (Philadelphia, 1873), I, 335–36. Thomas Hart Benton and Samuel Houston were not even invited, but Houston appeared to work against extreme pronouncements. Elbert B. Smith, *The Magnificent Missourian: The Life of Thomas Hart Benton* (Philadelphia, 1958), 245.

57. In the midst of the preparations for the Southern caucus, Senator George Badger of North Carolina wrote, "I am a friend to the Union—I have sworn to support the Constitution and will never concur in any movement which may, however remotely, endanger its continuance—certainly not for the privilege of carrying slaves to California or keeping up private gaols by slavedealers in this district." Quoted in Norman Brown, "Edward Stanly, Federal Whig" (Ph.D. diss., Univ. of N.C., 1963) 221. See also Howell Cobb et al., "To Our Constituents," in Brooks, ed., "Howell Cobb Papers," 156–57; Robert P. Brooks, "Howell Cobb and the Crisis of 1850," *Miss. Valley Hist. Rev.*, IV (December 1917), 283.

58. Henry Hilliard, Whig congressman from Alabama, "purposely or inadvertently, [had] franked into [his] district a speech of a Whig colleague comparing the Southern meeting with the Hartford Convention." Austin L. Venable, "Alabama's War of the Roses," *Alabama Review*, VIII (October 1955), 252. Some of the passionate anti-Calhoun feeling can be gathered from George Badger to John J. Crittenden, January 13, 1849, Robert Toombs to Crittenden, January 22, 1849, Crittenden Papers; Sam Houston to his constituents, March 2, 1849, Houston to Henderson Yoakum, January 31, 1849, Houston to James Gadsden, September 20, 1849, in Amelia W. Williams and Eugene C. Barker, eds., *The Writings of Sam Houston, 1813–1863* (Austin, 1938–1943), V, 86, 88, 71, 99; Thomas B. Stevenson to Caleb B. Smith, February 11, 1849, Caleb Smith Papers, Lib. Cong.; *Richmond Times* quoted by *Richmond Enquirer*, February 1, 1849.

59. Wiltse, *Calhoun, Sectionalist*, 382. The Whig feeling about Taylor's administration and Southern pressure can be seen in Leslie Coombs to John M. Clayton, January 22, 1849, John M. Clayton Papers, Lib. Cong. See also, Edward M. Steel, Jr., *T. Butler King of Georgia* (Athens, 1964), 64.

60. Milo M. Quaife, ed., *The Diary of James K. Polk During His Presidency, 1845–1849* (Chicago, 1910), IV, 249–50, 281, 283; Eugene I. McCormac, *James K. Polk: A Political Biography* (Berkeley, 1922), 649. Polk also intervened earlier when Southern reaction against the Wilmot Proviso had led to discussions of a possible move for sectional unity. See James K. Polk to Lewis Cass, August 24, 1848, Cass Papers.

61. The sources listed in note 54 are relevant here.

62. See Calhoun et al., *Address to Southern Constituents.*

63. The Democrats included Howell Cobb, Sam Houston, Andrew Johnson, Thomas Hart Benton, and many of the Democrats from Georgia, Tennessee, and North Carolina. The two Whigs were Patrick Tompkins of Mississippi and John Gayle of Alabama.

64. "The antipathies of Whig and Democrat are too strong in Washington and their exercise forms too much the habit of men's lives there." *Charleston Mercury*, January 22, 1849.

65. January 30, 1849.

CHAPTER EIGHT

1. Evidence of this debate can be drawn from the following: John C. Calhoun to James Hammond, February 14, 1849, Hilliard M. Judge to Calhoun, April 29, 1849, Herschel V. Johnson to Calhoun, July 20, 1849, all in J. Franklin Jameson, ed., "Correspondence of John C. Calhoun," *Annual Report of the American Historical Association for 1899* (Washington, 1900), 762–63, 1195, 1198; David L. Yulee to Calhoun, July 10, 1849, quoted in Arthur Thompson, "David L. Yulee, A Study of Nineteenth Century Politics and Enterprise" (Ph.D. diss., Columbia Univ., 1954), 290; Herschel V. Johnson to R. A. L. Atkinson, June 29, 1849, in Percy S. Flippen, ed., "Herschel V. Johnson Correspondence," *N.C. Hist. Rev.*, IV (April 1927), 184; other collections of correspondence, various newspapers, and such secondary works as Charles Wiltse, *John C. Calhoun, Sectionalist, 1840–1850* (Indianapolis, 1951), 404 ff.

2. John C. Calhoun to Andrew Pickens Calhoun, July 24, 1849, Jameson, ed., "Calhoun Correspondence," 769; Ulrich B. Phillips, *The Course of the South to Secession* (New York, 1939), 138–39; Dallas T. Herndon, "The Nashville Convention of 1850," *Transactions of Ala. Hist. Soc.*, V (1904), 203–37.

3. Representative Edward Stanly of North Carolina referred to the Southern sectionalists at this time as "the chivalry destructionaries of the South." Quoted in Norman D. Brown, "Edward Stanly, Federal Whig" (Ph.D. diss., Univ. of N.C., 1963), 239. The opposition of Southerners to the convention can be followed up to its meeting, in the *National Intelligencer* (Washington), January and February, 1850, various issues; Athens (Ga.) *Southern Banner*, February 7, 28, 1850.

4. Alexander H. Stephens of Georgia wrote to his brother just as Congress opened that "I never saw greater sectional feeling exhibited—the

North is insolent and unyielding." Alexander H. Stephens to Linton Stephens, December 2, 1849, Alexander H. Stephens Correspondence, Manhattanville College of the Sacred Heart, New York.

5. Although Howell Cobb, the Democratic candidate, and Robert Winthrop, the Whig candidate, each received a solid bloc of party votes, the House was so closely divided with 112 Democrats and 109 Whigs, that the decision of several congressmen not to vote for their party's candidate for sectional reasons made a decision impossible. *Cong. Globe*, 31 Cong., 1 Sess., 2–66. Some of the bitterness that erupted as a result of the failure to organize the House can be seen in the *Charleston Courier*, December 20, 1849; *Raleigh Standard*, January 16, 1850; William H. Bissell to William Martin, February 5, 1850, Miscellaneous Papers, Ill. State Hist. Soc.; John A. Quitman to Robert J. Walker, February 13, 1850, Robert J. Walker Papers, N.Y. Hist. Soc.; *Cong. Globe*, 31 Cong., 1 Sess., 29 ff. The same sort of sectional hostility erupted in the election for minor officers of the House. Thomas L. Harris to Isaac Lanphier, January 12, 1850, Lanphier Papers, Ill. State Hist. Soc.

6. Holman Hamilton has written a full scale survey of the crisis of 1850 in Congress, *Prologue to Conflict: The Crisis and Compromise of 1850* (Lexington, 1964). His book is particularly useful for its coverage of the debates in Congress, the problems of leadership, and the pressures operating to influence the representatives and senators.

7. Robert Rayback, *Millard Fillmore, Biography of a President* (Buffalo, 1959), 223; Gerald Capers, *Stephen A. Douglas, Defender of the Union* (Boston, 1959), 61; Holman Hamilton, *Zachary Taylor, Soldier in the White House* (Indianapolis, 1951), 50. Meetings were held by these men to work out a compromise. See Hamilton, *Prologue to Conflict*, 65–67; Allan Nevins, *Ordeal of the Union* (New York, 1947), i, 303, 342.

8. Henry Clay declared "I owe no allegiance to any one section—East, North, West or South. And I know . . . of but two sovereignties to whom I owe allegiance—the one the Union, and the other my own state." *Cong. Globe*, 31 Cong., 1 Sess., 371. He and others pushed through a resolution that created a Committee of Thirteen in the Senate to work out the details of the compromise proposals. Ibid., 770 ff. Their efforts received support in various newspapers: "We stand ready to accept the Compromise as a noble and patriotic offering on the shrine of Union.", Montgomery *Alabama Journal*, quoted by *Charleston Courier*, May 17, 1850; *Augusta Constitutionalist*, May 16, 1850; *Nashville True Whig*, May 24, 1850; Springfield *Illinois State Register*, May 16, 1850; *Chicago Journal*, June 5, 1850.

9. "The admission of California as a state would be the practical triumph

of the Wilmot Proviso." *Augusta Constitutionalist,* January 8, 1850; L. J. Glenn to Howell Cobb, January 15, 1850, in R. P. Brooks, ed., "Howell Cobb Papers," *Ga. Hist. Qtly.,* v (September 1921), 36; *Cong. Globe, 31* Cong., 1 Sess., *Appendix,* 343.

10. Columbus *Ohio State Journal,* January 30, 1850; Milwaukee *Weekly Wisconsin,* May 22, 1850.

11. *Chicago Democrat,* May 3, August 26, 1850; *Ohio State Journal,* February 12, 1850; "Resolutions of the Legislature of the State of Michigan," U.S. Congress, House, 31 Cong., 1 Sess., *House Miscellaneous Documents,* no. 10.

12. The compromise legislation problem was further complicated by the position of President Taylor. He had set himself to bring California into the Union unencumbered by any other legislation. Contemporary students of the subject believe that Taylor exercised effective power over many Whig congressmen and made them stand against compromise. See Holman Hamilton, "Democratic Senate Leadership and the Compromise of 1850," *Miss. Valley Hist. Rev.,* XLI (December 1954), 403–18.

13. This scale contained additional proposals giving free Negroes the right of habeus corpus if seized as a fugitive slave, an amendment to divide the state of California at the line 36° 30′ , another to fix the Texas boundary at what it had been in 1845, as well as similar sectionally-oriented demands.

14. This scale contained votes on the various proposals making up the Omnibus bill as well as related resolutions. See note 24.

15. The three moderates were Senators Spruance and Wales of Delaware, and Clay of Kentucky.

16. The Democrats divided:

	Northeast	*Northwest*
Pro-North	2	2
Moderate	1	7
Pro-South	2	1

The senators in each position were: Pro-North—Dodge and Walker of Wisconsin, Hale of New Hampshire, and Hamlin of Maine. Moderate—Shields and Douglas of Illinois, Bright and Whitcomb of Indiana, Jones and Dodge of Iowa, Norris of New Hampshire, and Felch of Michigan. Pro-South—Cass of Michigan, Dickinson of New York, and Sturgeon of Pennsylvania.

17. See Chapters 5 and 6.

18. After the failure of the "Southern Address," Southern Whigs were strongly attacked for not being true to their section. *Raleigh Standard,* May

23, 1849. Northern Whigs and Free-Soilers similarly assailed the Northern Democrats.

19. This scale contained the same type of votes as in the Senate. See note 13.

20. Of the Southern Whigs, 4 of 25 (from Virginia, Tennessee, North Carolina and Delaware) were in a moderate position. They were joined by 2 of 56 Southern Democrats, both of whom were from Missouri.

21. The representatives, of course, had to face more frequent elections in smaller constituencies than did the senators and this may have made them more responsive to public pressure. See Lewis N. Froman, Jr., *Congressmen and Constituency* (New York, 1963), for suggestions along this line.

22. Congressman William Bissell of Illinois wrote that the slavery question was "embarrassing and retarding the proper business of Congress" and that it was obliterating party lines but "we must try to preserve the integrity of our party." Bissell to William Martin, February 5, 1850, Miscellaneous Papers, Ill. State Hist. Soc.

23. Such "national" Democrats as Stephen Douglas, Lewis Cass, and Isaac Walker of Wisconsin, found themselves continually hampered in their voting by anti-Southern instructions from their state legislatures as well as by popular sentiment. U.S., Congress, House, 30 Cong., 1 Sess., *House Miscellaneous Documents*, no. 96; ibid., Senate, 30 Cong., 1 Sess., *Senate Miscellaneous Documents*, nos. 38, 41.

24. This scale included votes on the various parts of what was considered to be the compromise proposal: the yeas and nays on the intermediate stages and final passage of the Omnibus bill, and on attempts to separate the component parts of the bill so as to destroy the compromise scheme.

25. The exception was James Cooper of Pennsylvania. The attitude of Northern anti-compromisers was perhaps best summed up by the statement of Salmon P. Chase, elected to the Senate by a combination of Whig and Free-Soil votes in Ohio, that the compromise was "sentiment for the North, substance for the South." Salmon P. Chase to E. S. Hamlin, February 2, 1850, Salmon P. Chase Papers, Lib. Cong.

26. The one Southern Democrat in the anti-compromise position was Thomas Hart Benton of Missouri. The three moderates on the issue were Yulee of Florida, Davis of Mississippi, and Turney of Tennessee.

27. In neither case did the fragments in any of the voting positions reflect particular subregional groupings.

28. This scale included votes on the various parts of the Omnibus bill. See note 24.

29. Some examples of this splintering were:

	Va.	N. C.	Ala.	Mass.
Pro-compromise	8	5	3	3
Moderate	—	1	—	—
Anti-compromise	5	3	4	3

30. The Senate also voted on several other matters, but there were not enough votes to form a scale on anything other than the slavery and compromise issues.

31. See Chapter 6.

32. Roy M. Robbins, *Our Landed Heritage: The Public Domain, 1776–1936* (2d ed., New York, 1950), 156–57.

33. The issues on the scale were mainly concerned with taking up the bill or delaying it, moderating its provisions, and final passage. The term "liberal" in the chart is, once again, a subjectively selected descriptive adjective.

34. The outstanding example of this was the Ohio delegation: 8 in favor, 4 moderate, and 5 opposed.

35. See Chapters 4–6.

36. This scale included votes on various land grants to states for railroad construction, on different components of the Illinois Central bill, and on a lighthouse construction bill.

37. For instance, of 27 Whig congressmen from New York, 10 were pro-improvements, 11 were moderates, and 6 were opposed. Such splintering was not uncommon.

38. Ohio Democrats split, 3 pro, 1 moderate, and 5 against. Other state divisions of a similar nature included Kentucky where the Democrats split 2 pro, 2 anti, and Tennessee and South Carolina where the divisions were 2 pro, 4 against.

39. Note their votes on the internal improvements issue in Chapters 4–6.

40. Regional division on internal improvements:

	South Atlantic	Southwest
Pro (govt. intervention)	4	20
Moderate	1	2
Anti	22	6

Local variations of note included the South Carolina delegation where 2 of 6 Democrats were in the pro-intervention position, and the Tennessee Democratic group in which 4 of 6 voted against intervention.

41. Thus the Northern Whigs in the Senate were united on both issues. But the Northern Whigs in the House were never united. The Southern Democrats in the Senate were united but the Southern House Democrats

were so only once of four times. The Southern Whigs were united in the House on the sectional and compromise scales but not on the two others. In the Senate Southern Whigs split twice. The Northern Democrats were only united on the improvements issue in the House of Representatives.

CHAPTER NINE

1. Joshua Giddings to Thomas Bolton, December 17, 1850, Miscellaneous Collections, N.Y. Hist. Soc.; *Washington Union*, January 3, 1851; Eufaula, Alabama *Spirit of the South* quoted by the *Union*, January 2, 1851. This feeling continued well into the year. See *Cincinnati Gazette*, November 10, 1851, quoted by *National Intelligencer* (Baltimore), November 15, 1851.

2. *Washington Union*, January 18, 1851; Springfield *Illinois State Journal*, March 15, August 18, 1851.

3. Thomas Hart Benton happily combined his long-standing anti-Whiggism with the holdover of the recent slavery controversy by writing to a friend that "the fugitive slave law has done good service: it has cut the throat of Whiggery, i.e. Clay Whiggery, in three great states and six small ones; and tho I cannot say, may it live a thousand years, yet I want it to live long enough to cut the throat of Clay Whiggery in all the rest of the states." Thomas Hart Benton to Montgomery Blair, August 29, 1851, Blair Family Papers, Lib. Cong. I am grateful to Professor Ari Hoogenboom for calling my attention to this particular letter.

4. This debate can be conveniently followed in Allan Nevins, *The Ordeal of the Union* (New York, 1947), I, Chaps. 11, 12. Chap. 11 is entitled: "Southern Acquiescence—With Conditions," while Chap. 12 is "Northern Acquiescence—With Reservations."

5. The idea of the compromise as a Southern loss was stressed repeatedly throughout 1850 and 1851. See for example, *Resolutions and Address Adopted by the Southern Convention Held at Nashville, Tennessee . . . 1850* (Charleston, S.C., 1850); J. A. Woodward's address to his constituents in the Columbia *South Carolinian*, quoted by *Charleston Mercury*, October 8, 1850; *Memphis Daily Appeal*, February 22, 1851; *Huntsville Democrat* quoted by *Charleston Mercury*, October 19, 1850; *Cong. Globe*, 32 Cong., 1 Sess., Appendix, 43; resolutions of the Democrats of the Fourth Congressional District of Louisiana, quoted in Leslie M. Norton, "A History of the Whig Party of Louisiana" (Ph.D. diss., La. State Univ., 1940), 332.

6. *Cleveland Plain Dealer*, October 10, 21, 1850. See also the *Chicago*

Journal, October 2, 1850, April 29, 1851; Centreville *Indiana True Democrat,* February 27, 1851.

7. *Cong. Globe,* 31 Cong., 2 Sess., *Appendix,* 186; Daniel Webster to Edward Everett, April 13, 1851, Edward Everett Papers, Mass. Hist. Soc. In this letter Webster complained of the malignity with which the Free-Soilers and abolitionists attacked on this issue. The moderates found the Fugitive Slave Law quite embarrassing and destructive to them. There is much evidence for this in the Everett Papers as well as in E. Conner to Thomas Corwin, November 16, 1850, Thomas Corwin Papers, Lib. Cong.

8. Nevins, *Ordeal,* 380–90.

9. See for example, Vroman Mason, "The Fugitive Slave Law in Wisconsin, with Reference to Nullification Sentiment," *Proceedings,* State Hist. Soc. of Wisc., 1895, (Madison, 1895), 117–144; Nevins, *Ordeal.*

10. Larry Gara, *The Liberty Line: The Legend of the Underground Railroad* (Lexington, 1961), 141.

11. *Illinois State Journal,* December 19, 1850.

12. Milwaukee *Weekly Wisconsin,* November 6, 1850; *Detroit Free Press,* October 16, 1850; Columbus *Ohio State Journal,* November 1, 1850; *Cong. Globe,* 31 Cong., 2 Sess., 16.

13. Ibid., 32 Cong., 1 Sess., 700; *Washington Union,* March 3, 1852; Arthur C. Cole, *The Era of the Civil War, 1848–1870. The Centennial History of Illinois,* Vol. III (Springfield, 1919), 74.

14. A Union party of Democrats and Whigs was formed in Georgia to fight for acceptance of the Compromise. See Horace Montgomery, *Cracker Parties* (Baton Rouge, 1950), 28 ff. See also the Huntsville *Advocate* quoted by *National Intelligencer,* November 21, 1850; *Fort Smith Herald,* March 21, 1851; Sam Houston to John Letcher, January 24, 1851, in Amelia M. Letcher and Eugene C. Barker, eds., *The Writings of Sam Houston, 1813–1863* (Austin, 1938–1943), v, 263–66; speech of Aaron V. Brown before the Nashville Convention, November 15, 1850, in *Speeches, Congressional and Political, of Ex-Governor Aaron V. Brown of Tennessee* (Nashville, 1854), 317.

15. *Cong. Globe,* 32 Cong., 1 Sess., 35–36; *National Intelligencer,* February 26, 1852; *Washington Union,* March 3, 1852.

16. *Cong. Globe,* 31 Cong., 2 Sess., 12; 32 Cong., 1 Sess., 35, 976–78.

17. See for example, the speech of Senator Butler of South Carolina, ibid., 32 Cong., 1 Sess., 36, and the *Indiana True Democrat,* February 27, 1851.

18. See the speech of Lewis Cass on December 23, 1851, in *Cong. Globe,* 32 Cong., 1 Sess., 146.

19. These planks were successfully incorporated in the platforms of both

parties. The Democratic finality resolution read, in part: "*Resolved*, That the Democratic Party will resist all attempts at renewing . . . the agitation of the slavery question." The Whigs said they would "discountenance all efforts to continue or renew such agitation whenever, wherever, or however the attempt may be made." Kirk H. Porter and Donald B. Johnson, eds., *National Party Platforms, 1840–1956* (Urbana, 1956), 17, 21.

20. The *Charleston Mercury* throughout 1851 reported in detail on the contests between moderates and extremists. See for example, the issues of February 12, August 12, October 14, 29, 1851. See also Dallas T. Herndon, "The Nashville Convention of 1850," *Transactions of Ala. Hist. Soc.*, v (1904); Montgomery, *Cracker Parties*, 28 ff; Chauncey S. Boucher, "The Secession and Cooperation Movement in South Carolina, 1848–1852," *Washington Univ. Studies*, v (April 1918), 67–138; Arthur C. Cole, "The South and the Right of Secession in the Early Fifties," *Miss. Valley Hist. Rev.*, i (December 1914), 376–99.

21. See for example, the clash between Henry W. Hilliard and William L. Yancey, in the Montgomery, Alabama, Congressional district. Henry W. Hilliard, *Politics and Pen Pictures at Home and Abroad* (New York, 1892); Lewy Dorman, "Party Politics in Alabama from 1850 through 1860," *Publications of the Alabama State Department of Archives and History, Historical and Patriotic Series*, no. 13 (Wetumpka, 1935), 48–60. In North Carolina the Whig Edward Stanly was re-elected to Congress by an increased majority despite sectionalist attacks on him for his support of the Compromise of 1850.

22. *Indiana True Democrat*, August 7, 1851; George Julian to Joshua Giddings, August 22, 1851, Giddings-Julian Papers, Lib. Cong.; Annette M. Sheel, "The Congressional Career of John Wentworth," (M.A. thesis, Univ. of Chicago, 1935), 67. The Alabama Southern Rights Convention summed up the position of the South by resolving, "That, in consideration of the fact that the people of Alabama had decided against resistance to the compromise measures, the Southern Rights party could no longer make that an issue, but would guard the future." *National Intelligencer*, March 9, 1852.

23. In Georgia Joseph E. Brown, the future Governor and a staunch Southern rights man in 1850, chaired a committee in 1851 "which . . . urged reunion of the two wings of the party." In 1852 Brown served as an elector on the national Democratic ticket. Louise Hill, *Joseph E. Brown and the Confederacy* (Chapel Hill, 1939), 11–12. Similarly, many members of the Union party in Georgia demonstrated a strong desire to return to the national parties. In several Northern states coalitions of antislavery Whigs, Democrats and Free-Soilers began to break up, as many men returned to

their old parties. See for example, Richard Sewell, *John P. Hale and the Politics of Abolition* (Cambridge, 1965), 142–43.

24. See for example, the exchange between Senators Andrew P. Butler and Henry S. Foote, December, 1851, *Cong. Globe*, 32 Cong., 1 Sess., 35–39, 95–96.

25. These involved two separate groups of items: one including various resolutions and proposals to end all further agitation on the slavery issue; the other including resolutions calling on the country to carry out all parts of the compromise measures of 1850, including the Fugitive Slave Law.

26. These involved receiving and debating petitions in favor of repealing the law, and an amendment to an appropriation bill preventing the expenditure of government money in the capture of fugitive slaves.

27. Wade had been elected with Free-Soil help. Paul I. Miller, "Thomas Ewing, Last of the Whigs" (Ph.D. diss., Ohio State Univ., 1933), 245.

28. *Cong. Globe*, 31 Cong., 2 Sess., 14.

29. This has some interest since Brown was considered a moderate on the slavery issue and Wentworth a militant antislaveryite.

30. *Cong. Globe*, 31 Cong., 2 Sess., 14–16.

31. See Chapter 2.

32. See for example, the *Chicago Journal*, February 25, March 25, April 25, 1851; U.S., Congress, House, 31 Cong., 1 Sess., *House Miscellaneous Documents*, no. 3; *Cong. Globe*, 31 Cong., 2 Sess., 394–97, *Appendix*, 787; 32 Cong., 1 Sess., 950–51, 1303, 2073.

33. Although there had been continuous concern with internal improvements since 1846. See Chapters 5–8.

34. *Nashville True Whig*, March 7, 1851; *Weekly Wisconsin*, March 12, 1851; *Cong. Globe*, 31 Cong., 2 Sess., 530–32, 549–51.

35. Ibid., 366–67, *Appendix*, 212, 234; 32 Cong., 1 Sess., 506; J. G. Butler to Thomas Corwin, February 15, 1851, William D. Wilson to Corwin, August 9, 1851, Corwin Papers; "Report of the Secretary of the Treasury," U.S., Congress, Senate, 31 Cong., 2 Sess., *Senate Executive Documents*, no. 4; *Georgia Enquirer* quoted by Athens (Ga.) *Southern Banner*, February 20, 1851; *Cleveland Plain Dealer*, July 12, 1851.

36. Railroad demands are recorded in the *Cong. Globe*, 31 Cong., 2 Sess., *Appendix*, 157–58; 32 Cong., 1 Sess., *Appendix*, 184; demands for improved mail service are recorded ibid., 31 Cong., 2 Sess., 223; U.S., Congress, House, 31 Cong., 2 Sess., *House Miscellaneous Documents*, no. 3, 8, 9. See also, Robert R. Russel, "A Re-evaluation of the Period before the Civil War: Railroads," *Miss. Valley Hist. Rev.*, xv (December 1928), 346–47.

37. *Cong. Globe*, 31 Cong., 2 Sess., 22, 125, 316, 720, *Appendix*, 35–

36; 32 Cong., 1 Sess., 12, 684, 1018, 2100; *Washington Union*, March 14, 1852.

38. Although the subject of railroad land grants was comparatively new to Congress, the debates on it included many of the same arguments for and against legislation calling for federal government aid as had the earlier debates on rivers and harbors improvements. Some people wanted the federal government to take a direct hand in the economy through federal aid, while others opposed such direct intervention. See the *Cong. Globe*, 31 Cong., 2 Sess., 127–30; 32 Cong., 1 Sess., 672, 704, *Appendix*, 232–33, 272–74.

39. The scales included votes on various provisions of a rivers and harbors bill, on canal construction, on land grants to states for railroad construction, and on steamship line subsidies.

40. Senate, improvements issue, Whig party breakdown:

	31st Congress			32nd Congress		
	North	South	West	North	South	West
Pro	9	8	1	5	5	—
Moderate	1	1	—	1	3	—
Anti	—	—	—	—	—	—

41. See Chapters 4 and 5.

42. It might be noted here that the sectional positions on this issue were badly scattered and were shaped by the party membership of each section's members.

43. As in the Senate, these included rivers and harbors legislation, railroad land grants, and steamship subsidies.

44. Western breakdown, House of Representatives, improvements issue:

	31st Congress		32nd Congress	
	Old Northwest	Whole West	Old Northwest	Whole West
Pro	24	35	33	59
Moderate	2	7	9	14
Anti	11	35	3	10

45. An interesting difference here which may tie in with the localistic nature of the voting, was that in the 31st Congress the House was concerned primarily with the traditional river and harbor legislation, while in the 32d the focus was primarily on land grants to railroads. In the Senate this had not been true.

46. These included amendments involving the cost of postage, whether or not newspapers would be subsidized through the mails, and whether or not to pass the bill. The use of the terms "expansive" and "limited" is a subjective description implying acceptance or rejection of increased federal government activity to develop and cheapen postal service.

47. This internal dissent was not of a partisan nature. The sectional party breakdowns were:

	North		South		West	
	Dems.	*Whigs*	*Dems.*	*Whigs*	*Dems.*	*Whigs*
Expansive	1	5	—	—	5	1
Moderate	2	4	5	3	4	—
Limited	1	2	11	6	—	—

Regional groupings, both partisan and nonpartisan, were similarly scattered.

48. The scale included both a postage bill and a bill to establish branch mints in various cities.

49. House, government operations scale, sectional voting by party:

	North		South		West	
	Dems.	*Whigs*	*Dems.*	*Whigs*	*Dems.*	*Whigs*
Expansive	36	3	5	3	6	7
Moderate	19	8	7	1	8	7
Limited	1	7	9	48	1	8

50. They included a bill making bounty-land warrants assignable, and various maneuvers to bring homestead legislation before Congress. The background and maneuvering on this legislation can be followed in Roy M. Robbins, *Our Landed Heritage, The Public Domain, 1776–1936* (2d ed., New York, 1950), 114–16. The word "liberal" in the chart is a subjective description of the position taken.

51. The Western Democrats divided as follows: 5 in favor, 5 moderate, and 2 against.

52. This scale included votes on various parts of the Homestead bill as well as on the military land warrant bill.

53. House, land issue, Old Northwest:

	Whigs	*Democrats*
Liberal	5	19
Moderate	1	5
Conservative	6	1

54. See Chapters 4–6.

55. It had been the Democrats who were willing to push the English aggressively in Oregon and who welcomed the war with Mexico. The Whigs had been more cautious in these areas.

56. Kossuth's background and subsequent tour can be followed in Arnold Whitridge, *Men In Crisis: The Revolutions of 1848* (New York, 1949), 255–81.

57. Ibid., 281–82, 323–25.

58. The American people's attitude toward Kossuth is described in Eddie

William Schodt, "American Policy and Practice with Respect to European Liberal Movements, 1848–1853" (Ph.D. diss., Univ. of Colo., 1951). See also, *Chicago Democrat*, December 31, 1851; Merle Curti, "The Impact of the Revolutions of 1848 on American Thought," in Edward N. Saveth, ed., *Understanding the American Past* (Boston, 1954), 242–58.

59. Schodt, "American Policy," 260; speech of Joshua Giddings, January 28, 1852, *Cong. Globe*, 32 Cong., 1 Sess., *Appendix*, 143–45.

60. Washington Hunt to Robert Winthrop, December 26, 1851, Robert Winthrop Papers, Mass. Hist. Soc.; *National Intelligencer*, December 13, 1851; "Resolutions of the Legislature of Georgia," U.S., Congress, Senate, 32 Cong., 1 Sess., *Senate Miscellaneous Documents*, no. 48.

61. *Cleveland Plain Dealer*, January 2, 1852.

62. *Cong. Globe*, 32 Cong., 1 Sess., 324, 672; *National Intelligencer*, January 20, 1852; Daniel Webster to Edward Everett, November 21, 1851, Everett Papers. Secretary of State Webster asked Everett to draw up a note pointing out America's traditional principle of neither intervening nor meddling in Europe's internal affairs. Webster to Everett, October 20, 1850, Everett Papers.

63. Curti, "Revolutions of 1848," 253; Schodt, "American Policy," 333. Some contemporary comments along this line were made also. See the speech of Representative Taylor of Ohio, January 20, 1852, *Cong. Globe*, 32 Cong., 1 Sess., 325. He was challenged immediately by Representative Campbell of Ohio, ibid.

64. They included the matter of how friendly to be towards Kossuth, as well as resolutions in favor of an American nonintervention policy in world affairs, and a memorial against Louis Napoleon. The terms "aggressive," etc. are a subjective description of the positions taken.

65. Although the senators from the Old Northwest were all united in the most aggressive voting-position on this scale, they were all Democrats with the exception of Salmon P. Chase, Free-Soiler and former Democrat.

66. Senate, foreign relations issue, Southern voting breakdown:

	Democrats	Whigs
Aggressive	3	—
Moderate	1	—
Nonaggressive	5	3

The Democratic divisions here did not reflect a regional breakdown within the South either, since the 3 senators in the aggressive position were from Florida, Louisiana, and Mississippi; the moderate was from South Carolina; and the nonaggressive senators included the other Florida Democrat, both senators from Alabama and one senator each from Virginia and Georgia.

67. The scale included, in addition to the Kossuth matter, a recurrence of earlier resolutions declaring the Mexican War to have been Mexico's fault, as well as resolutions of sympathy towards the American "filibusters" captured in Cuba, and resolutions calling for and opposing our interference in Cuban affairs.

68. House, foreign relations issue, Southern voting breakdown:

	Democrats	Whigs
Aggressive	28	4
Moderate	14	15
Nonaggressive	5	5

CHAPTER TEN

1. Frank Lawrence Owsley, "Sectionalism," *Dictionary of American History* (New York, 1940), v, 53–55. This quote is on page 54.

2. Avery O. Craven, *The Coming of the Civil War* (2d. ed., Chicago, 1957), Chaps. 8–10, and *The Growth of Southern Nationalism* (Baton Rouge, 1953), 25–26; Charles Wiltse, *John C. Calhoun, Sectionalist, 1840–1850* (Indianapolis, 1951), 164–65, 234–37; Frederick Jackson Turner, *The United States, 1830–1850: The Nation and Its Sections*, (New York, 1935), 225, 559.

3. Henry Clyde Hubbart, *The Older Middle West, 1840–1880* (New York, 1936), 4–5; John Barnhart, "Sources of Southern Migration into the Old Northwest," *Miss. Valley Hist. Rev.*, xxii (June 1935), 49–62, and "The Southern Element in the Leadership of the Old Northwest," *Jour. of Southern Hist.*, i (May 1935), 186–97; Joel H. Silbey, "Proslavery Sentiment in Iowa, 1838–1861," *Iowa Jour. of Hist. and Politics*, x (October 1957), 289–318.

4. Louis B. Schmidt, "The Internal Grain Trade of the United States, 1850–1860," *Iowa Jour. of Hist. and Politics*, xviii (January 1920), 14–24.

5. Douglass C. North, *The Economic Growth of the United States, 1790–1860* (Englewood Cliffs, 1961), 67; William Appleman Williams, *The Contours of American History* (Cleveland, 1961), 258.

6. "It was this effort to extend political power by the formation of alliances and the creation of satellites that produced a state of fear and tension. . . . It began when the South attempted to draw the young and growing Northwest into its orbit. . . . To the building of that alliance, John C. Calhoun gave as much attention as he did to the unification of the South itself, and on its foundations Stephen A. Douglas . . . built his political career. Its success gave the South control of the Democratic party

and made that party the dominant political power in the nation." Avery O. Craven, "Democracy in Crisis," *Alabama Review*, VIII (October 1955), 269.

7. Charles Wiltse perhaps deals with this most extensively in his chapters beginning with "A New South-West Alliance" to his discussions of Manifest Destiny and the Wilmot Proviso. See Wiltse, *Sectionalist*, 233–302. Other treatments are located in the works cited in note 2.

8. "Traditionally, the Northwest had close economic and political ties with the South, so it was no surprise to find most of the Democratic Northwesterners willing to go along with Whig border-staters in a compromise direction." Holman Hamilton, *Prologue to Conflict: The Crisis and Compromise of 1850* (Lexington, 1964), 33. See also, Charles Wiltse, *The New Nation, 1800–1845* (New York, 1961), 188–89.

9. Clark Persinger, "The 'Bargain of 1844' As the Origin of the Wilmot Proviso," *Annual Report of the American Historical Association for 1911* (Washington, 1913), I, 187–95.

10. "If we express sectional contests, in national party conventions and in the federal House and Senate, in such European phrases as 'diplomatic congresses,' 'ententes,' 'alliances,' and the attempts at 'balance of power,' we shall not go altogether wrong in the description of what actually occurs, and we shall find that the rival sections of the United States have played parts not entirely different from those played by European states." Frederick Jackson Turner, *The Significance of Sections in American History* (New York, 1932; reprinted, 1950), 319–20.

It is interesting to note the pervasiveness of this idea among historians even when they discuss other periods. Professor C. Vann Woodward, for example, characterizes the political maneuvering of Southern political leaders in the 1890's as a revival of the "ante-bellum sectional diplomacy of a Western alliance." C. Vann Woodward, *Origins of the New South, 1877–1913* (Baton Rouge, 1951), 48.

11. Craven, *Coming of Civil War*, Chap. 10.

12. Ray Allen Billington, *Westward Expansion* (New York, 1960), 386.

13. Craven, *Growth of Southern Nationalism*, 21.

14. See Chapter 3.

15. Duff Green to John C. Calhoun, September 24, 1845, in J. Franklin Jameson, ed., "Correspondence of John C. Calhoun," *Annual Report of the American Historical Association for 1899* (Washington, 1900), II, 1055. This quote is found in Wiltse, *Calhoun, Sectionalist*, 235; Craven, *Coming of Civil War*, 212; Turner, *U.S., 1830–1850*, 225.

16. Quoted in Wiltse, *Calhoun, Sectionalist*, 236.

17. See, for example, Craven, *Coming of Civil War*, 213 ff.

18. Most sectional historians have been quite imprecise about just what was the Southern-Western alliance. A study of the different authorities cited in this chapter reveals a great deal of vagueness and many different conclusions concerning the extent and nature of the relationship.

19. See Chapter 4.

20. See Chapter 5. The position of John C. Calhoun in these Congresses is quite interesting. He voted with the Democrats on most issues. But this placed him in opposition to the bulk of the Southern Whigs. On two issues he broke with most of the other Southern Democrats. Obviously, the Southern congressmen as a bloc were not following Calhoun.

21. This conclusion is drawn from the scales of the roll-call votes in the first session of the 29th Congress.

22. See the scales in Chapter 5.

23. Craven, *Coming of Civil War*, 213 ff.

24. The editorial columns of the *Chicago Democrat*, as one example of the Western point of view, were filled with bitter and vituperative comments against the South after the middle of 1846. Perhaps even more significant was the comment of Representative James Hunt, Democrat of Michigan, to the abolitionist leader James Birney on June 2, 1846, that "I have learned to agree with you in your estimate of Southern men and as a body have but little confidence in them." Dwight L. Dumond, ed., *Letters of James Gillespie Birney 1831–1857* (New York, 1938), II, 1024.

25. See the scales on the slavery-extension issue in the 29th and 30th Congresses in Chapter 6.

26. See Chapter 6.

CHAPTER ELEVEN

1. James Seddon of Virginia, in returning to the Democratic party in 1852, commented that the "cursed bonds of party paralyzed our strength and energy when they might have been successfully exerted, and now as some partial compension must sustain and uphold us from dispersion and prostration." Seddon to R. M. T. Hunter, February 7, 1852, in Charles Ambler, ed., "Correspondence of R. M. T. Hunter, 1826–1876," *Annual Report of the American Historical Association for 1916* (Washington, 1918), 137. Northern Barnburner–Free-Soil elements also returned to their party in 1852.

2. Rhett continued, "the fact is that, from party contact at Washington, the courage of Southern representatives . . . oozes out." Quoted in Harold Schultz, *Nationalism and Sectionalism in South Carolina, 1852–1860* (Durham, 1950), 213–14 n.

3. I have described and analyzed the arguments of one group of national party advocates in the antebellum crisis in Joel H. Silbey, "The Southern National Democrats, 1846–1861," *Mid-America*, XLVII (July 1965), 176–90.

4. This conclusion is based on some of the results of the work of Mr. Gerald Wolff of the University of Iowa who is engaged in a full-scale study of the Kansas-Nebraska bill in which he makes extensive use of the Guttman scalogram. See, for example, his "The Slavocracy and the Homestead Problem of 1854," *Agricultural Hist.*, XL (April 1966), 101–11.

5. In 1860, Senator Jefferson Davis of Mississippi offered a set of resolutions which would have committed the federal government to protect slave property in the territories of the United States. There was much Southern opposition to these resolutions during the debates. *Cong. Globe*, 36 Cong., 1 Sess., 1480–90, 1962–66, and elsewhere. In addition, a scale of the roll-call votes on the resolution indicates that there was not complete Southern unity. The important thing here is that the Southern Democratic opponents of the Davis resolutions argued against them in the interest of maintaining national party unity. See Silbey, "Southern National Democrats."

6. See George Daniels, "Immigrant Vote in the 1860 Election: The Case of Iowa," *Mid-America*, XLIV (July 1962), 146–62; and Robert Swierenga, "The Ethnic Voter and the First Lincoln Election," *Civil War History*, XI (March 1965), 27–43.

7. Joel H. Silbey, "The Civil War Synthesis in American Political History," *Civil War History*, X (June 1964), 130–40.

8. Lee Benson's careful analysis of voting in New York State between the 1820's and 1844, *The Concept of Jacksonian Democracy: New York As a Test Case* (Princeton, 1961), is an example of the type of studies of political behavior that we need. Other such studies include the Daniels and Swierenga articles referred to in note 6. Several of these are discussed in Silbey, "Civil War Synthesis."

9. For a discussion of the opportunities opened to historians by such recent advances see William O. Aydelotte, "Quantification in History," *Amer. Hist. Rev.*, LXXI (April 1966), 803–25. See also his "Some Notes on the Problem of Historical Generalization," in Louis Gottschalk, ed., *Generalization in the Writing of History* (Chicago, 1963), 145–77, especially 172–77.

10. Quoted by John Brooke in "Namier and Namierism," *History and Theory*, III (1963–1964), 333.

11. The quote is from the Milledgeville (Ga.) *Federal Union*, January 30, 1849. For the context in which it was written see note 65 of Chapter 7.

BIBLIOGRAPHIC NOTE

Although the major portion of this work is based on a statistical analysis of almost two thousand Congressional roll-calls, a wide variety of monographs, articles, newspapers, manuscripts, and other traditional historical sources were also extensively used. The following notes only the most important of the works consulted during the course of my research, beginning with the publications of the United States government and its agencies during the 1840's and since. The relevant volumes of the *Congressional Globe* contain a somewhat uneven record of the day-to-day debates and activities of both houses. Although the *Globe* has many of the roll-call votes taken, the most complete collection of them is in the House and Senate *Journals*, the official record of the proceedings of Congress. Biographical information about the members of Congress came primarily from the *Biographical Directory of the American Congress, 1774–1961* (Washington, 1961). *The Whig Almanac* (New York, 1841–1852) was a useful supplement to the *Directory*, particularly for party affiliation, districts represented, and a variety of election statistics. In addition, the collected documents and reports of each Congress, contained in the Congressional Serial Set (House and Senate *Executive Documents, Miscellaneous Documents,* and *Reports,* each issued by Congress and session), were useful in tracing ideological positions, constituency points of view, and the general framework in which votes were cast. The U.S. Bureau of the Census, *Historical Statistics of the United States from Colonial Times to 1957* (Washington, 1960), conveniently supplied economic and miscellaneous political statistics of different types.

In tracing the background of the period under study to establish the day-to-day situation in which Congress acted and, most particularly, to help explain the Congressional voting patterns, I used newspapers and manuscript collections. In the case of the former I endeavored to spread a wide net, sectionally and politically, in an effort to recapture the many points of view present. Particularly helpful in this connection were the Washington-based party organs, each of which contained numerous local and state reports of conventions, reactions to legislation, election campaigns, etc., as well as reprints of editorials from many newspapers not otherwise available. The Democratic newspapers were the *Daily Globe* (1841–April, 1845), and its successor, the *Daily Union*. The *National Intelligencer* expressed the Whig point of view at the Capitol and the *Madisonian* briefly upheld the Tylerites in the early 1840's. In addition, *Niles National Register*, published at Baltimore, contained a great amount of useful material beyond its local scene. In the Southern states, the *Richmond Enquirer*, the *Raleigh Standard*, and the Milledgeville, Georgia *Federal Union*, best reflected the Democratic outlook. The Whigs had able organs in such papers as the Augusta *Daily Chronicle and Sentinel*, the *Charleston Courier*, and the *Richmond Whig*. The Southern sectional viewpoint was consistently maintained by the *Charleston Mercury* throughout the decade and by several others over a briefer span. Particularly pertinent in the North and West were such Democratic newspapers as the Columbus *Ohio Statesman*, the Springfield *Illinois State Register*, and the Detroit *Democratic Free Press*. The *New York Tribune, Chicago Journal*, and the Columbus *Ohio State Journal* were the most important Whig newspapers. Representative John Wentworth's *Chicago Daily Democrat* was the best newspaper source of the Great Lakes sectional viewpoint.

There are extensive collections of surviving manuscripts of contemporary political figures. At the Library of Congress, the most important for this study were the James K. Polk and Martin Van Buren Papers, both containing many letters from political observers throughout the country. Some of the collections of Congressional leaders were almost as useful, particularly the John Clayton, Caleb B. Smith, and John Jordan Crittenden Papers. In other depositories, the most helpful collections were the Alexander H. Stephens Letters at Manhattanville College of the Sacred Heart, Purchase, New York, and the Robert Winthrop and Edward Everett Papers at the Massachusetts Historical Society. The other collections consulted varied in quality, scope, and usefulness, but many of them supplied important items of one kind or another. Unpublished collections were supplemented by frequent reference to published collections of letters. The most important of these were Ulrich B. Phillips, ed., "The Correspondence of Robert Toombs, Alexander H. Stephens, and Howell Cobb," *Annual Report of the American Historical Association for the Year 1911* (Washington, 1913); Chauncey S. Boucher and Robert P. Brooks, eds., "Correspondence Addressed to John C. Calhoun, 1837–1849," *Annual Report*

of the American Historical Association for 1929 (Washington, 1930);
J. Franklin Jameson, ed., "Correspondence of John C. Calhoun," *Annual
Report of the American Historical Association for 1899* (Washington,
1900); Robert Johannsen, *The Letters of Stephen A. Douglas* (Urbana,
1961); Robert Brooks, ed., "Howell Cobb Papers," *Ga. Hist. Qtly.,* v
(1921). In a slightly different category, Milo M. Quaife, ed., *The Diary
of James K. Polk During His Presidency, 1845–1849* (Chicago, 1910),
supplied much pertinent information.

Among collections of miscellaneous sources contributing valuable
material were Kirk H. Porter and Donald Bruce Johnson, eds., *National
Party Platforms, 1840–1956* (Urbana, 1956); and James Richardson, ed.,
A Compilation of the Messages and Papers of the Presidents, 1789–1905
(Washington, 1907). There are, in addition, some compilations of state
party platforms and the papers and messages of the governors of various
states. In several libraries, particularly the Library of Congress and the
New York Public Library, are many printed addresses of congressmen
to their constituents, reports of meetings such as the rivers and harbors
meetings at Chicago and Memphis, and the Nashville Convention, and a
miscellany of political party compaign statements, all of which were useful at some point.

Any study of the sectional thesis in American historiography begins with
Frederick Jackson Turner, *The Significance of Sections in American
History* (New York, 1932) and *The United States, 1830–1850* (New
York, 1935). Avery Craven's contribution can be followed primarily in
such works as *The Coming of the Civil War* (New York, 1942; 2d ed.,
Chicago, 1957), *The Growth of Southern Nationalism, 1848–1861* (Baton
Rouge, 1953), and *Civil War in the Making, 1815–1860* (Baton Rouge,
1959). Other material on the sectional thesis is in Merrill Jensen, ed.,
Regionalism in America: A Symposium (Madison, 1951). The application
of the thesis by historians can be typically seen in such works as Henry
Clyde Hubbart, *The Older Middle West, 1840–1880* (New York, 1936),
and Charles Sydnor, *The Development of Southern Sectionalism, 1819–
1848* (Baton Rouge, 1948). In contrast, Charles G. Sellers, Jr., "Who
Were the Southern Whigs?" *Amer. Hist. Rev.,* LIX (January 1954), 335–
46; Thomas P. Govan, "Americans Below the Potomac," in Charles G.
Sellers, Jr., ed., *The Southerner as American* (New York, 1960), 19–39;
and Chauncey S. Boucher, "*In Re*: That Aggressive Slavocracy," *Miss.
Valley Hist. Rev.,* VIII (June–September 1921), 13–79, serve to put the
sectional thesis in a somewhat different perspective.

The starting point for a historical analysis of Congress should be the old but still useful contribution of Orrin G. Libby, "A Plea for the Study of Votes in Congress," *Annual Report of the American Historical Association for 1896* (Washington, 1897), I, 323–34. The scalogram technique is fully set forth in Louis Guttman's essay in volume 4 of Samuel Stouffer, *Measurement and Prediction* (Princeton, 1949). Its application to legislative analysis is described in George Belknap, "A Method of Analyzing Legislative Behavior," *Midwest Jour. of Pol. Sci.*, II (November 1958), 377–402; and Duncan MacRae, *Dimensions of Congressional Voting* (Berkeley, 1958). William O. Aydelotte has made the most extensive use of the scalogram in historical studies. See his "A Statistical Analysis of the Parliament of 1841: Some Problems of Method," Inst. for Hist. Res. *Bulletin*, XXXVII (1954), 141–45, and "Voting Patterns in the British House of Commons in the Early 1840's," *Comparative Studies in Society and History*, V (January 1963), 134–63.

The great mass of secondary material, both published and unpublished, relating to the background of the 1840's, the problems of that decade, the story of Congressional activity, and the slavery crisis, has been consulted throughout the research for this book. My dependence upon the work of earlier analysts can best be seen in the notes to the text. Several of the more extensively consulted works should be especially cited here, however. Although I disagree with much of his analysis, the last volume of Charles Wiltse's magnificent biography, *John C. Calhoun, Sectionalist, 1840–1850* (Indianapolis, 1951), has been constantly referred to as an unparalleled source of the politics of the 1840's as well as a prime statement of a particular point of view concerning those politics. Robert Rayback, *Millard Fillmore, Biography of a President* (Buffalo, 1959); Charles Grier Sellers, Jr., *James K. Polk, Jacksonian, 1795–1843* (Princeton, 1957); William Nisbet Chambers, *Old Bullion Benton, Senator from the New West* (Boston, 1956); George Rawlings Poage, *Henry Clay and the Whig Party* (Chapel Hill, 1936); and Holman Hamilton, *Zachary Taylor, Soldier in the White House* (Indianapolis, 1951) were other biographies whose merit and scope made an understanding of the 1840's easier. Such standard works on the economic situation of the period as George Rogers Taylor, *The Transportation Revolution, 1815–1860* (New York, 1951); Paul Wallace Gates, *The Farmer's Age, 1815–1860* (New York, 1960), and Douglass C. North, *The Economic Growth of the United States, 1790–1860* (Englewood Cliffs, 1961), supplied a large part of the material contained in Chapters 2 and 3. In addition to the biographies cited above, other works of political history used included, Lee Benson *The Concept of Jacksonian Democracy: New York As a Test Case* (Princeton, 1961);

Allan Nevins, *Ordeal of the Union*, 2 vols., (New York, 1947); George Fort Milton, *The Eve of Conflict: Stephen A. Douglas and the Needless War* (Boston, 1934); and the old, relatively outmoded, but still quite useful, Arthur C. Cole, *The Whig Party in the South* (Washington, 1913). For the period of the slavery crisis and its aftermath a particularly relevant study of a single state's politics is Horace Montgomery, *Cracker Parties* (Baton Rouge, 1950).

Finally, there is a great mass of useful, undigested, and otherwise difficult-to-find material in the many unpublished doctoral dissertations located in university libraries throughout the country. Obviously they vary in quality, scope, and usefulness but, as an indicator example, Herbert Pegg, "The Whig Party in North Carolina, 1834–1861" (Univ. of N.C., 1932), supplied quite pertinent material at many points in this study.

INDEX